New York / St. Louis / Dallas / San Francisco
Auckland / Bogotá / Düsseldorf / Johannesburg / London
Madrid / Mexico / Montreal / New Delhi / Panama / Paris
São Paulo / Singapore / Sydney / Tokyo / Toronto

Library of Congress Cataloging in Publication Data

Gregg, John Robert, date.
Gregg shorthand, series 90.

Includes indexes.
1. Shorthand–Gregg. I. Leslie, Louis A., date. joint author. II. Zoubek, Charles E., date. joint author. III. Title.
Z56.G813 1978 653'.427 77-4161
ISBN 0-07-024471-5

Gregg Shorthand,
Series 90

2 3 4 5 6 7 8 9 0 DODO 7 8 6 5 4 3 2 1 0 9 8

Preface

Gregg Shorthand, the universal system

Gregg Shorthand was first published in 1888 and has been learned and used successfully by millions of writers throughout the entire world. Gregg Shorthand was written in English but has been successfully adapted to numerous other languages, including French, Spanish, and Portuguese. To most people the terms *shorthand* and *Gregg* are synonymous. Gregg Shorthand is truly the universal system of shorthand. It is used by more shorthand writers than any other system in the world.

Gregg Shorthand is used by stenographers and administrative secretaries as a vocational tool that enables them to obtain and hold interesting and rewarding positions. It is used by business and professional people who are relieved of the burden of writing longhand in making notes, preparing important papers, and drafting reports.

The success of any system of shorthand rests on the merits of its alphabet. The Gregg alphabet is the most logical, consistent, and efficient shorthand alphabet devised in more than 2,000 years of shorthand history. The fact that this alphabet, virtually without change, has been the basis of Gregg Shorthand for more than 90 years is a tribute to the genius of its inventor, John Robert Gregg.

Series 90

Objectives *Gregg Shorthand, Series 90,* is published in the ninetieth anniversary year of the invention of the Gregg system. This revision involves a small number of system changes which have been deemed desirable to make learning and writing Gregg Shorthand even easier and more consistent. A major change has been made in the order of presentation of the theory principles. This change was made to provide better, more logical business letters even in the very early lessons in the text. Teachers will find the system changes to be logical and the teaching and learning suggestions helpful. The major objectives of *Gregg Shorthand, Series 90,* are:

1 To teach the students to read and write Gregg Shorthand rapidly and accurately in the shortest time possible.

2 To provide the students with transcription readiness by building their vocabulary and developing their ability to spell and punctuate accurately.

Organization

Gregg Shorthand, Series 90, is divided into three parts—Principles, Reinforcement, and Shorthand and Transcription Skill Building. These parts are subdivided into 10 chapters and 70 lessons. The last new theory is presented in Lesson 47. The theory is presented in 40 lessons. Eight of the first 48 lessons are devoted to review.

Format

Gregg Shorthand, Series 90, is published in the same two-column format which proved popular in the last edition of Gregg Shorthand. This format makes it possible to present the shorthand practice material in columns that are approximately the width of the columns of the students' shorthand notebooks. The short lines make reading easier because the eye does not have to travel very far from the end of one line of shorthand to the beginning of the next. The format also makes it possible to highlight the words from the Reading and Writing Practice that are identified for spelling attention. The words are placed in the margins near the corresponding shorthand outline.

Building transcription skills

Gregg Shorthand, Series 90, continues to place great stress on the nonshorthand elements of transcription, which are taught concurrently with shorthand. It retains all the helpful transcription exercises of the former edition. These include:

Business Vocabulary Builders Beginning with Lesson 7, each lesson contains a Business Vocabulary Builder consisting of several business words or expressions for which meanings are provided. The words and expressions are selected from the Reading and Writing Practice. The Business Vocabulary Builders help to overcome a major student handicap—a limited vocabulary.

Spelling—Marginal Reminders Words singled out from the Reading and Writing Practice for special spelling attention appear in the margins of the shorthand. Usually each word appears on the same line as its shorthand outline. These words appear in a second color in the shorthand so that they are easy to see.

In *Gregg Shorthand, Series 90,* spelling is introduced in Chapter 4.

Spelling—Families An effective device for improving spelling is the study of words in related groups, or spelling families. In the Series 90 edition, the students study six spelling families, beginning with Lesson 45.

Similar-Words Drills These drills teach the students the difference in meaning between similar words that stenographers often confuse—*it's, its; addition, edition; there, their, they're,* etc.

Punctuation Beginning with Lesson 31, nine frequent usages of the comma are introduced. Only one comma usage is introduced in any given lesson. The commas are encircled and appear in the shorthand; the reason for the use of the comma is shown above the circle.

Common Prefixes An understanding of the meaning of common English prefixes is an effective device for developing the students' understanding of words. In *Gregg Shorthand, Series 90,* the students study five common English prefixes, beginning in Lesson 56.

Grammar Checkup In a number of lessons, drills are provided on rules of grammar that students often apply incorrectly.

Transcription Quiz Beginning with Lesson 57, each lesson contains a Transcription Quiz consisting of a letter in which the students have to supply internal punctuation. This quiz provides them with a daily test of how well they have mastered the punctuation rules presented in earlier lessons.

Reading and writing practice

In *Gregg Shorthand, Series 90,* there are 40,616 words of shorthand practice material in the Reading and Writing Practice exercises. Most of the material is new.

A brief-form letter is included in *every* lesson of Part 1 (except the review lessons), beginning with Lesson 5.

Other features

Shorthand spelling helps When a new letter in the shorthand alphabet or a theory principle is presented, the shorthand spelling is given.

Chapter openings Each chapter is introduced by a well-illustrated spread that not only paints for the students a picture of the life and duties of a secretary but also encourages them in their efforts to acquire the necessary skills.

Student helps To be sure that the students get the greatest benefit from each phase of their shorthand study, they are given step-by-step suggestions on how to handle each phase when it is first introduced.

Reading scoreboards At various points in the text, students are given an opportunity to determine their reading speed by means of a scoreboard. The scoreboard enables the students to calculate the number of words a minute they are reading. By comparing their reading speed from scoreboard to scoreboard, they see some indication of their shorthand reading growth.

Recall charts In the last lesson of each chapter in Part 1 a recall chart is provided. This chart contains illustrations of theory principles taught in the chapter. It also contains many illustrations of theory principles the students have studied up to that chapter.

Checklists To keep the students constantly reminded of the importance of good practice procedures, occasional checklists are provided. These checklists deal with writing shorthand, reading shorthand, homework, proportion, etc.

Appendix The Appendix contains a number of additional teaching aids. These include:

1 A brief-form chart giving all brief forms in Gregg Shorthand, Series 90, in the order of their presentation.

2 A list of common geographical expressions.

3 A chart showing Gregg outlines for common metric expressions.

Computer control

All of the connected matter in *Gregg Shorthand, Series 90,* has been checked by a carefully written computer program to ensure adequate, proper, and sequential coverage of the theory principles and brief forms. The computer program helped the authors of the book to ensure that the points were properly covered in the lessons in which they were presented as well as in the two lessons following their initial presentation.

• • •

Gregg Shorthand, Series 90, is published with pride and with the confidence that it will help teachers of Gregg Shorthand do an even more effective job of training rapid and accurate shorthand writers and transcribers.

The Publishers

Contents

Your Shorthand Practice Program

The speed with which you learn to read and write Gregg Shorthand will depend largely on two factors—the *time* you devote to practice and the *way* in which you practice. If you practice efficiently, you will be able to complete each lesson in the shortest possible time and derive the greatest possible benefit.

Here are some suggestions which will help you to get the maximum benefit from the time you invest in shorthand practice.

Before you begin, select a quiet place in which to practice. Do not try to practice while listening to music or watching television. Then follow the steps below.

Reading word lists

In each lesson there are a number of word lists that illustrate the principles introduced in the lesson. As part of your out-of-class practice, read these word lists in this way:

1 *With the type key available,* spell—aloud if possible—the shorthand characters in each outline in the list, thus: *"see, s-e; fee, f-e."* Reading aloud will help to impress the shorthand outlines firmly on your mind. Read all the shorthand words in the list in this way—with the type key exposed—until you feel you can read the shorthand outlines without referring to the key.

2 *Cover the type key* with a piece of paper and read aloud from the shorthand, thus: *"s-e, see; f-e, fee."*

3 If the spelling of a shorthand outline does not immediately give you the meaning, refer to the key and determine the meaning of any outline you cannot read. Do *not* spend more than a few seconds trying to decipher an outline.

4 After you have read all the words in the list, read them again if time permits.

Note: In reading brief forms for common words and phrases, which first occur in Lesson 3, do not spell the shorthand outlines.

Study the word lists by placing a slip of paper over the type key and reading the shorthand words aloud.

Reading sentences, letters, and articles

Each lesson contains a Reading Practice (Lessons 1-6) or a Reading and Writing Practice (Lessons 7-70) in which sentences, letters, or articles are written in shorthand. Proper practice on this material will help you develop your shorthand ability. First, *read* the material. Two procedures are suggested for reading shorthand—one with a *Student's Transcript* and one without a *Student's Transcript.*

Procedure With Student's Transcript If you have a *Student's Transcript* to the shorthand in this textbook, you should follow this procedure:

1 Place the *Student's Transcript* to the right of your textbook and open it to the key to the Reading Practice or the Reading and Writing Practice you are about to read.

2 Place your left index finger under the shorthand outline in the text that you are about to read and your right index finger under the corresponding word in the *Student's Transcript.*

3 Read the shorthand outlines aloud until you come to a word you cannot read. Spell the shorthand strokes in that outline. If this spelling does not *immediately* give you the meaning, anchor your left index finger on the outline and look at the transcript, where your right index finger is resting near the point at which you are reading.

4 Determine the meaning of the outline you cannot read and place your right index finger on it.

5 Return to the shorthand from which you are reading—your left index finger has kept your place for you—and continue reading in this manner until you have completed the material.

6 If time permits, read the material a second time.

Refer to your *Transcript* whenever you cannot read an outline. Keep your left index finger anchored in the shorthand; the right index finger, on the corresponding place in the *Transcript.*

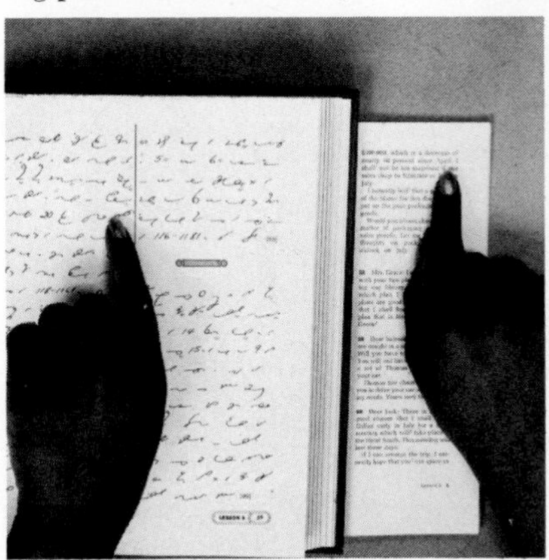

By following this procedure, you will lose no time finding your place in the shorthand and in the transcript when you cannot read an outline.

Procedure Without Student's Transcript If you do not have a *Student's Transcript,* you should follow this procedure:

1 Before you start reading the shorthand, have a blank piece of paper or a blank card handy.

2 Read the shorthand aloud.

3 When you come to a shorthand outline that you cannot read, spell the shorthand strokes in the outline. If the spelling gives you the meaning, continue reading. If it does not, write the outline on your sheet of paper or card and continue reading. Do not spend more than a few seconds trying to decipher the outline.

4 After you have gone through the entire Reading and Writing Practice in this way, repeat this procedure if time permits. On this second reading you may be able to read some of the outlines that gave you trouble the first time. When that happens, cross those outlines off your sheet or card.

5 Finally—and very important—at the earliest opportunity ask your teacher or a classmate the meaning of the outlines that you could not read.

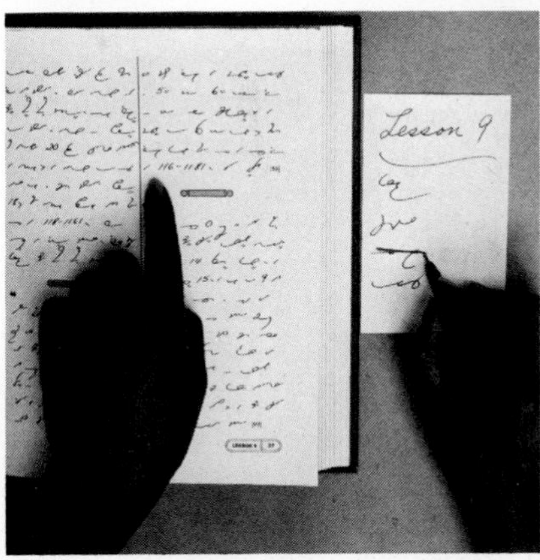

Read the Reading and Writing Practice, writing on the card any outlines that you cannot read after spelling them.

Remember, during the early stages your shorthand reading may not be very rapid. That is only natural, as you are, in a sense, learning a new language. If you practice regularly, however, you will find your reading rate increasing almost daily.

Writing the Reading and Writing Practice

Before you do any writing of shorthand, you should give careful consideration to the tools of your trade—your notebook and your writing instrument.

Your notebook The best notebook for shorthand writing is one that measures 6 x 9 inches and has a vertical rule down the center of each page. It should have a spiral binding so that the pages lie flat at all times. The paper should, of course, take ink well.

Your writing instrument A pen is a satisfactory instrument for writing Gregg Shorthand. *A pencil is not recommended.* Because writing with a pen requires little pressure, you can write for long periods of time without becoming fatigued. A pencil, however, requires considerable pressure. In addition, the pencil point quickly becomes blunt. The blunter it gets, the more effort you have to expend to write with it. Penwritten notes remain legible almost indefinitely; pencil notes become blurred and hard to read. In addition, penwritten notes are also easier to read under artificial light.

Having selected your writing tools, follow these steps in writing the Reading and Writing Practice:

1 Read the material you are going to copy. *Always* read the Reading and Writing Practice before copying it.

2 When you are ready to start writing, read a convenient group of words from the printed shorthand; then write the group, reading aloud as you write. Keep your place in the shorthand with your left index finger if you are right-handed or with your right index finger if you are left-handed.

In the early stages your writing may not be very rapid, nor will your notes be as well written as those in the book. With regular practice, however, your notes will rapidly improve.

Good luck with your study of Gregg Shorthand.

When copying, read a convenient group of words aloud and then write that group in your notebook. Keep your place in the shorthand with your left index finger.

PART

Part 1 Principles

CHAPTER

Why Study Shorthand?

"Why should I study to perfect my shorthand skills?" "Is shorthand really necessary in today's business?" "In the world of automation, is manual shorthand skill still needed?" These are some of the questions students ask today as they prepare for careers. The answers are very clear:

Today there are more shorthand writers than ever before, and the number grows continually. Even so, the demand for secretaries in business exceeds the supply. The ability to take shorthand is a vital skill in the fast-paced world of business, a world in which recording data quickly and accurately is a necessity. So much of all business is transacted on written communications—letters, memorandums, reports, minutes—that the secretary who can take shorthand is in great demand.

Knowing shorthand is important not only when someone wants to dictate a letter or a report, but also when the phone rings and you must take a long, involved message. And what a help it is, when composing your own letters, to be able to jot down all your thoughts before they escape.

When you begin looking for your first job, you will find that the ability to take shorthand will increase your chances of getting just the position you want. The ability to use shorthand will also increase the size

of your paycheck. Whether your job is as a beginning worker or is on an advanced level, in almost every case, business pays more to the secretary who can take shorthand than to the one who cannot.

The dividends continue to pay off. After you have been on a job for a while, you will discover that your shorthand ability will very likely put you in line for a promotion. Good, above-average stenographic skill combined with language ability and a desire to work will put you at the top of the list when there is a chance for a promotion.

You are now starting to learn the basics of Gregg Shorthand. Take time to learn shorthand well. Spend some out-of-class time every day studying the current lesson. You will find that your ability to read and write shorthand will grow rapidly. Follow your teacher's instructions, and you will soon have a marketable skill which you can put to work in a business office.

Shorthand is a valuable skill that can open many doors for you. The time you spend in learning shorthand is well invested.

GREGG SHORTHAND IS EASY TO LEARN

As you leaf through the pages of this book and see the hooks and circles and straight lines in the shorthand outlines, you may wonder whether you can learn shorthand. Be assured that you can, just as millions of others have learned it. If you can write longhand—and of course you can!—you can learn to write Gregg Shorthand. The strokes you will write in Gregg Shorthand are the same strokes that you are accustomed to writing in longhand.

Actually, you will find Gregg Shorthand easier to learn than longhand. Skeptical? Well, the following illustration should convince you of the truth of that statement. In longhand there are many ways to write *f*. Here are six of them:

What is more, in many words the sound of *f* is expressed by combinations of other letters in the alphabet—for example, *ph*, as in *phase*; *gh*, as in *rough*.

In Gregg Shorthand there is one way—and only one way—to express the sound of *f*, as you will learn later in this lesson.

With Gregg Shorthand you can attain almost any speed goal you set for yourself. All it takes is regular, intelligent practice.

Principles

GROUP A

1 **S-Z**

The first shorthand stroke you will learn is *s*, one of the most frequently used letters in the English language. The shorthand *s* is a tiny downward curve that resembles the longhand comma.

Because in English *s* often has the sound of *z*, as in *saves*, the same tiny downward curve is used to express *z*.

S-Z

2 A

The second stroke you will learn is the shorthand *a*, which is simply the longhand *a* with the final connecting stroke omitted.

A

3 Silent Letters Omitted

In the English language many words contain letters that are not pronounced. In Gregg Shorthand these silent letters are not written.

For example, the word *say* would be written *s-a*; the y would not be written because it is not pronounced. The word *face* would be written *f-a-s*; the *e* would not be written because it is not pronounced, and the *c* would be represented by *s* because it is pronounced *s*.

In the following words, what letters would not be written because they are not pronounced?

right	*same*	*day*	*steam*
main	*save*	*snow*	*aid*

4 S-A Word

With the strokes for *s* and *a*, you can form the shorthand outline for a very useful word.

say, s-a

5 F, V

The shorthand stroke for *f* is a downward curve the same shape as *s*, but it is somewhat larger—about half the height of the space between the lines of your shorthand notebook.

The shorthand stroke for v is also a downward curve the same shape as *s* and *f*, but it is very large—almost the full height of the space between the lines of your shorthand notebook.

▶ Notice the difference in the sizes of *s, f, v*.

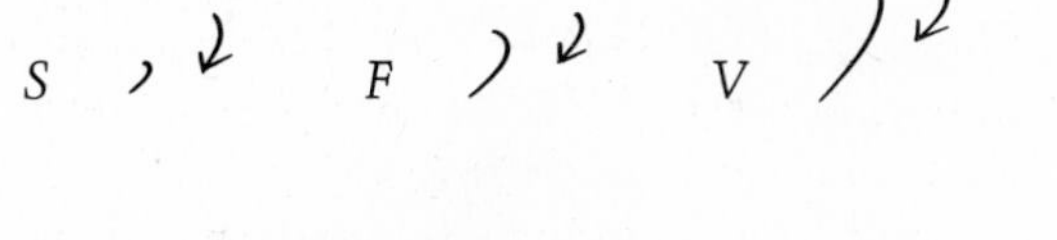

F

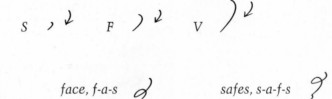

safe, s-a-f | *face, f-a-s* | *safes, s-a-f-s*

▶ Notice that the c in *face* is represented by the *s* because it has the *s* sound.

V

save, s-a-v *vase, v-a-s* *saves, s-a-v-s*

▶ Notice that the final *s* in *saves* has the *z* sound, which is represented by the *s* stroke.

6 E

The shorthand stroke for *e* is a tiny circle. It is simply the longhand *e* with the two connecting strokes omitted.

E

▶ Notice the difference in the sizes of *a* and *e*.

A E

see, s-e *sees, s-e-s* *ease, e-s*

fee, f-e *fees, f-e-s* *easy, e-s-e*

▶ Notice that the *y* in *easy* is pronounced *e*; therefore, it is represented by the *e* circle.

Suggestion At this point take a few moments to read the procedures outlined for practicing word lists on page 10.

GROUP B

7 N, M

The shorthand stroke for *n* is a very short forward straight line.
The shorthand stroke for *m* is a longer forward straight line.

N M

N

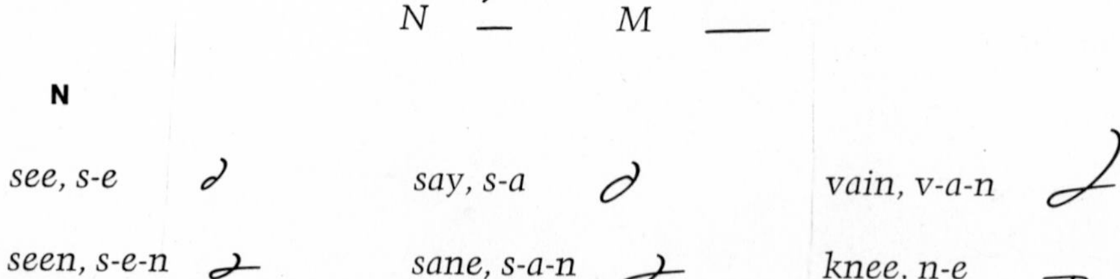

▶ Notice that the *k* in *knee* is not written because it is not pronounced.

M

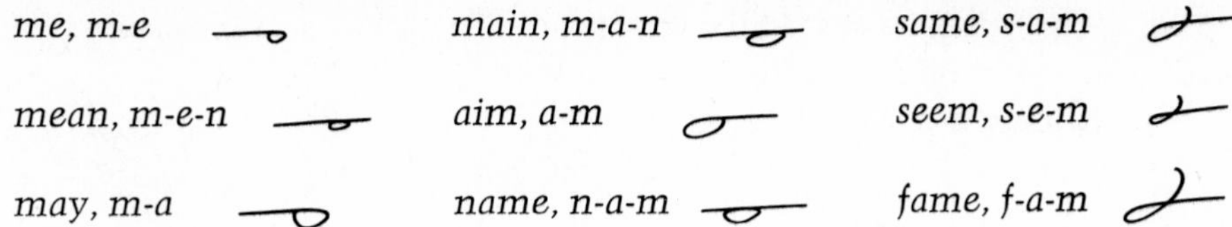

8 T, D

The shorthand stroke for *t* is a short upward straight line.
The shorthand stroke for *d* is a longer upward straight line.

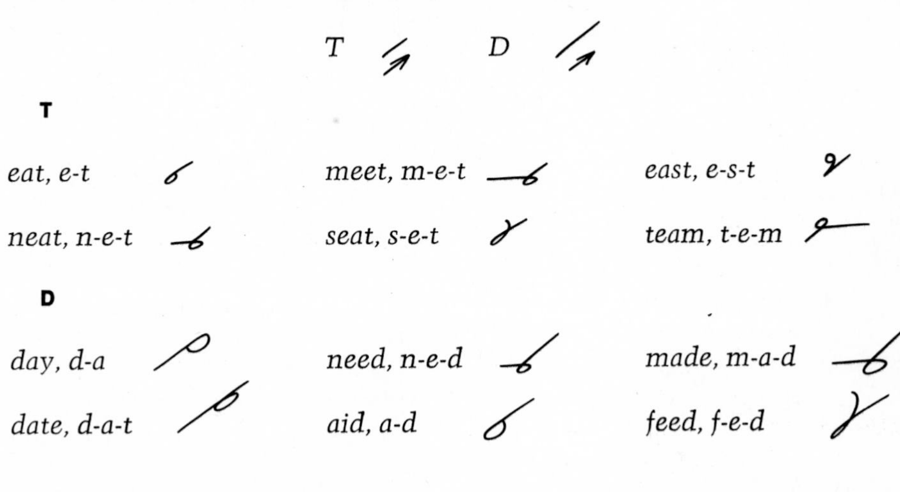

9 Punctuation and Capitalization

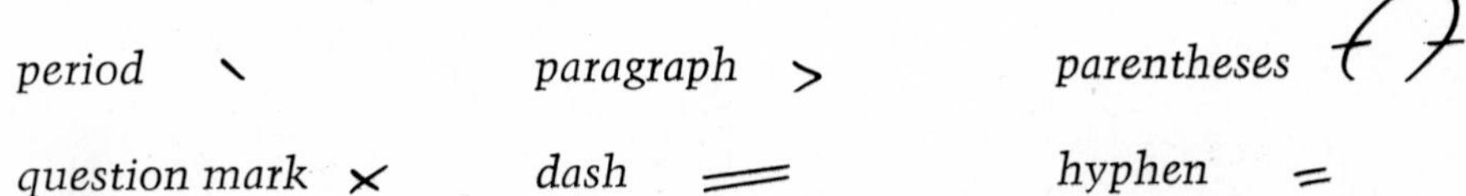

The regular longhand forms are used for all other punctuation marks.

Capitalization is indicated by two upward dashes placed underneath the word to be capitalized.

Fay *Dave* *May*

Reading Practice

With the help of an occasional word written in longhand, you can already read complete sentences.

Read the following sentences, spelling each shorthand outline aloud as you read it thus: *F-a, Fay; m-a-d, made; t-e, tea.* If you cannot read a shorthand outline after you have spelled it, refer to the key which follows the Reading Practice.

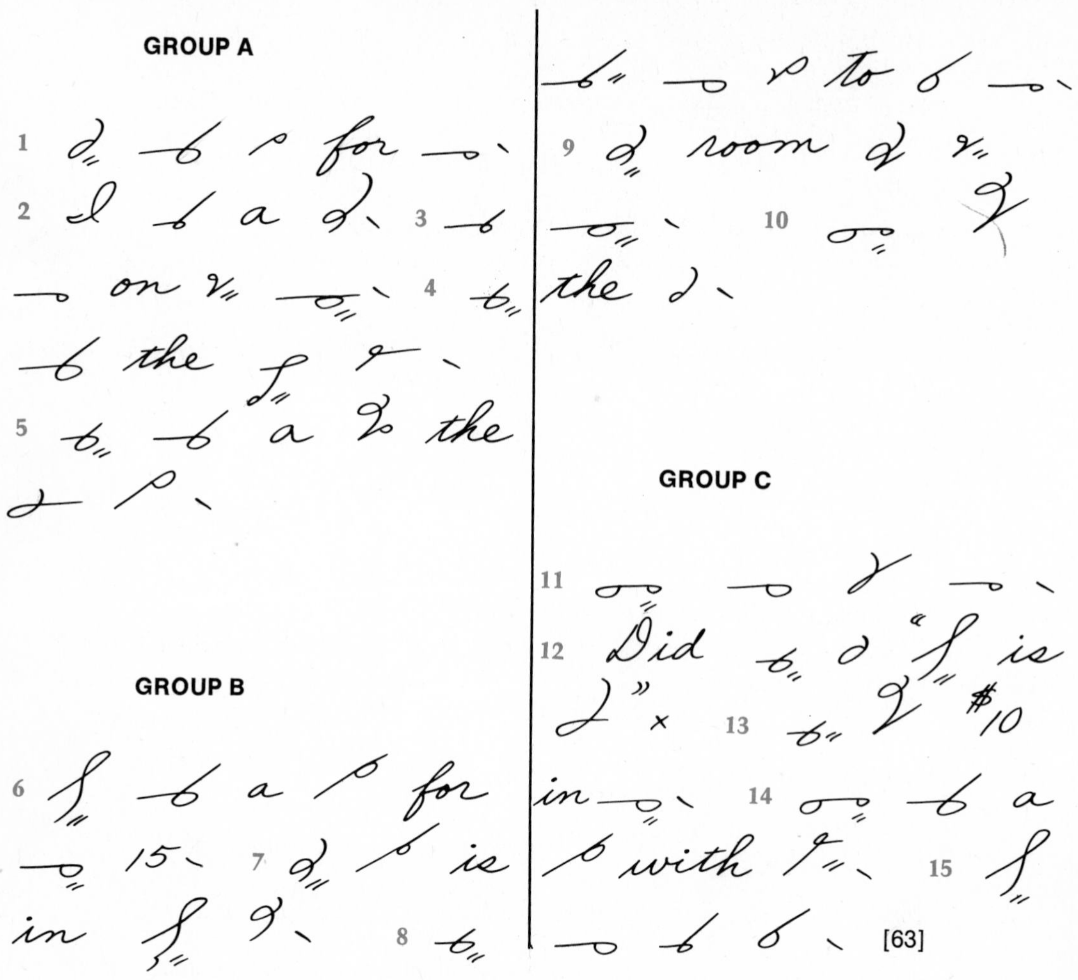

GROUP A 1. *Fay made tea for me.* 2. *I need a vase.* 3. *Meet me on East Main.* 4. *Nate made the Navy team.* 5. *Nate made a safety the same day.* GROUP B 6. *Dave made a date for May 15.* 7. *Fay's deed is in Dave's safe.* 8. *Nate Meade may stay to aid me.* 9. *Fay's room faced East Main.* 10. *Amy saved the fee.* GROUP C 11. *Amy may feed me.* 12. *Did Nate say, "Dave is vain"?* 13. *Nate saved $10 in May.* 14. *Amy made a date with Dean.* 15. *Dave may need aid.*

Principles

10 Alphabet Review

In Lesson 1 you studied the following nine shorthand strokes. How rapidly can you read them?

11 O, R, L

The shorthand stroke for *o* is a small deep hook.
The shorthand stroke for *r* is a short forward curve.
The shorthand stroke for *l* is a longer forward curve about three times as long as *r*.

▶ Note how these strokes are derived from their longhand forms.

O R L

O

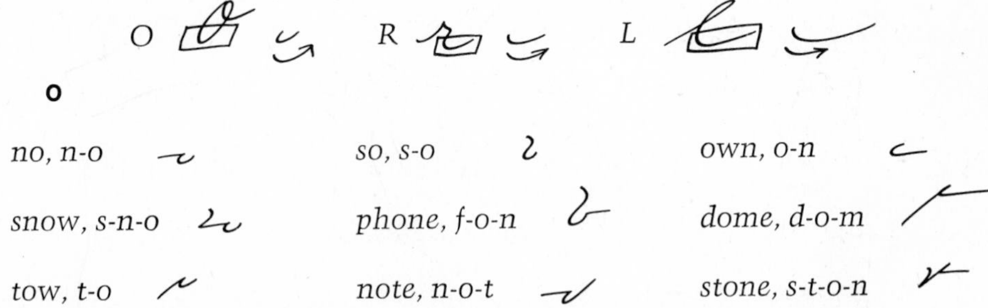

no, n-o | *so, s-o* | *own, o-n*
snow, s-n-o | *phone, f-o-n* | *dome, d-o-m*
tow, t-o | *note, n-o-t* | *stone, s-t-o-n*

▶ Notice that in *own, dome,* and *stone* the o is placed on its side. By placing o on its side before *n* or *m* in these and similar words, we obtain smoother joinings than we would if we wrote the o upright.

R

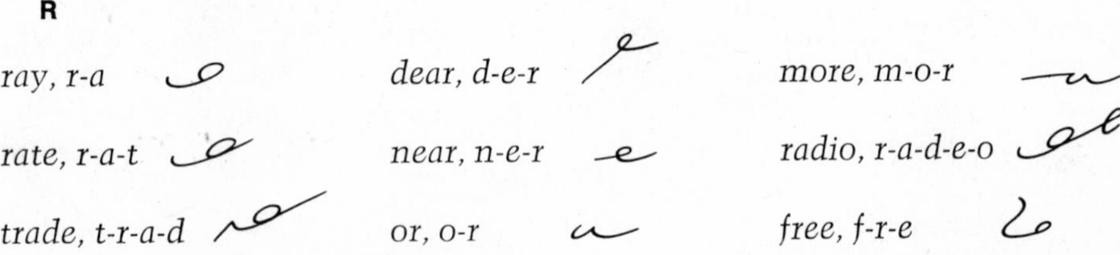

ray, r-a | *dear, d-e-r* | *more, m-o-r*
rate, r-a-t | *near, n-e-r* | *radio, r-a-d-e-o*
trade, t-r-a-d | *or, o-r* | *free, f-r-e*

L

lay, l-a | *mail, m-a-l* | *leaves, l-e-v-s*

late, l-a-t | *deal, d-e-l* | *low, l-o*

ail, a-l | *feel, f-e-l* | *flow, f-l-o*

▶ Notice that *f-r*, as in *free*, and *f-l*, as in *flow*, are written with one sweep of the pen, with no stop between the *f* and the *r* or *l*.

free *flow*

12 H, -ing

The letter *h* is simply a dot placed above the vowel. With few exceptions, *h* occurs at the beginning of a word.

Ing, which almost always occurs at the end of a word, is also expressed by a dot.

H

he, h-e | *hear, h-e-r* | *hole, h-o-l*

-ing

reading, r-e-d-ing | *hearing, h-e-r-ing* | *heeding, h-e-d-ing*

13 Long Ī

The shorthand stroke for the long sound of *ī*, as in *high*, is a large broken circle.

I

high, h-ī | *write (right), r-ī-t* | *fine, f-ī-n*

tire, t-ī-r | *my, m-ī* | *side, s-ī-d*

light, l-ī-t | *might, m-ī-t* | *line, l-ī-n*

14 Omission of Minor Vowels

Some words contain vowels that are slurred or not pronounced at all in ordinary speech. For example, the word *even* is really pronounced *e-vn*; the word *meter* is pronounced *met-r*. These vowels may be omitted if they do not contribute to speed or readability.

even, e-v-n | *reader, r-e-d-r* | *later, l-a-t-r*

meter, m-e-t-r *motor, m-o-t-r* *dealer, d-e-l-r*

Reading Practice

With the aid of a few words written in longhand, you can now read the following sentences. Remember to spell each shorthand word aloud as you read it. Refer to the key when you cannot read a word.

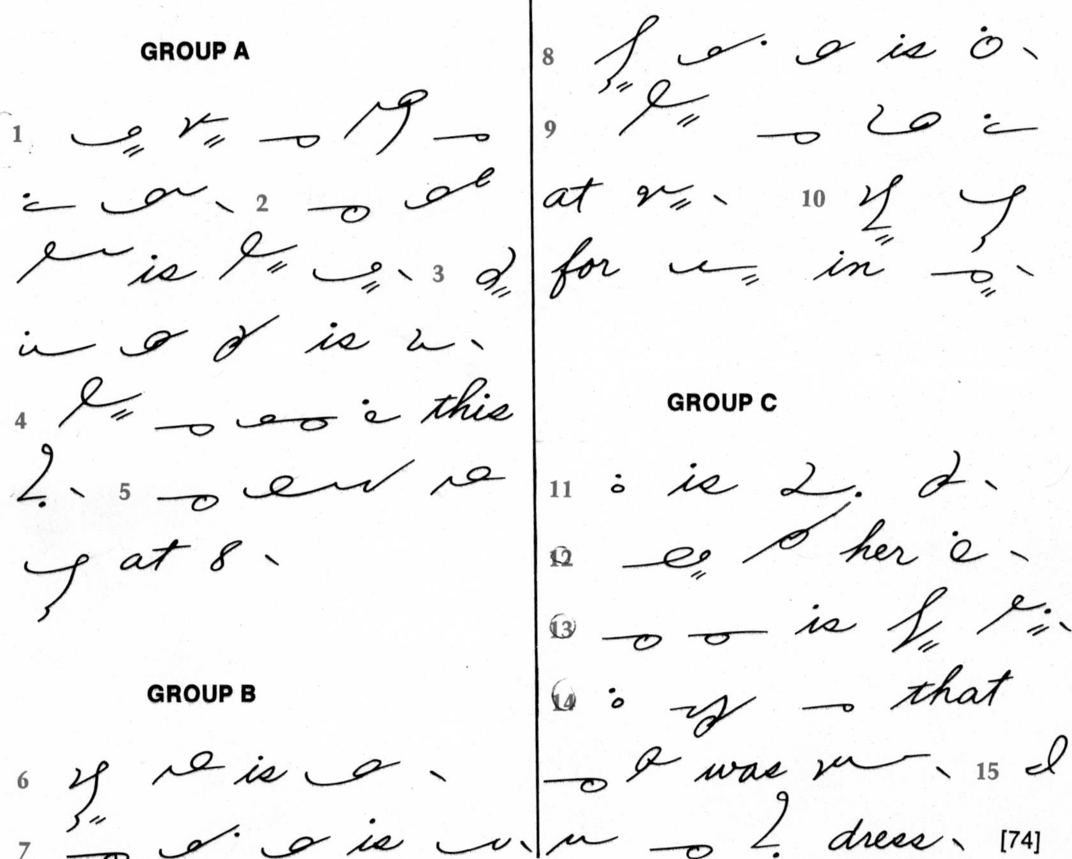

GROUP A 1. *Lee Stone may drive me home later.* 2. *My radio dealer is Dale Lee.* 3. *Fay's whole right side is sore.* 4. *Dale may remain here this evening.* 5. *My railroad train leaves at eight.* GROUP B 6. *Steve's train is late.* 7. *My reading rate is low.* 8. *Dave's reading rate is high.* 9. *Dale may fly home at Easter.* 10. *Steven leaves for Rome in May.* GROUP C 11. *He is feeling fine.* 12. *Mary dyed her hair.* 13. *My name is David Dearing.* 14. *He notified me that my tire was stolen.* 15. *I tore my evening dress.*

Principles

15 Alphabet Review

Here are the strokes you studied in Lesson 1 and 2. How fast can you read them?

16 Brief Forms

The English language contains many words that are used over and over again. As an aid to rapid shorthand writing, special abbreviations, called *brief forms,* are provided for some of these words. For example, we write *m* for *am,* v for *have.*

You are already familiar with the process of abbreviation in longhand—you write Mr. for *Mister, Dr.* for *Doctor.*

Because these brief forms occur so frequently, you will be wise to learn them well!

I	*are, our, hour*	*am*
Mr.	*will, well*	*it, at*
have	*a, an*	*in,* not*

**In* is also used as a word beginning in such words as:

invite, in-v-ī-t   *indeed, in-d-e-d*   *inside, in-s-ī-d*

▶ Did you notice that some shorthand outlines have two or more meanings? You will have no difficulty selecting the correct meaning of a brief form when it appears in the sentence. The sense of the sentence will give you the answer.

17 Phrasing

By using brief forms for common words, we are able to save writing time. Another device that helps save writing time is called *phrasing,* or the writing of two or more shorthand outlines together. Here are a number of useful phrases built with the brief forms you have just studied.

I have	*I will not*	*he will not*
I have not	*I am*	*are not*
I will	*he will*	*in our*

18 Left S-Z

In Lesson 1 you learned one stroke for *s* and *z*. Another stroke is also used for *s* and *z* in order to provide an easy joining in any combination of strokes—a backward comma, which is also written downward. For convenience, it is called the *left s.*

At this point you need not try to decide which *s* stroke to use in any given word; this will become clear to you as your study of shorthand progresses.

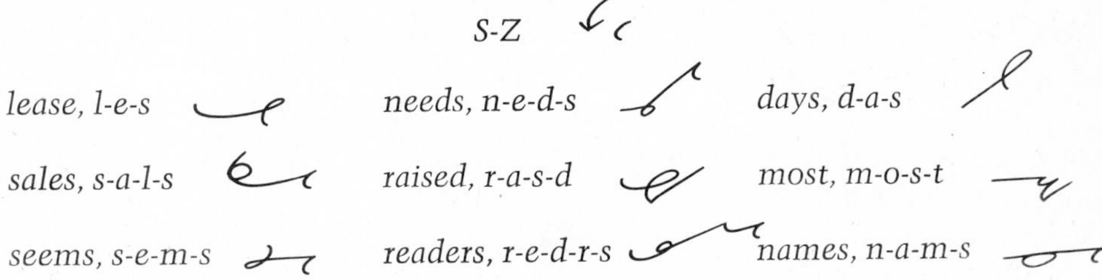

S-Z
lease, l-e-s
needs, n-e-d-s
days, d-a-s
sales, s-a-l-s
raised, r-a-s-d
most, m-o-s-t
seems, s-e-m-s
readers, r-e-d-r-s
names, n-a-m-s

19 P, B

The shorthand stroke for *p* is a downward curve the same shape as the left *s* except that it is larger—approximately half the height of the space between the lines in your shorthand notebook.

The shorthand stroke for *b* is also a downward curve the same shape as the left *s* and *p* except that it is much larger—almost the full height of the space between the lines in your shorthand notebook.

▶ Notice the difference in the sizes of the left *s*, *p*, and *b*.

S P B

P

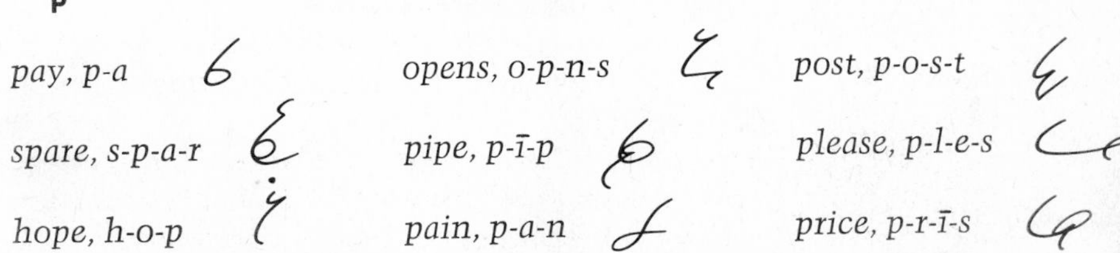

pay, p-a
opens, o-p-n-s
post, p-o-s-t
spare, s-p-a-r
pipe, p-ī-p
please, p-l-e-s
hope, h-o-p
pain, p-a-n
price, p-r-ī-s

B

bay, b-a	*beat, b-e-t*	*blame, b-l-a-m*
base, b-a-s	*bright, b-r-ī-t*	*neighbor, n-a-b-r*
boat, b-o-t	*brief, b-r-e-f*	*label, l-a-b-l*

▶ Notice that the combinations *p-r*, as in *price*; *p-l*, as in *please*; *b-r*, as in *brief*, and *b-l*, as in *blame*, are written with one sweep of the pen without a pause between the *p* or *b* and the *r* or *l*.

price *please* *brief* *blame*

Reading Practice

You can already read sentences written entirely in shorthand.

Suggestion Before you start your work on this Reading Practice, read the practice procedures for reading shorthand on page 10.

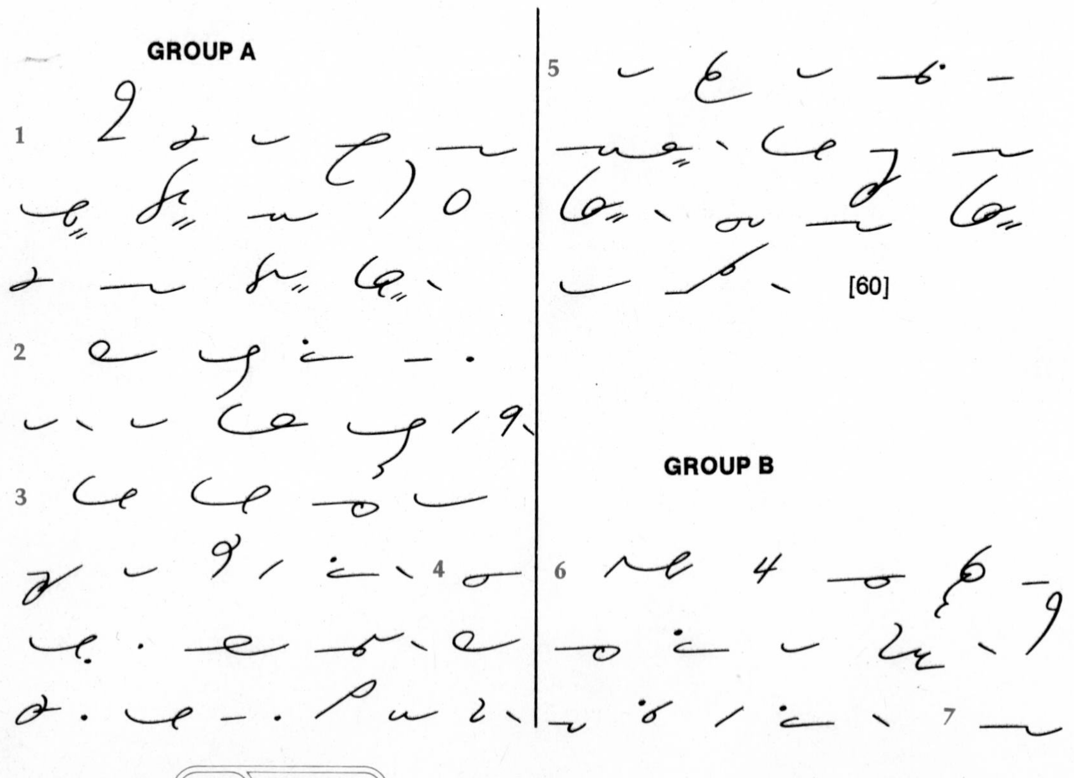

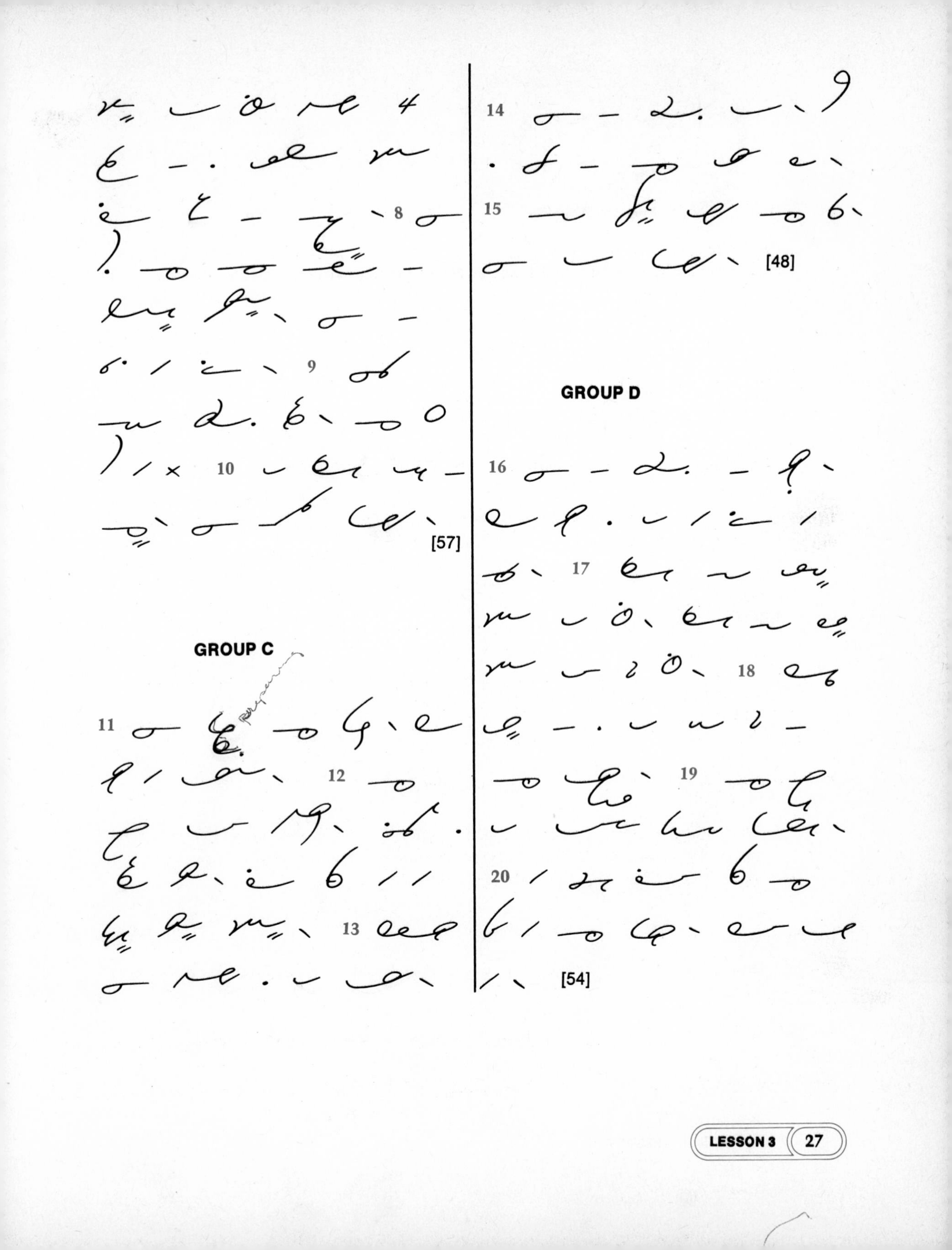

8

9

10

[57]

GROUP C

11

12

13

14

15

[48]

GROUP D

16

17

18

19

20

[54]

Principles

20 Alphabet Review

Here is a review of the 17 shorthand strokes you studied in Lessons 1 through 3. How fast can you read them?

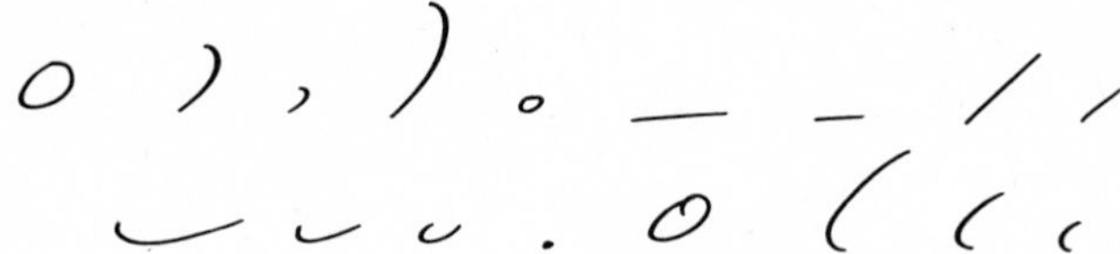

21 OO

The shorthand stroke for the sound of *oo,* as in *to,* is a tiny upward hook.

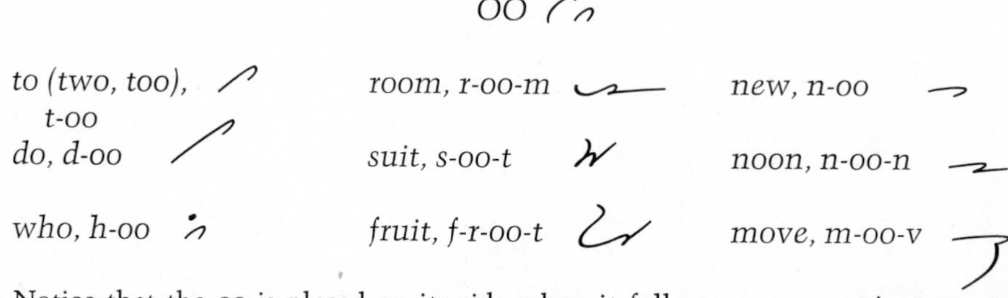

▶ Notice that the *oo* is placed on its side when it follows *n* or *m,* as in *new, noon, move.* By placing the hook on its side in these combinations rather than writing it upright, we obtain smooth joinings.

22 W, Sw

At the beginning of words *w,* as in *we,* is represented by the *oo* hook; *sw,* as in *sweet,* by *s-oo.*

we, oo-e   *wait, oo-a-t*   *sweet, s-oo-e-t*

way, oo-a   *waste, oo-a-s-t*   *swear, s-oo-a-r*

23 Wh

Wh, as in *why* and *while,* is also represented by the *oo* hook.

why, oo-ī — *white, oo-ī-t* — *while, oo-ī-l*

24 Useful Phrases

Here are a number of useful phrases that employ the *oo* hook.

we are — *we have* — *I do*

we will — *we may* — *I do not*

25 K, G

The shorthand stroke for *k* is a short forward curve.
The shorthand stroke for the hard sound of *g,* as in *game,* is a much longer forward curve. It is called *gay.*

Notice the difference in the size and shape of *oo, k,* and *gay.*

OO — *K* — *Gay*

K

take, t-a-k — *like, l-ī-k* — *week, oo-e-k*

make, m-a-k — *keep, k-e-p* — *clean, k-l-e-n*

cake, k-a-k — *care, k-a-r* — *increase, in-k-r-e-s*

Gay

gain, gay-a-n — *great, gay-r-a-t* — *go, gay-o*

game, gay-a-m — *grade, gay-r-a-d* — *goal, gay-o-l*

gave, gay-a-v — *green, gay-r-e-n* — *legal, l-e-g-l*

Notice that *k-r,* as in *increase,* and *gay-l,* as in *legal,* are written with a smooth, wave-like motion.

increase — *legal*

But *k-l,* as in *clean,* and *gay-r,* as in *green,* are written with a hump between the *k* and the *l* and the *gay* and the *r.*

clean — *green*

Reading Practice

The following sentences contain many illustrations of the new shorthand strokes you studied in Lesson 4. They also review the shorthand strokes, brief forms, and phrases you studied in Lessons 1 through 3.

Read these sentences aloud, spelling each shorthand outline that you cannot immediately read.

GROUP A

1

2

3

4

5

[43]

GROUP B

6

7

8

9

10

[41]

GROUP C

11

12

13

14

15

[48]

GROUP D

16

17

18

19

20

[51]

GROUP E

21

22

23

24

25

[47]

GROUP F

26

27

28

29

[29]

Principles

26 Alphabet Review

Here are all the shorthand letters you studied in Lessons 1 through 4. See how rapidly you can read them.

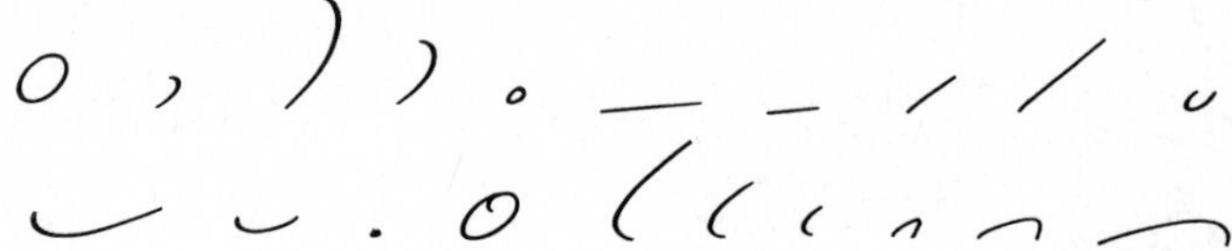

27 A, Ä

The large circle that represents the long sound of *ā,* as in *main,* also represents the vowel sounds heard in *as* and *park.*

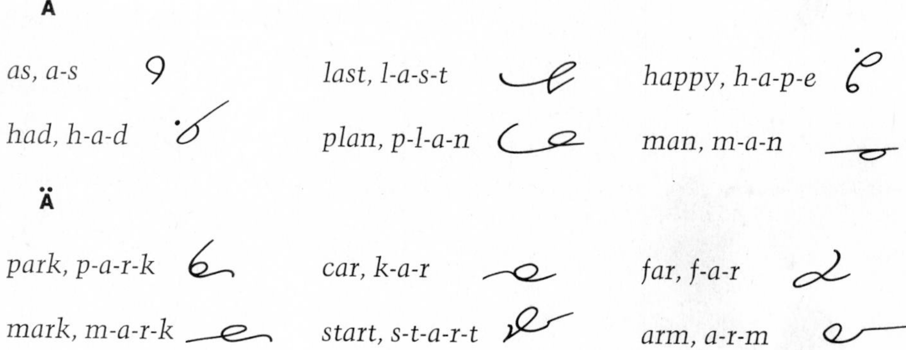

28 E, I, Obscure Vowel

The tiny circle that represents the sound of *ē,* as in *heat,* also represents the vowel sounds heard in *best, him,* and the obscure vowel sound heard in *her, hurt.*

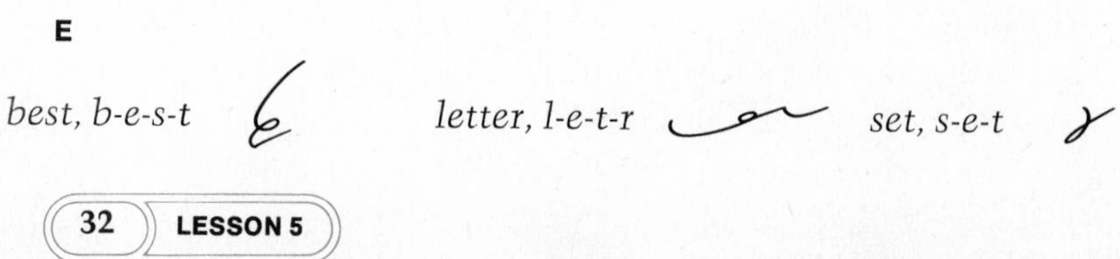

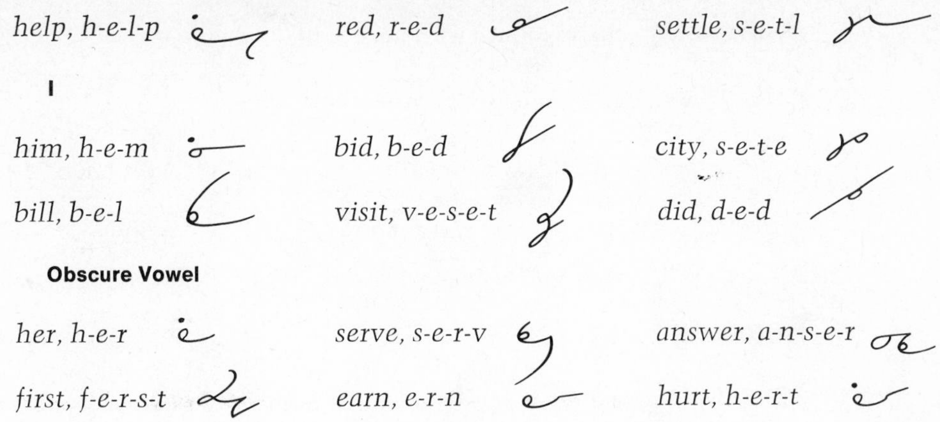

29 Th

Two tiny curves, written upward, are provided for the sounds of *th*. These curves are called *ith*.

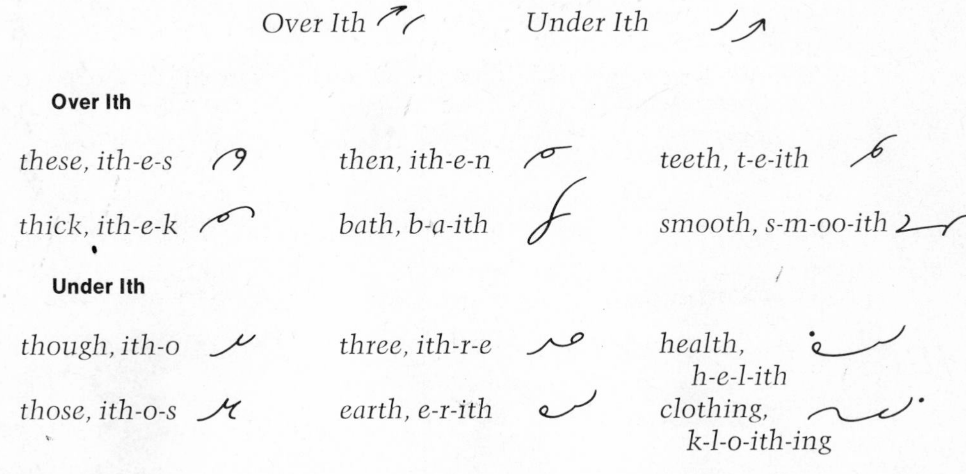

30 Brief Forms

Here is another group of brief forms for very frequently used business words. Learn them well.

is, his   *can*   *of*

the   *you, your*   *with*

that   *Mrs.*   *but*

31 Phrases

Here are useful phrases formed with some of these brief forms.

in the	*with you*	*do you*
of the	*you can*	*you have*
with the	*I cannot*	*you are*

Reading Practice

Your progress has been so rapid that you can already read business letters written entirely in shorthand.

32 Brief-Form Letter

This letter contains one or more illustrations of all the brief forms in this lesson.

[74]

33

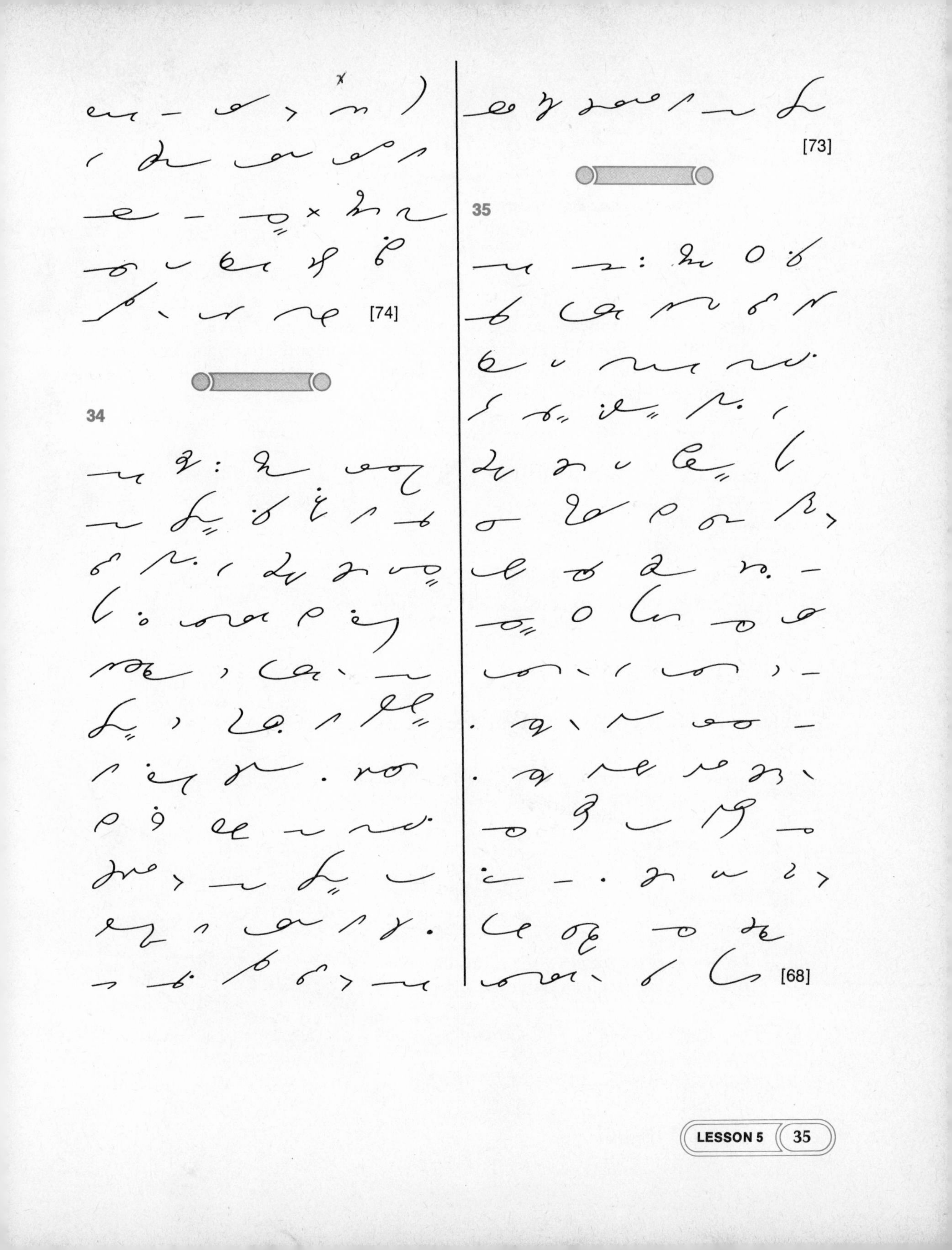

[74]

34

[73]

35

[68]

RECALL

Lesson 6 is a "breather." It contains no new strokes for you to learn. In this lesson you will find an Alphabet Review, a simple explanation of the principles that govern the joining of the strokes you studied in Lessons 1 through 5, a Recall Chart, and a Reading Practice employing the shorthand devices of Lessons 1 through 5.

36 Alphabet Review

Here are the shorthand strokes you studied thus far. Can you read them in 20 seconds or less?

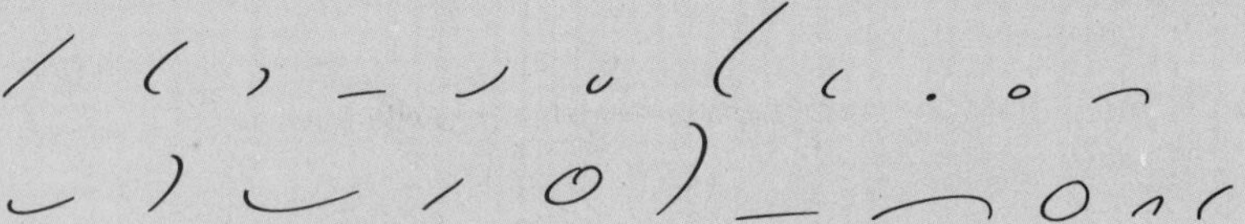

Principles of Joining

As a matter of interest, you might like to know the principles by which the words you have already learned are written. Notice the groups into which the joinings naturally fall.

37 Circles are written inside curves and outside angles.

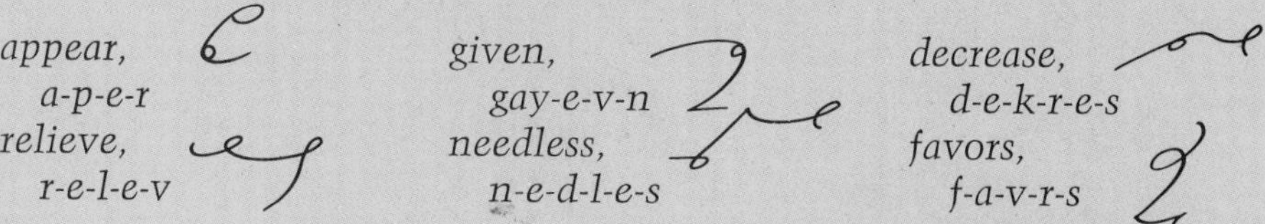

appear, *a-p-e-r* — *given,* *gay-e-v-n* — *decrease,* *d-e-k-r-e-s*

relieve, *r-e-l-e-v* — *needless,* *n-e-d-l-e-s* — *favors,* *f-a-v-r-s*

38 Circles are written clockwise (in this direction) on a straight line or between two straight strokes in the same direction.

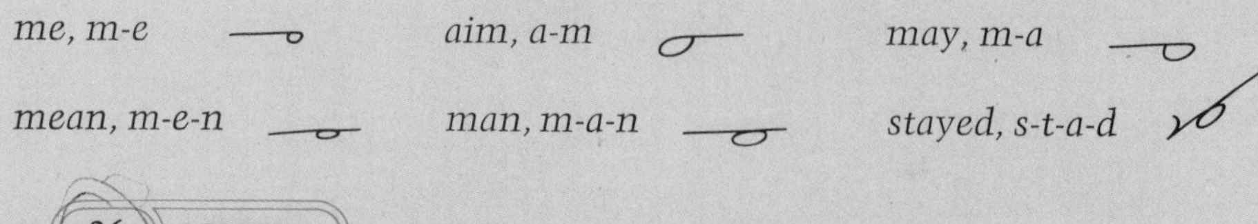

me, m-e — *aim, a-m* — *may, m-a*

mean, m-e-n — *man, m-a-n* — *stayed, s-t-a-d*

39 Between two curves written in opposite directions, the circle is written on the back of the first curve.

gear, gay-e-r   *wreck, r-e-k*   *pave, p-a-v*

care, k-a-r   *leg, l-e-gay*   *vapor, v-a-p-r*

40 The *o* hook is written on its side before *n, m* unless a downward character comes before the hook.

owns, o-n-s   *loan, l-o-n*   *homes, h-o-m-s*

but

bone, b-o-n   *zone, s-o-n*   *phone, f-o-n*

41 The *oo* hook is written on its side after *n, m.*

news, n-oo-s   *noon, n-oo-n*   *moved, m-oo-v-d*

42 The over *ith* is used in most words, but when *ith* is joined to *o, r, l,* the under *ith* is used.

these, ith-e-s   *both, b-o-ith*   *throw, ith-r-o*

43 Recall Chart

The following chart reviews the shorthand devices you studied in Lessons 1 through 5. It is divided into three parts: words, brief forms, and phrases.

Spell each word aloud thus: *ith-r-o, throw.* You need not spell the brief forms and phrases.

There are 84 shorthand outlines in the chart. Can you read the entire chart in 10 minutes or less?

WORDS

1						
2						
3						
4						

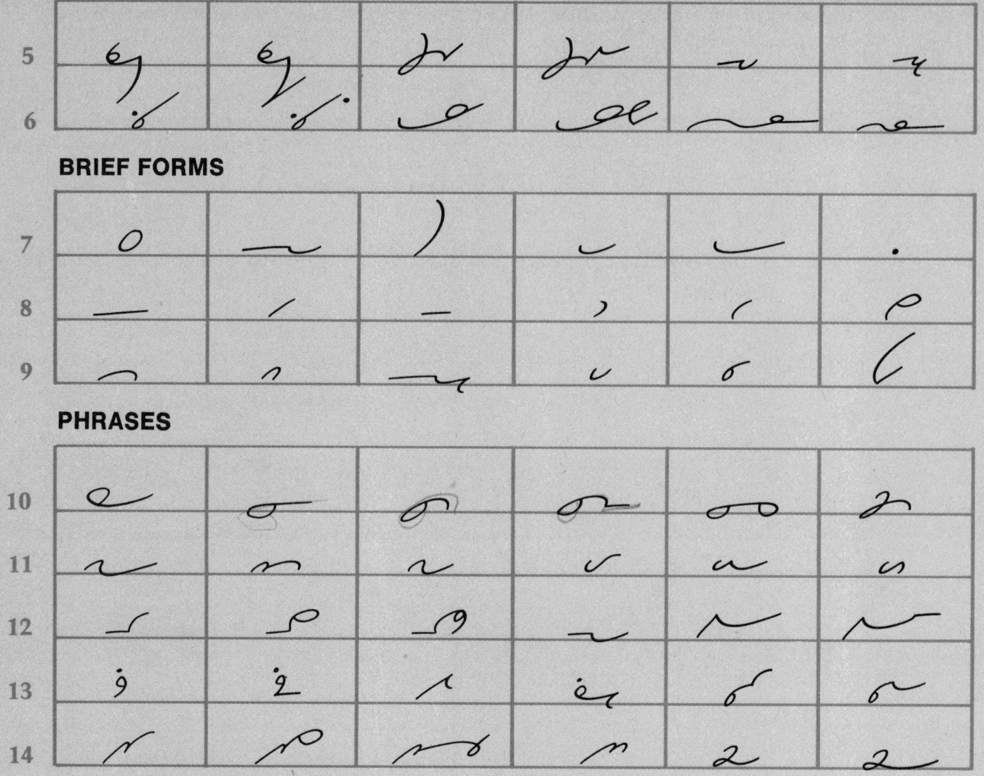

Reading Practice

44

[75]

45

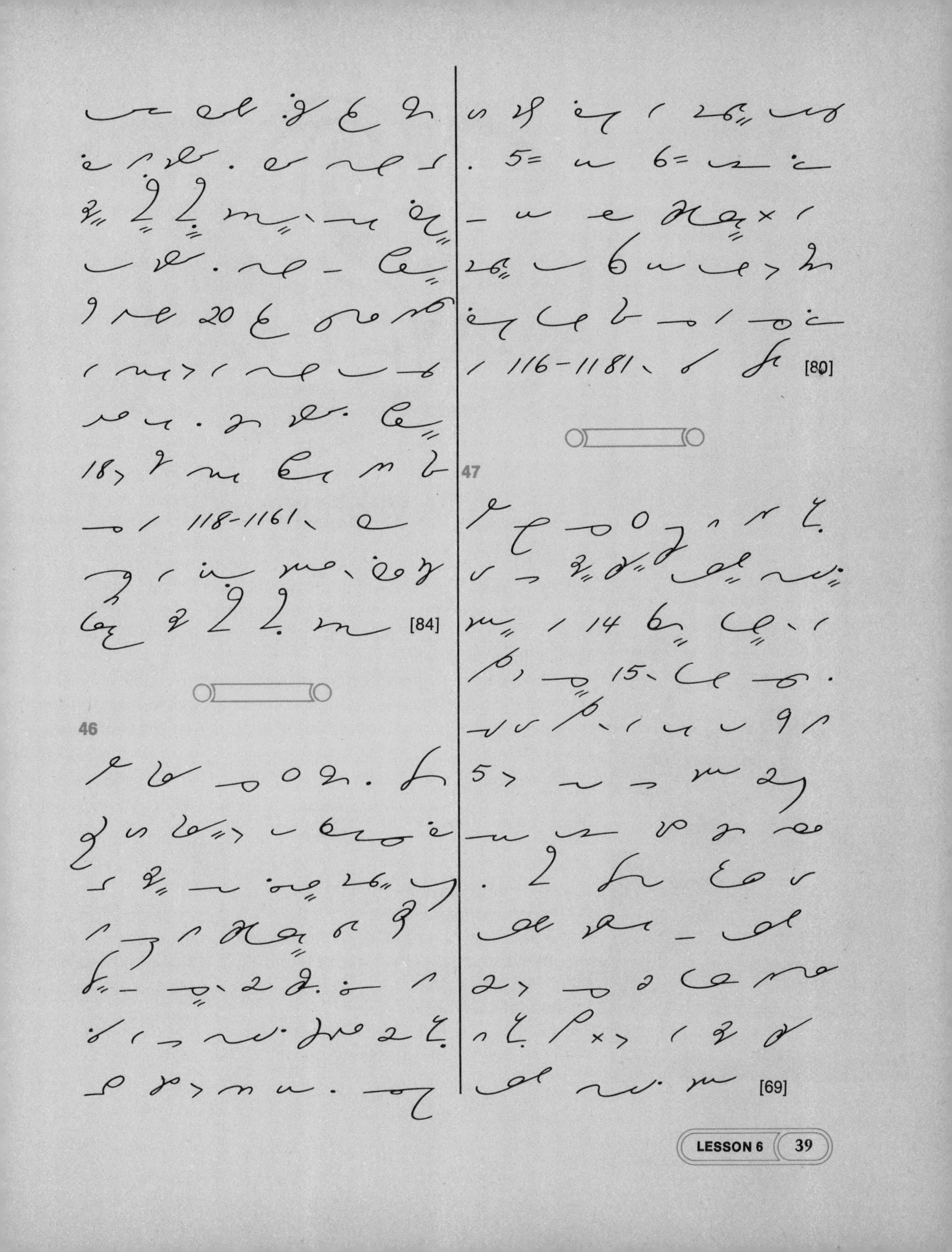

[84]

46

[80]

47

[69]

CHAPTER

Shorthand
A Vital Office Skill

Speedy communications are the heart of every modern business office. To keep business running smoothly, it is absolutely necessary to get information from one location to another quickly and accurately. Shorthand is the first step in the process of recording and transmitting information.

Let's take a peek at the activities in an office on an ordinary business day. We are listening to Mr. Johnson, the national product manager for a large distributor of electronic calculators, and his secretary, Ms. Rubin.

"Ms. Rubin, I have Mr. O'Brien on the phone from Los Angeles. Would you take down the revised specifications he has for the new line of calculators and then come into my office.

"Now, those specifications will have to be incorporated into the report, and copies of the revised report will have to be sent to all the regional managers immediately.

"Get a letter off special delivery to Mrs. Walters in Chicago and ask her to have her top engineer ready to revise the plans as soon as we get the specifications. After she has had a chance to discuss them with the engineer, ask her to let me know how extensive the changes will be.

"Ask Chuck to tell Lee Johnson that the final specs are in and will be ready for the national meeting next week. Make sure to send five copies by tomorrow afternoon.

"Get Albini and Pierce on the phone and tell them that they should be here the day before the meeting so that we can discuss the warehousing problems. I'll pick them up at the airport Monday afternoon.

"Call Mrs. Lopez in public relations and tell her that as soon as she gets the new specs, she can release the national campaign. Ask her if she needs any more pictures of the machine."

All this happened in less than three minutes. If the instructions given are not carried out correctly, many problems could arise. Since the flow of information may be like this all day in an office, these instructions must not be entrusted to memory. So many people and so many facts are involved, it would be too easy to confuse what Mr. Johnson just said. The information should be written. But in that short space of time, how can it all be recorded correctly?

The answer is with shorthand!

With the fast pace of business today, everyone who works in an office would benefit from the ability to take shorthand. For a secretary, however, it is a must! Whether working for an accountant or a zoologist, a secretary has to be prepared to listen to, to record, and to act upon an enormous amount of information daily. What office skill could make this task easier than shorthand?

Principles

48 Sh, Ch, J

The shorthand stroke for *sh* (called *ish)* is a very short downward straight stroke.
The shorthand stroke for *ch* (called *chay*) is a longer downward straight stroke approximately half the height of the space between the lines in your shorthand notebook.
The shorthand stroke for the sound of *j*, as in *jail* and *age,* is a long downward straight stroke almost the full height of the space between the lines in your shorthand notebook.

Note carefully the difference in the sizes of these strokes.

Ish *Chay* *J*

Ish

she, ish-e	*showed, ish-o-d*	*share, ish-a-r*
show, ish-o	*ship, ish-e-p*	*insure, in-ish-oo-r*

Chay

each, e-chay	*attach, a-t-a-chay*	*chair, chay-a-r*
teach, t-e-chay	*church, chay-e-r-chay*	*check, chay-e-k*

J

age, a-j	*page, p-a-j*	*change, chay-a-n-j*
large, l-a-r-j	*charge, chay-a-r-j*	*jail, j-a-l*

49 O, Aw

The small deep hook that represents the sound of *o,* as in *no,* also represents the vowel sounds heard in *hot* and *all.*

O

hot, h-o-t	*lot, l-o-t*	*stock, s-t-o-k*

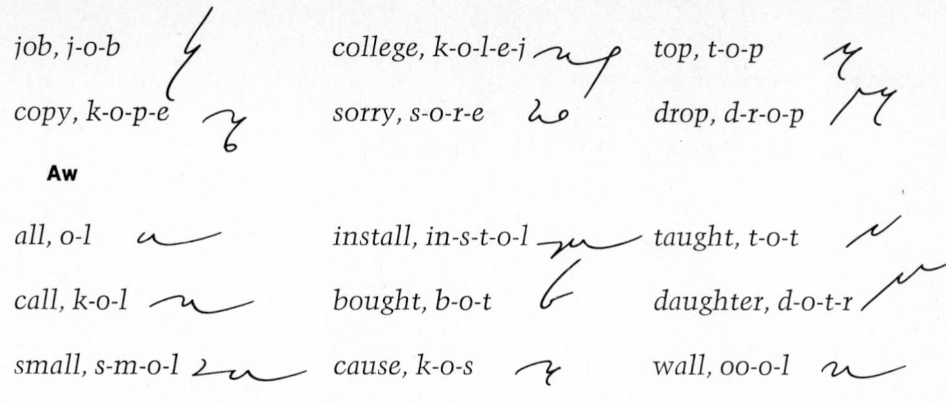

50 Common Business Letter Salutations and Closings

Dear Sir — *Yours truly* — *Yours very truly*

Dear Madam — *Sincerely yours* — *Very truly yours*

▶ Note: While the expressions *Dear Sir, Dear Madam,* and *Yours truly* are considered too impersonal by experts in letter writing, they are still used by many dictators. Therefore, special abbreviations are provided for them.

Building Transcription Skills

51 BUSINESS VOCABULARY BUILDER As a stenographer and secretary, you will constantly be working with words. Consequently, the larger the vocabulary you have at your command, the easier will be your task of taking dictation and transcribing.

To help you build your vocabulary at the same time that you are learning shorthand, a Business Vocabulary Builder is provided in Lesson 7 and in many other lessons that follow. The Business Vocabulary Builder consists of brief definitions of business words and expressions, selected from the Reading and Writing Practice, that should be part of your everyday vocabulary.

Be sure you understand the meaning of the words and expressions before you begin to work on the Reading and Writing Practice of the lesson.

Business Vocabulary Builder

vital Very important.

copier A machine for making printed copies.

obligate Bind; commit.

Reading and Writing Practice

Suggestion Before you begin your work on the letters in this Reading and Writing Practice, turn to page 10 and read the procedures outlined there for reading and writing shorthand. By following those key suggestions you will derive the greatest benefit from your practice.

52 Brief-Form Review Letter

This letter reviews the brief forms you studied in Lessons 3 and 5.

20 15 118-1151 25 [104]

53

[84]

54

18

[83]

55

[51]

56

20

1977

[61]

Principles

57 Brief Forms

Here is the third group of brief forms for frequently used words. Learn them well.

for	*this*	*which*
would	*good*	*them*
there (their)	*they*	*be,* by*

Be is also used as a word beginning in words such as *begin* and *believe.*

Spell: *be-gay-e-n, begin*

begin *believe* *because*

58 Word Ending -ly

The common word ending *-ly* is represented by the *e* circle.

Spell: *n-e-r-lē, nearly*

nearly	*fairly*	*sincerely*
only	*properly*	*mainly*
early	*mostly*	*daily*

Notice that the circle for *ly* in *daily* is added to the other side of the *d* after the *a* has been written.

59 Amounts and Quantities

In business you will frequently have to take dictation in which amounts and quantities are used. Here are some devices that will help you write them rapidly.

400	*$4*	*4 o'clock*
4,000	*$4,000*	*$4.50*
400,000	*$400,000*	*4 percent*

Notice that the *n* for *hundred* and the *ith* for *thousand* are placed underneath the figure.

Building Transcription Skills

60 Business Vocabulary Builder

brochure Booklet.

dry goods Textiles; ready-to-wear clothing.

cassettes Small plastic cartridges containing magnetic tape on reels.

Reading and Writing Practice

61 Brief-Form Letter

The following letter contains one or more illustrations of the brief forms presented in this lesson.

[97]

62

[93]

63

[102]

64

[52]

Principles

65 Word Ending -tion

The word ending *-tion* (also spelled *sion, cian,* or *shion*) is represented by *ish*.

Spell: s-e-k-shun, section

section · *vacation* · *national*

operation · *occasion* · *fashion*

collection · *nation* · *physician*

66 Word Endings -cient, -ciency

The word ending *-cient* (or *-tient*) is represented by *ish-t*; *-ciency*, by *ish-s-e*.

Spell: e-f-e-shun-t, efficient

p-r-o-f-e-shun-s-e, proficiency

efficient · *patient* · *proficiency*

67 T for To in Phrases

In phrases, *to* is represented by *t* when it is followed by a downstroke.

to be · *to plan* · *to place*

to have · *to fill* · *to see*

to pay · *to check* · *to say*

Building Transcription Skills

68 Business Vocabulary Builder

authorize To give permission to.

staggering Alternating.

sectional Local; regional.

collection agency An organization that collects past-due accounts.

Reading and Writing Practice

69 Brief-Form Review Letter

The following letter reviews the brief forms in Lesson 8 as well as many of the brief forms in Lessons 3 and 5.

[100]

70

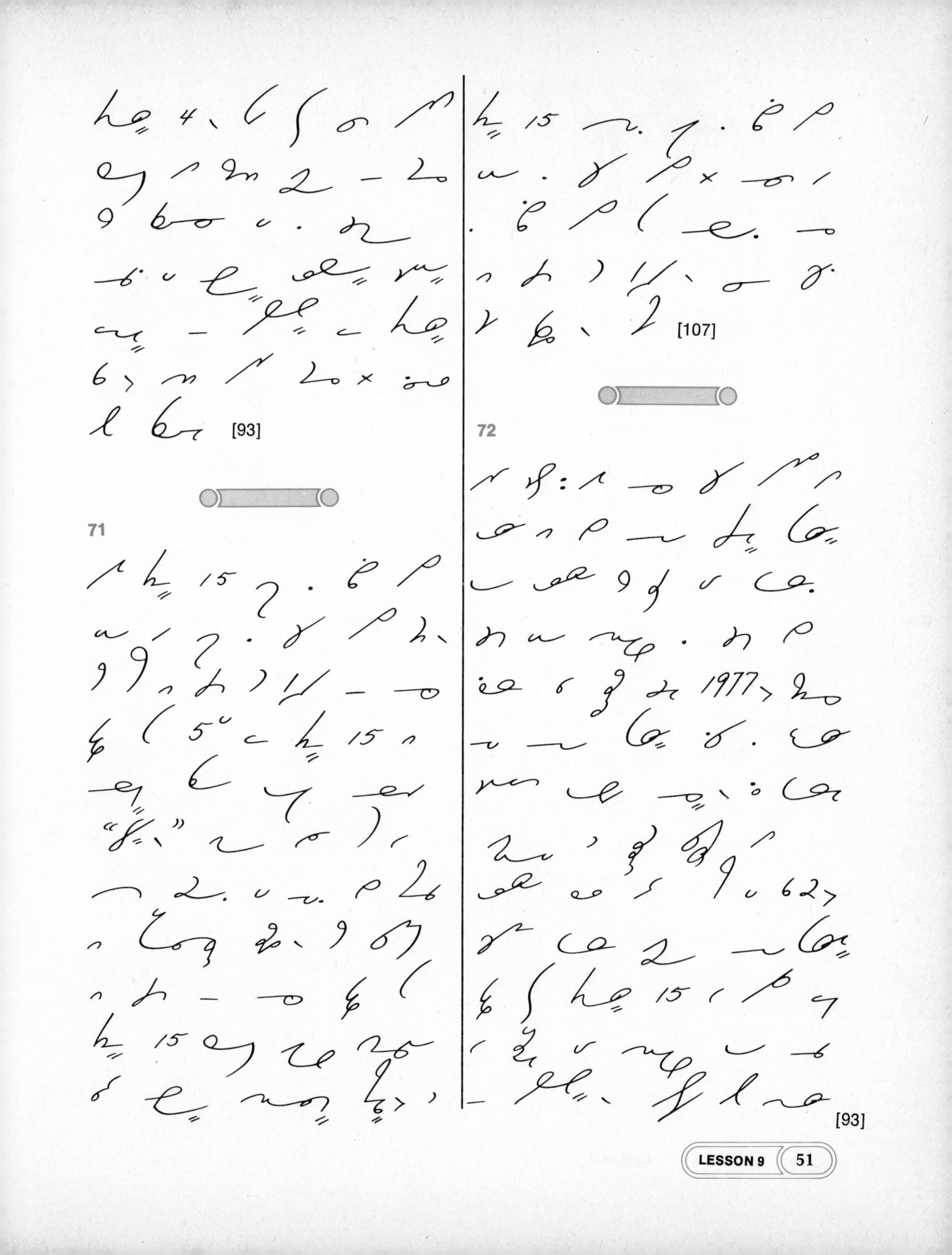

[93]

[107]

71

72

[93]

Principles

73 Nd

The shorthand strokes for *n-d* are joined without an angle to form the *nd* blend, as in *trained.*

Nd

Compare: *train* *trained*

Spell: *t-r-a-end, trained*

signed *land* *friend*

assigned *planned* *spend*

find *kind* *lined*

74 Nt

The stroke that represents *nd* also represents *nt,* as in *sent.*

Spell: *s-e-ent, sent; ent-oo, into*

sent *central* *agent*

print *current* *into*

rental *apparent* *entirely*

75 Ses

The sound of *ses,* as in *senses,* is represented by joining the two forms of *s.*

Compare: *sense* *senses*

face *faces*

Spell: s-e-n-sez, senses

senses	*services*	*necessary*
processes	*offices*	*promises*

76 Sis, Sus

The similar sounds of *sis,* as in *sister,* and *sus,* as in *versus,* are also represented by joining the two forms of *s.*

Spell: sez-t-r, sister; v-e-r-sez, versus

sister	*basis*	*assist*
analysis	*insist*	*versus*

Building Transcription Skills

77 Business Vocabulary Builder

processes *(noun)* Methods; procedures.

went astray Lost.

current Most recent.

● Reading and Writing Practice

78 Brief-Form Review Letter

This letter reviews all the brief forms you studied in Lesson 8.

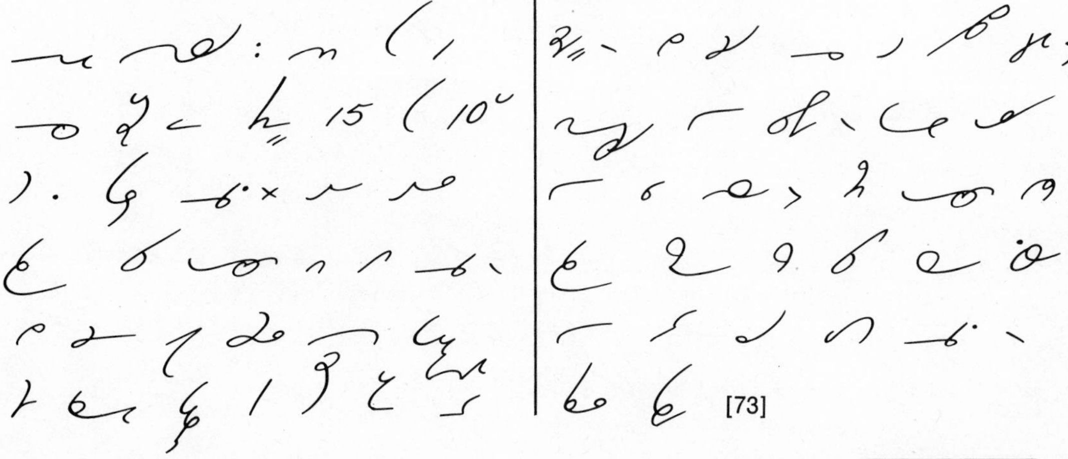

[73]

79

[98]

80

[64]

81

[94]

82

[48]

83

[76]

SHORTHAND READING CHECKLIST

When you read shorthand, do you—

- 1 Read aloud so that you know that you are concentrating on each outline that you read?
- 2 Spell each outline that you cannot immediately read?
- 3 Reread each Reading and Writing Practice a second time?
- 4 Occasionally reread the suggestions for reading shorthand given on pages 10 and 11?

Principles

84 Brief Forms

and	*should*	*after*
when	*could*	*street*
from	*send*	*were*

85 Rd

The combination *rd* is represented by writing *r* with an upward turn at the finish.

Compare: answer *answered*

Spell: a-n-s-e-ärd, answered; h-e-ärd, heard

prepared	*heard*	*record*
assured	*hard*	*recorded*
ignored	*harder*	*toward*

86 Ld

The combination *ld* is represented by writing the *l* with an upward turn at the finish.

Compare: call *called*

Spell: k-o-eld, called; o-eld, old

called	*failed*	*children*
held	*old*	*billed*
child	*told*	*folded*

87 Been in Phrases

The word *been* is represented by *b* after *have, has, had.*

had been · *I have been* · *it has been*

have been · *I have not been* · *should have been*

88 Able in Phrases

The word *able* is represented by *a* after *be* or *been.*

have been able · *has been able*

I have been able · *I should be able*

you have not been able · *you will be able*

Building Transcription Skills

89 **Business Vocabulary Builder**

plight Bad state or condition.

asset Advantage.

"on the drawing boards" In the planning stage.

ignored Neglected.

Reading and Writing Practice

90 Brief-Form Letter

The following letter contains one or more illustrations of every brief form in paragraph 84.

18 10

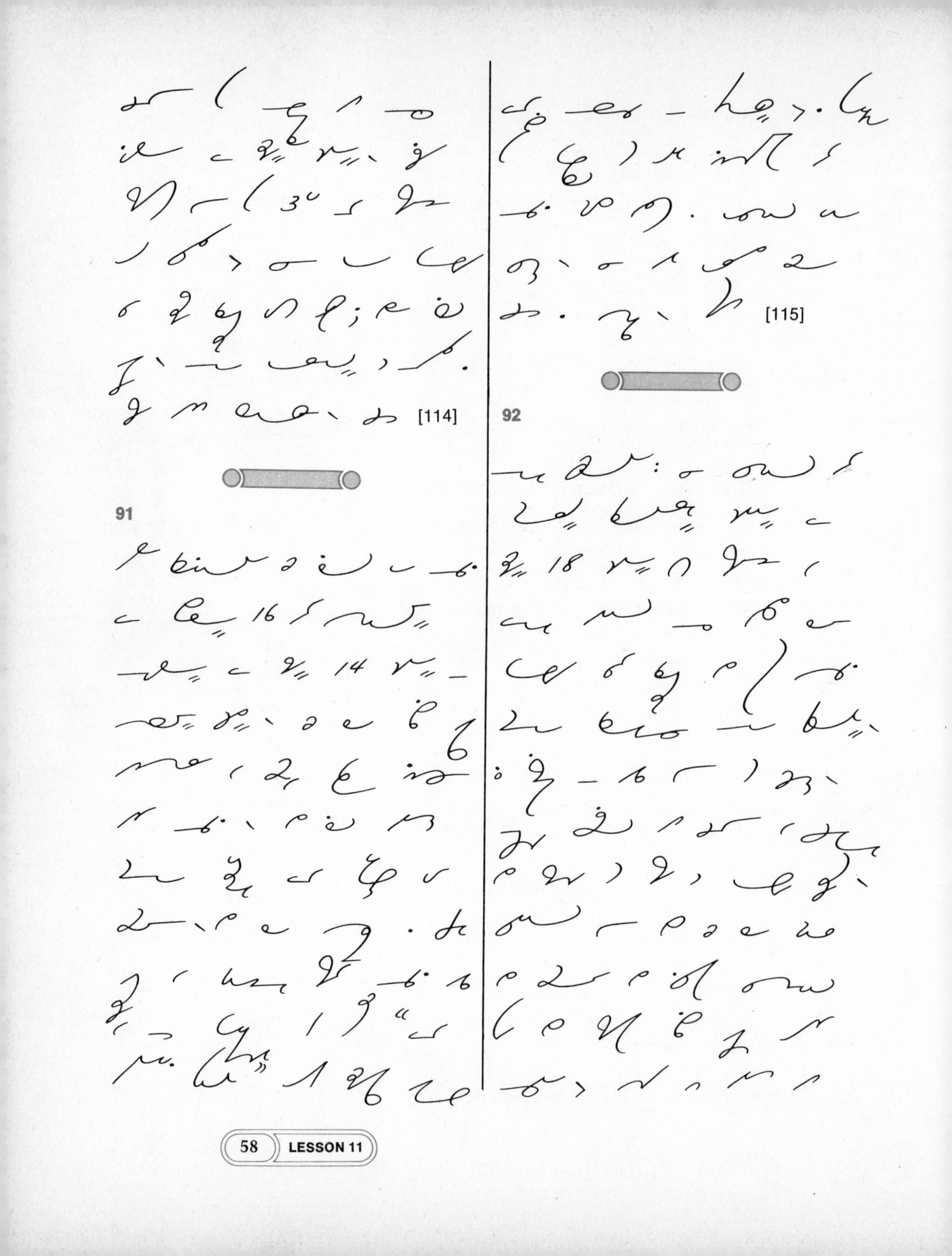

[114]

91

[115]

92

[92]

93

[77]

94

[65]

95

[56]

RECALL

Lesson 12 is another "breather" for you; it presents no new shorthand devices for you to learn. It contains a number of principles of joining, a helpful Recall Chart, and several short letters that you should have no difficulty reading.

Principles of Joining

96 At the beginning and end of words, the comma *s* is used before and after *f*, *v*, *k*, *g*; the left *s*, before and after *p*, *b*, *r*, *l*.

safes *globes* *sales*
sips *scares* *rags*

97 The comma *s* is used before *t*, *d*, *n*, *m*, *o*; the left *s* is used after those characters.

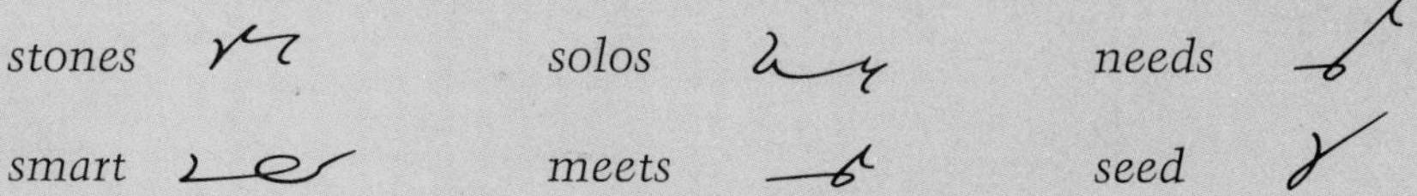

98 The comma *s* is used before and after *ish*, *chay*, *j*.

99 The comma *s* is used in words consisting of an *s* and a circle vowel or *s* and *ith* and a circle vowel.

see *these* *seethe*

100 Gregg Shorthand is equally legible whether it is written on ruled or unruled paper; consequently you need not worry about the exact placement of your outlines on the

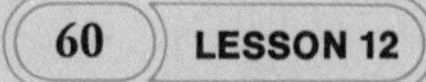

printed lines in your notebook. You will be able to read your outlines regardless of their placement on the printed line. The main purpose that the printed lines in your notebook serve is to keep you from wandering uphill and downhill as you write.

However, so that all outlines may be uniformly placed in the shorthand books from which you study, this general rule has been followed:

The base of the first consonant of a word is placed on the line of writing. When *s* comes before a downstroke, however, the downstroke is placed on the line of writing.

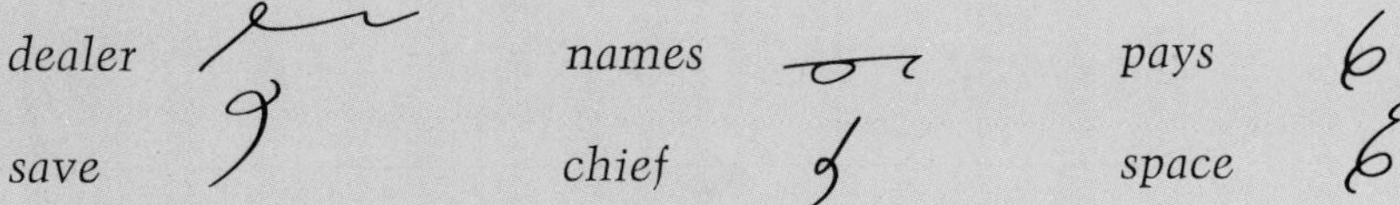

101 Recall Chart

The following chart contains all the brief forms presented in Chapter 2 and one or more illustrations of the shorthand principles you studied in Chapters 1 and 2.

Can you read the entire chart in 9 minutes or less?

BRIEF FORMS

1
2
3

PHRASES AND AMOUNTS

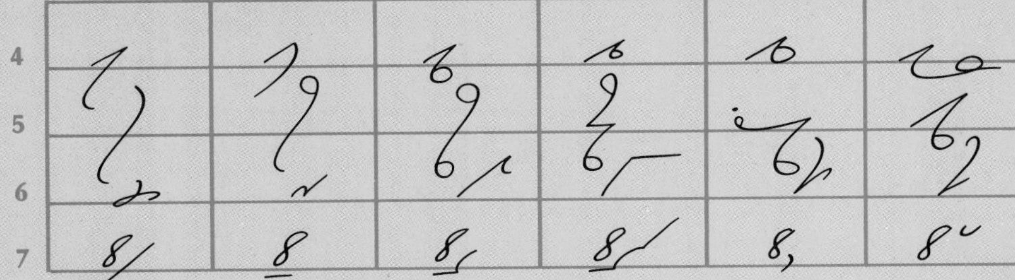

WORDS

8
9
10
11

12						
13						
14						

Building Transcription Skills

102 Business Vocabulary Builder

fee A charge.

leaflet A single printed sheet of paper.

glowing Showing elation or great satisfaction.

Reading and Writing Practice

103

[113]

104

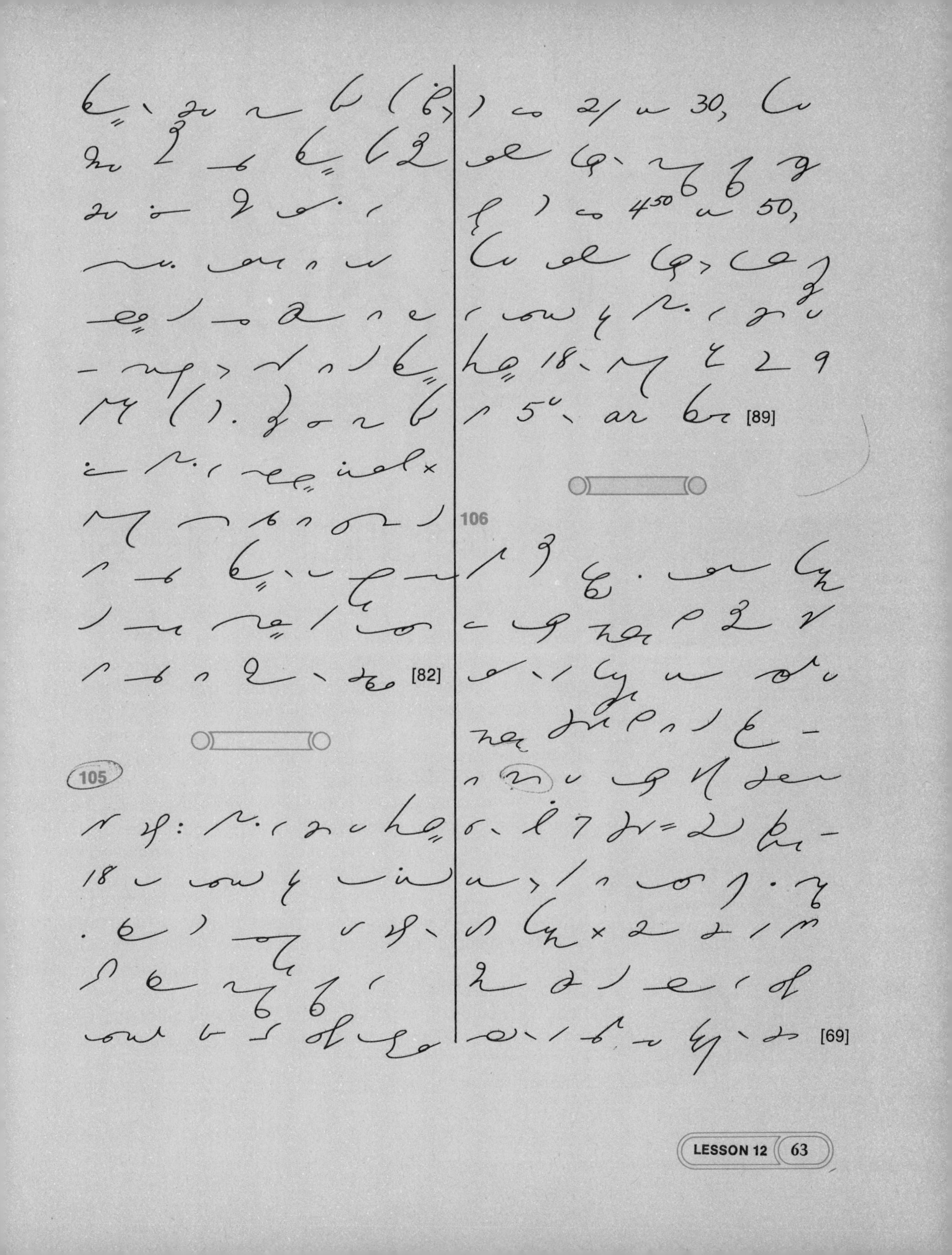

[82]

105

[89]

106

[69]

CHAPTER

3

The Secretarial Profession

A Brief History

The Bettmann Archive

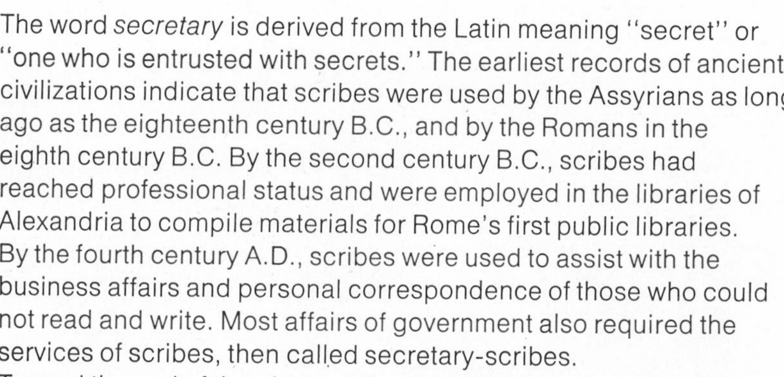

The word *secretary* is derived from the Latin meaning "secret" or "one who is entrusted with secrets." The earliest records of ancient civilizations indicate that scribes were used by the Assyrians as long ago as the eighteenth century B.C., and by the Romans in the eighth century B.C. By the second century B.C., scribes had reached professional status and were employed in the libraries of Alexandria to compile materials for Rome's first public libraries. By the fourth century A.D., scribes were used to assist with the business affairs and personal correspondence of those who could not read and write. Most affairs of government also required the services of scribes, then called secretary-scribes.

Toward the end of the nineteenth century, with the invention of the typewriter and the Gregg Shorthand system, many women became proficient in secretarial work and began to take over duties formerly performed by men. These "type-writers," as secretaries were then called, were trailblazers in business offices. They were eager to trade a life on the farm or in the factory for a very different life in a business office. Although their manner was quiet; their role, subservient; their dress, conservative; their pay, meager, the historical impact of these women was revolutionary. They were

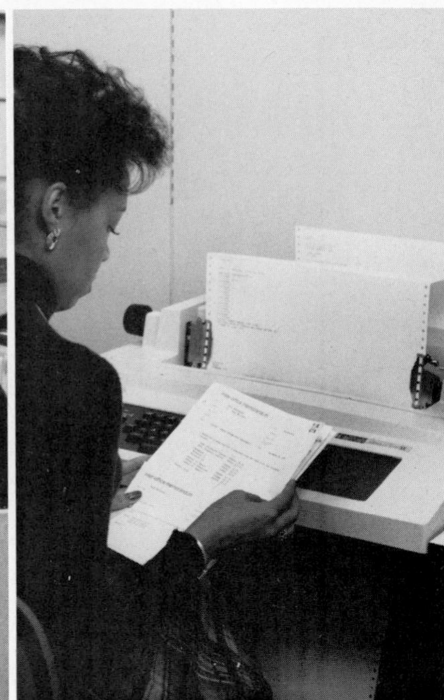

instrumental in changing the whole character of the business office. Today there are several million secretaries in the United States. Though the majority are women, many men are now choosing this as their profession. Secretaries' titles range from junior stenographer to administrative assistant; their work, from taking shorthand and transcribing verbatim notes on the typewriter to handling all administrative duties of a large modern business organization. Secretaries may work in many different kinds of places, from small, one-secretary offices to large communications centers in major cities. They may work for many executives or for only one. But their function is basically the same—keeping business running smoothly through the application of their secretarial skills and abilities.

The status of today's secretary ranks considerably higher than the status of a secretary 50 years ago. The secretary is really an executive aide who still does the traditional jobs of taking dictation, typing, filing, and handling calls and callers. But in many ways, today's secretary must know the job of the boss better than the boss does.

It has been said that behind every good executive there's a good secretary. Today there is a tremendous demand for good secretaries, and authoritative sources indicate that this demand will continue to grow. The secretary is an established and vital part of the structure of modern business.

Principles

107 Brief Forms

glad	circular	enclose
work	order	was
yesterday	soon	thank*

*In phrases, the dot is omitted from *thank*. *Thanks* is written with a disjoined left *s* in the dot position.

thank you	thank you for	thanks

108 U, OO

The hook that represents the sound of *oo*, as in *to*, also represents the vowel sounds heard in *does* and *book*.

U

Spell: d-oo-s, does

does	enough	us
drug	number	just
product	must	precious

▶ Notice: ■ 1 The hook in *enough, number,* and *must* is turned on its side;
■ 2 *oo-s* in *us, just, precious* join without an angle.

oo

Spell: b-oo-k, book

book		*full*		*took*	
put		*cook*		*foot*	
pull		*push*		*sugar*	

Building Transcription Skills

109 Business Vocabulary Builder

promotion pieces Circulars or bulletins advertising a company's products.

sketches Rough drawings.

major Greater in importance.

Reading and Writing Practice

110 Brief-Form Letter

All the brief forms in this lesson, or their derivatives, are used in this letter.

[98]

111

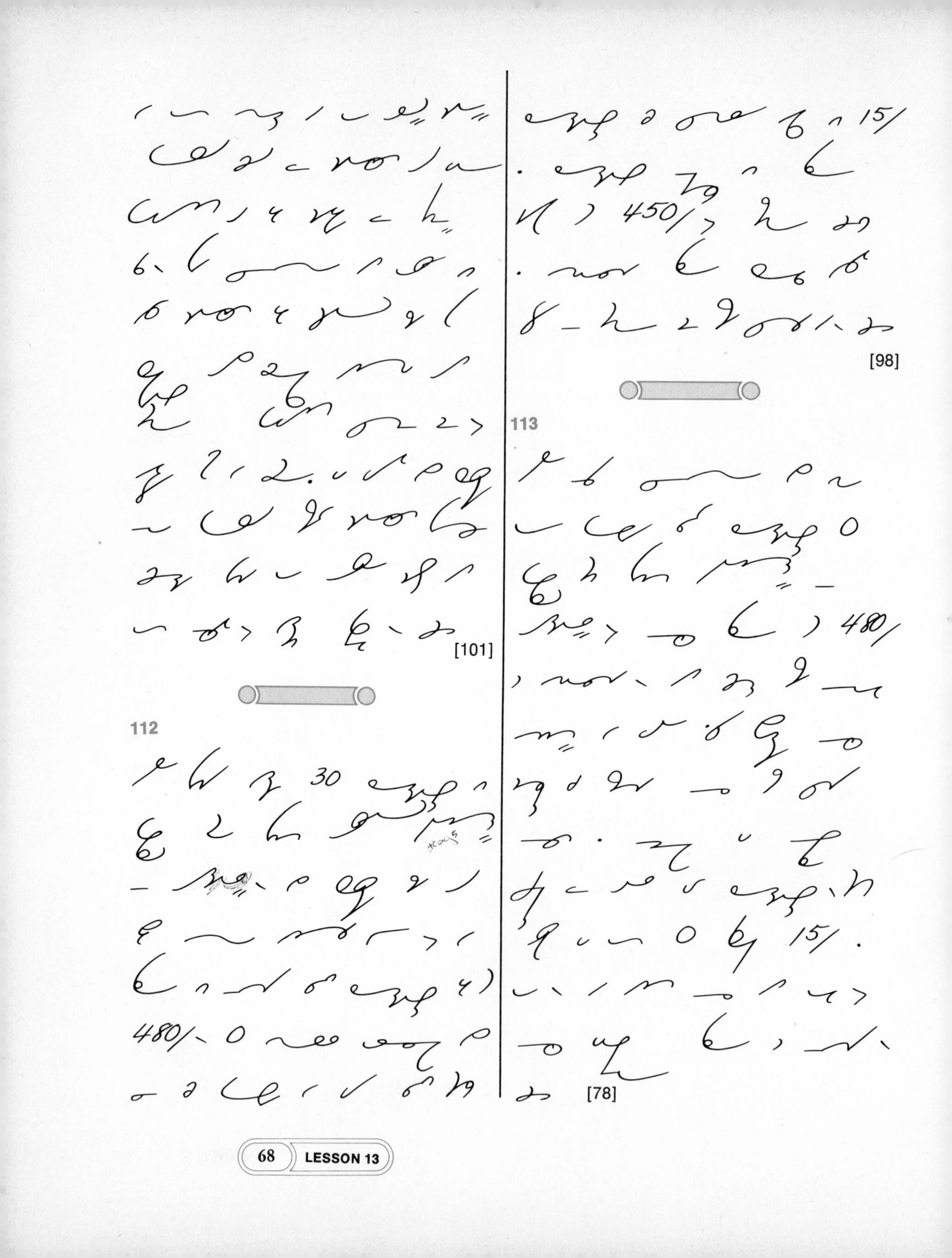

[101]

112

[98]

113

[78]

114

[66]

115

[109]

UP-AND-DOWN CHECKLIST *Do you always write the following strokes* upward?

■ 1 and   their (there)   ■ 2 it-at   would

Do you always write the following strokes downward?

■ 1 is-his   for   have   ■ 2 she   which

Principles

116 W in the Body of a Word

When the sound of *w* occurs in the body of a word, as in *quick,* it is represented by a short dash underneath the vowel following the *w* sound. The dash is inserted after the rest of the outline has been written.

Spell: k-oo-e-k, quick

quick	*between*	*qualify*
quit	*square*	*always*
quote	*hardware*	*Broadway*

117 Ted

The combination *ted* is represented by joining *t* and *d* into one long upward stroke.

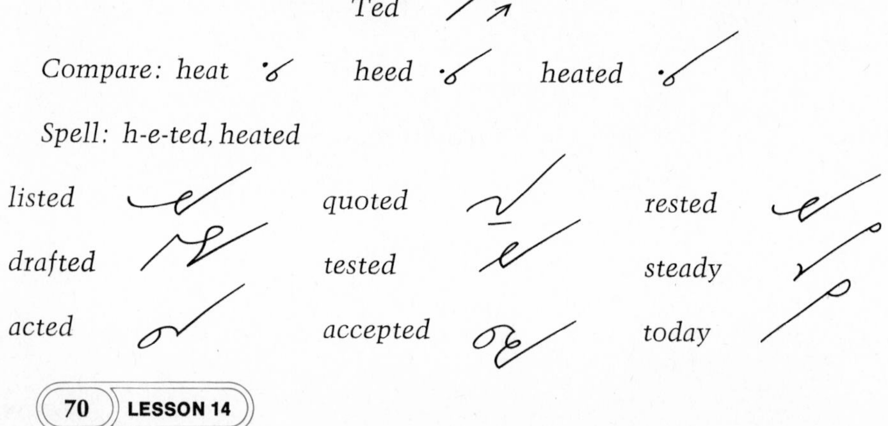

118 Ded

The long stroke that represents *ted* also represents *ded* and the similar sounds of *dit, det.*

Spell: gay-ī-ded, guided; det-a-l, detail

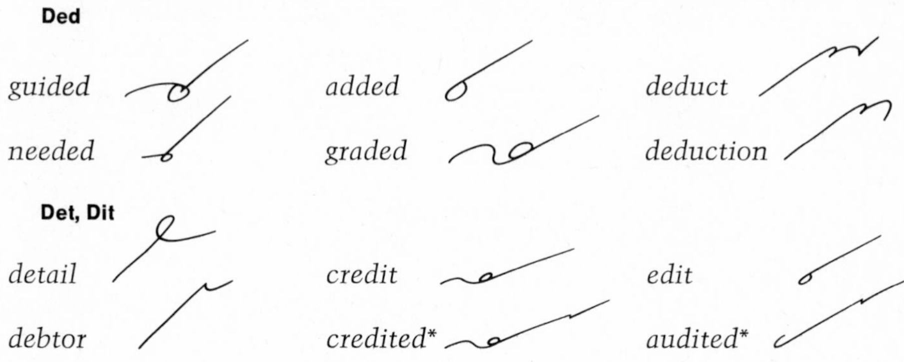

*Notice that the *d* representing the past tense is joined to *det* with a jog.

Building Transcription Skills

119 Business Vocabulary Builder

drafted Made a rough copy of.

applicant One who applies for a job.

fine arts Music, literature, painting, etc.

Reading and Writing Practice

120 Brief-Form Review Letter

This letter reviews all the brief forms you studied in Lesson 13 as well as many from earlier lessons.

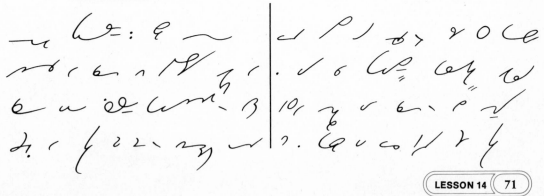

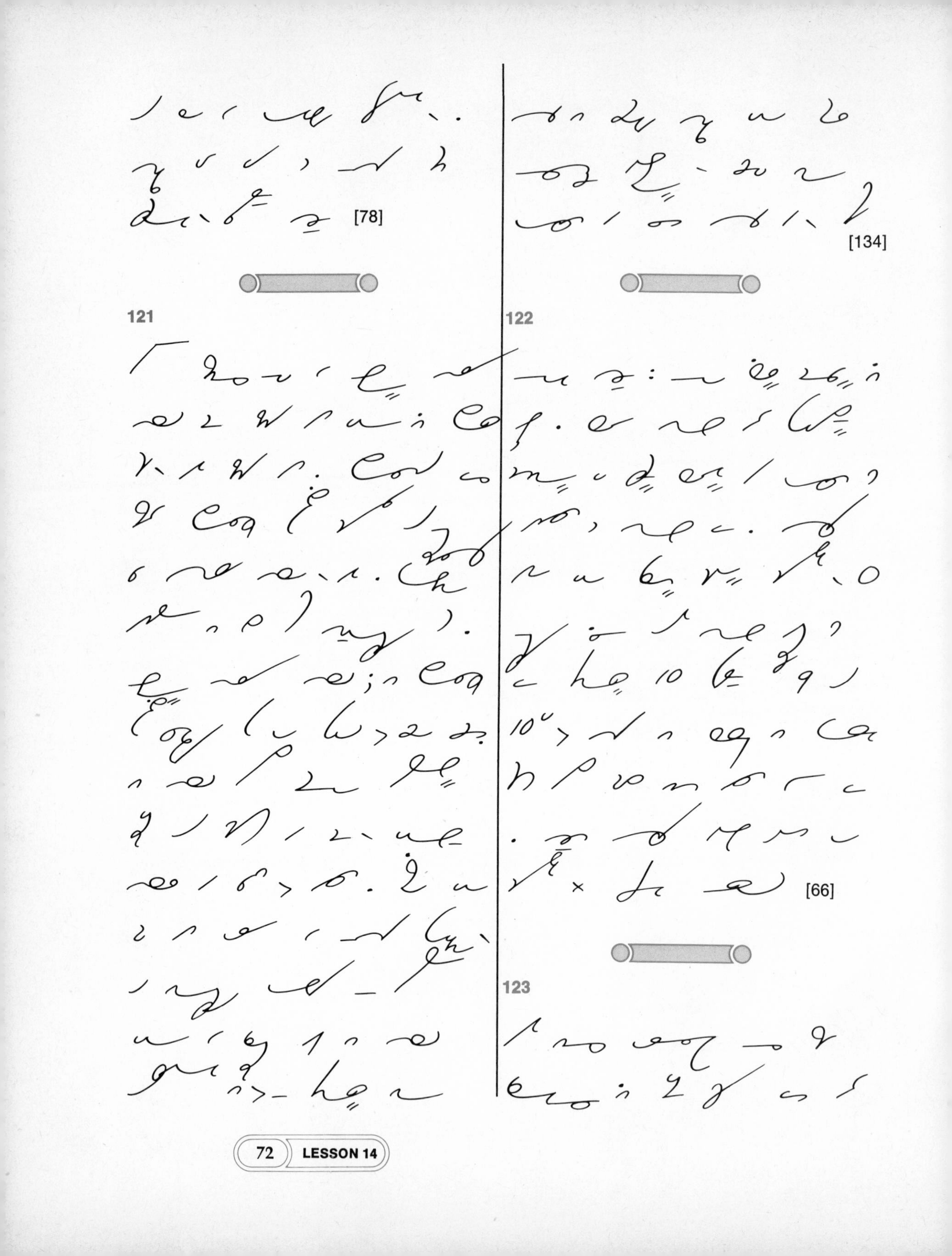

[78]

[134]

121

122

[66]

123

[90]

124

[139]

125

[39]

Principles

126 Brief Forms

value	*what*	*business*
than	*about*	*doctor*
one (won)	*thing, think*	*any*

127 Brief-Form Derivatives

once	*thinking*	*businessman*
things, thinks	*anything*	*businesses*

▶ Notice that a disjoined left *s* is used to express *things, thinks;* that the plural of *business* is formed by adding a left *s.*

128 Word Ending -ble

The word ending *-ble* is represented by *b.*

Spell: p-o-s-bul, *possible*

possible	*available*	*table*
capable	*favorable*	*trouble*
reliable	*sensible*	*troubled*

129 Word Beginning Re-

The word beginning *re-* is represented by *r*.

Spell: re-s-e-v, receive

receive	*resigned*	*reasonable*
replace	*reception*	*reappear*
research	*repairs*	*reopen*

Building Transcription Skills

130 Business Vocabulary Builder

queries Questions.

resigned Quit; gave up one's position.

patient *(adjective)* Bearing pains or trials without complaint.

Reading and Writing Practice

131 Brief-Form Letter

All the brief forms in Lesson 15, or derivatives of them, are used at least once in this letter.

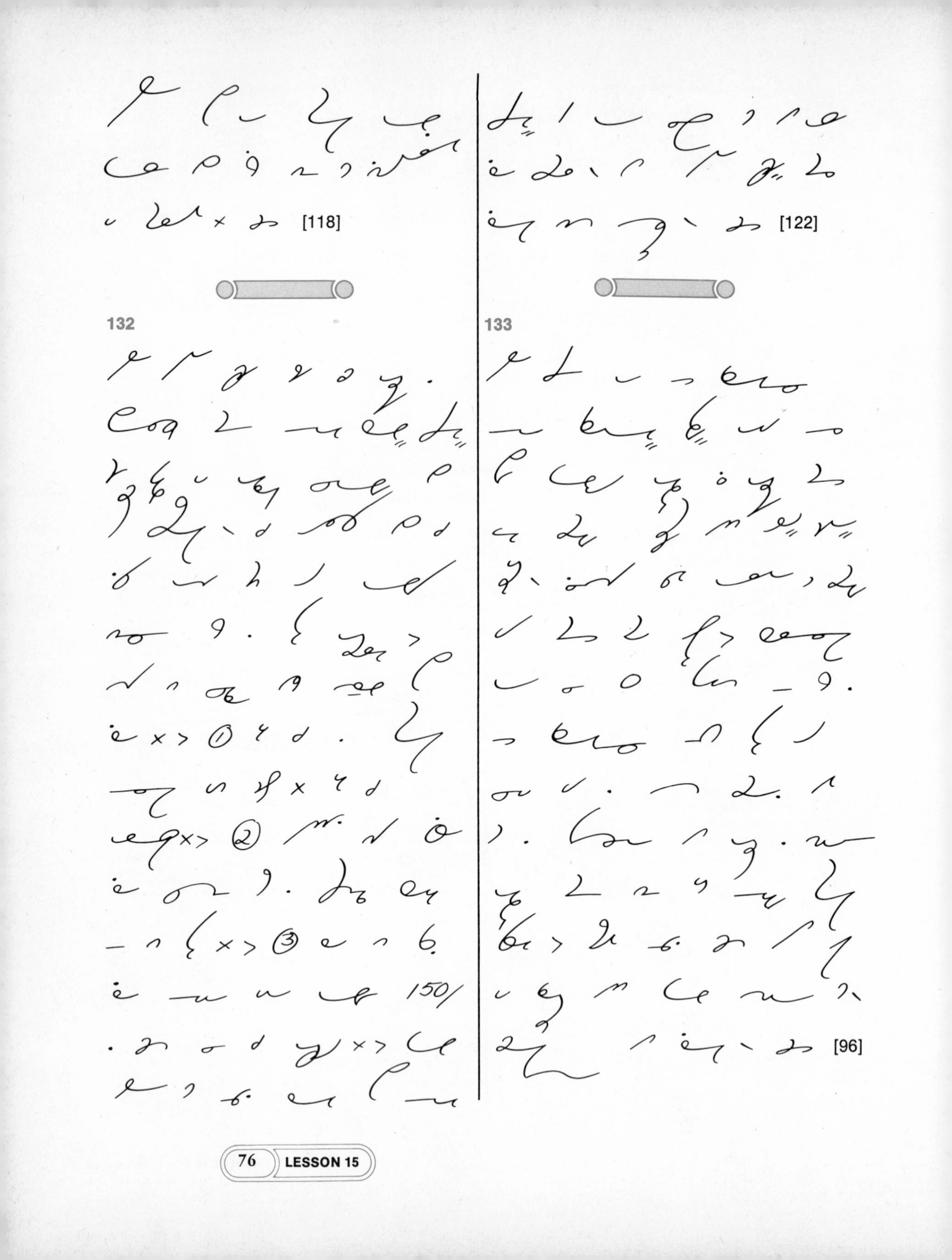

[118]

[122]

132

133

150

[96]

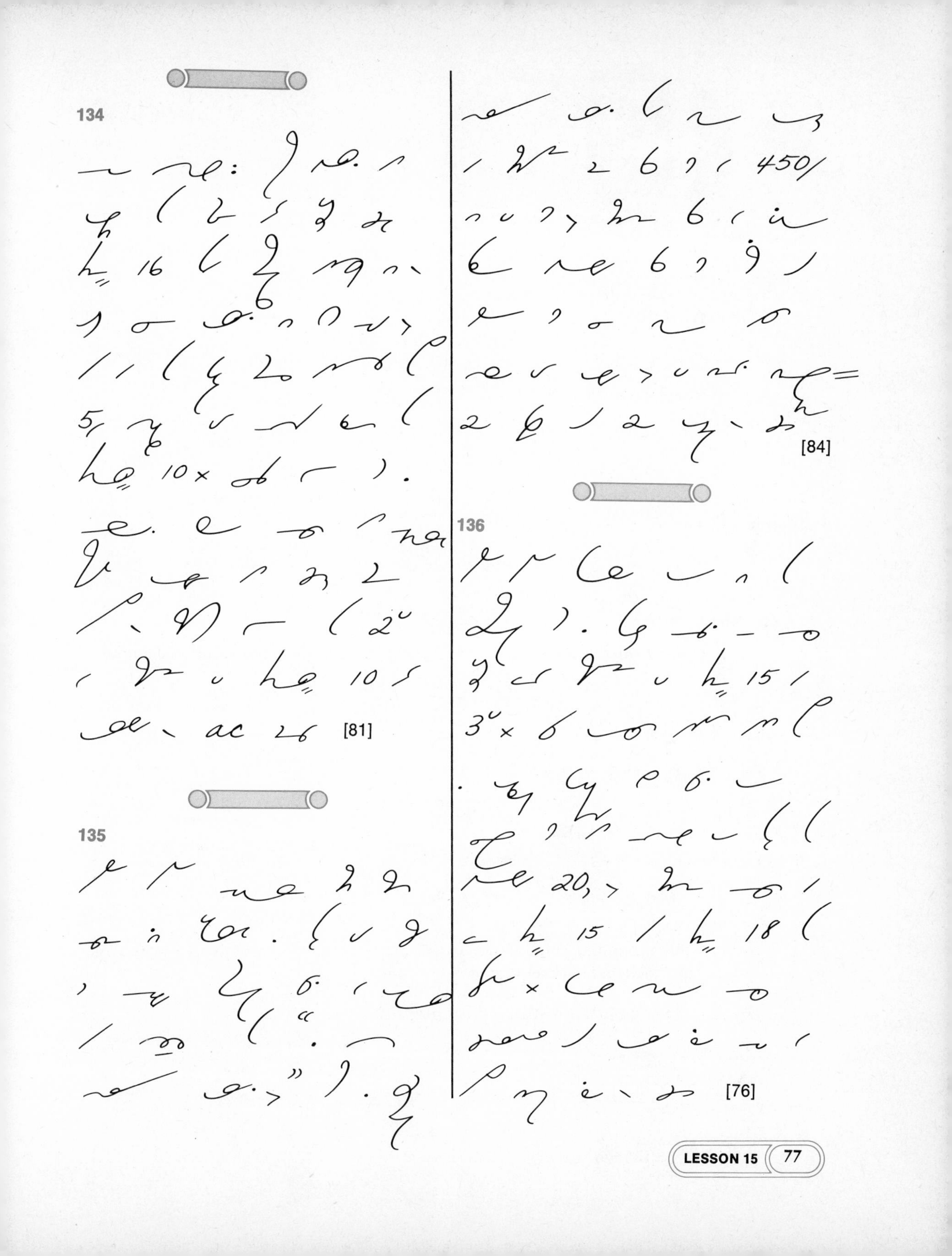

134

[81]

135

[84]

136

[76]

Principles

137 Oi

The sound of *oi,* as in *toy,* is represented by [shorthand].

Spell: *t-oi, toy*

toy	[shorthand]	*oil*	[shorthand]	*join*	[shorthand]
boy	[shorthand]	*soil*	[shorthand]	*noise*	[shorthand]
invoice	[shorthand]	*appoint*	[shorthand]	*royal*	[shorthand]

138 Men

The sound of *men* is represented by joining *m* and *n* into one long forward stroke.

Men [shorthand]

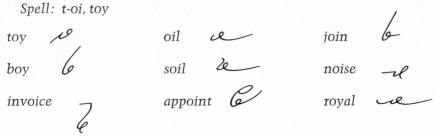

Compare: knee [shorthand] *me* [shorthand] *many* [shorthand]

Spell: *men-e, many*

men	[shorthand]	*mentioned*	[shorthand]	*mental*	[shorthand]
many	[shorthand]	*meant*	[shorthand]	*women*	[shorthand]

139 Min, Mon, Man

The similar sounding combinations *min, mon, man* are also represented by the long forward stroke that represents *men.*

Spell: *men-e-t, minute; men-r, manner*

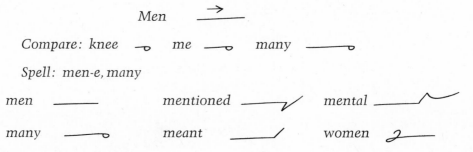

minute	[shorthand]	*monthly*	[shorthand]	*manager*	[shorthand]
month	[shorthand]	*money*	[shorthand]	*manner*	[shorthand]

140 Ye, Ya

Ye, as in *year,* is represented by the *e* circle; *ya,* as in *yard,* by the *a* circle.

Spell: e-r, year; a-ärd, yard

Ye

year	*yes*	*yield*
yet	*yellow*	*yielded*

Ya

yard	*yarn*	*Yale*

Building Transcription Skills

141 Business Vocabulary Builder

craftsmen Workers who practice a trade or handicraft.
net profit Amount remaining after the deduction of expenses.
sizable Fairly large; considerable.
decade Ten years.

● Reading and Writing Practice

142 Brief-Form Review Letter

This letter reviews all the brief forms you studied in Lesson 15 as well as many from earlier lessons.

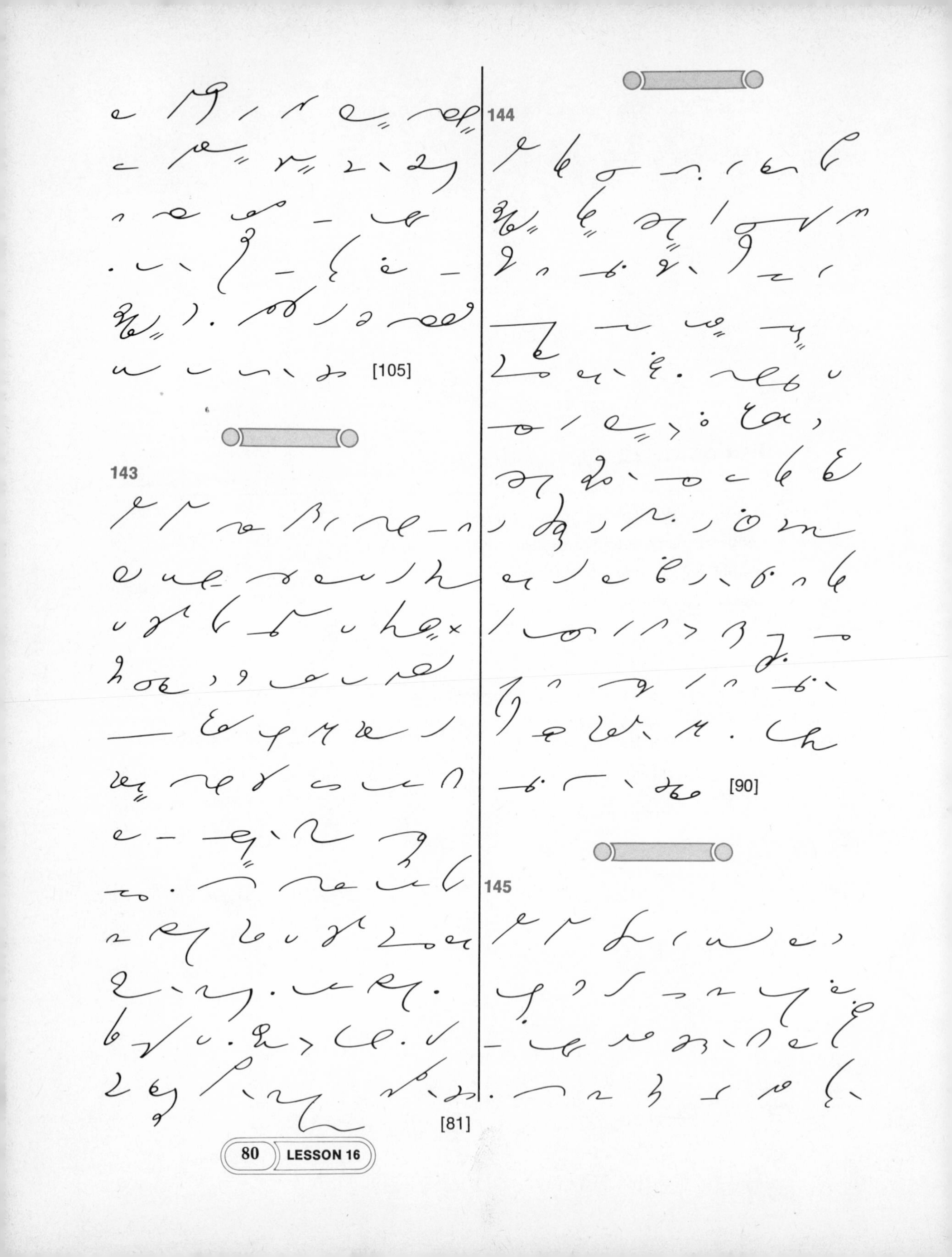

[105]

143

[81]

144

[90]

145

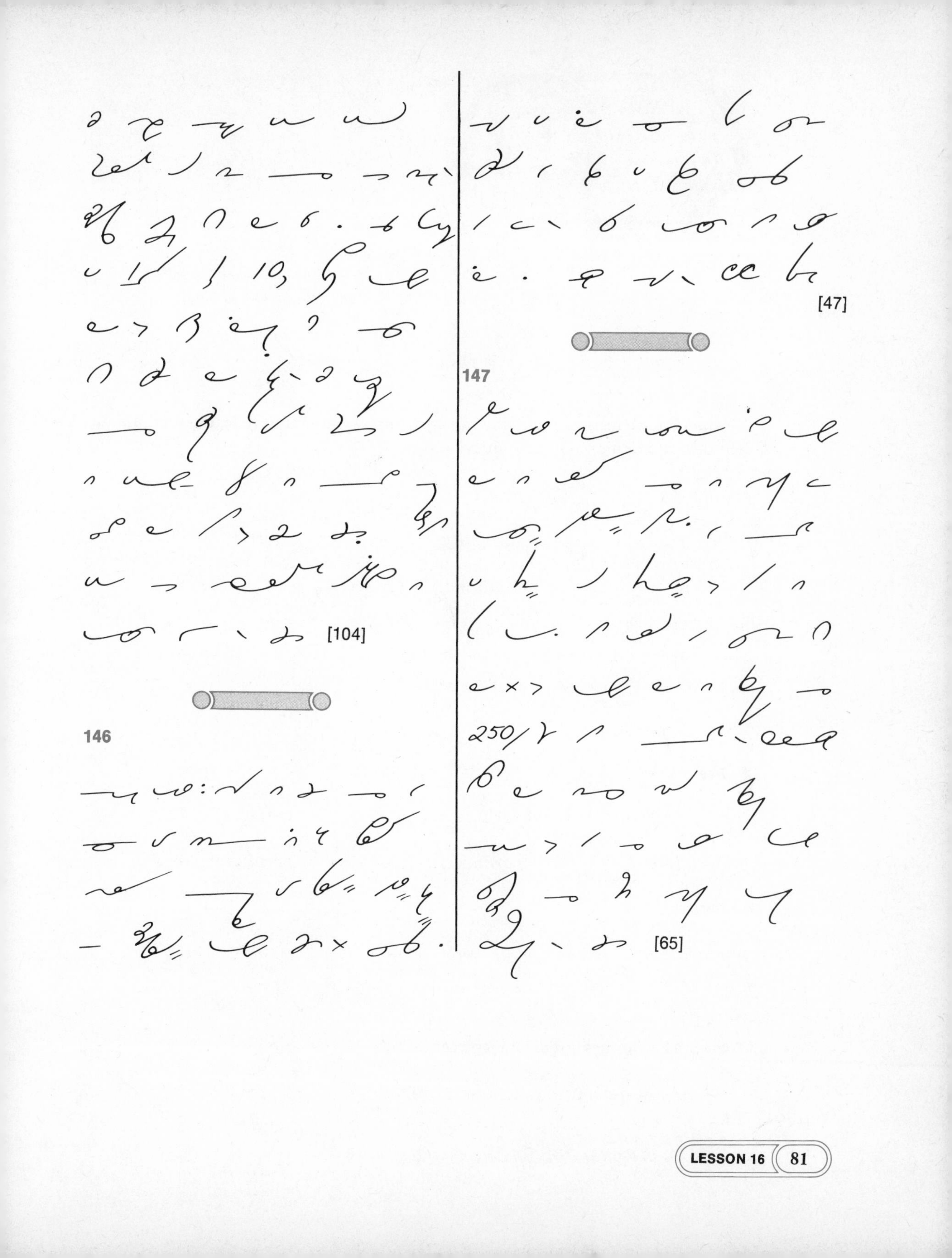

[104]

146

[47]

147

[65]

Principles

148 Brief Forms

When you have learned the following brief forms, you will have learned more than half the brief forms of Gregg Shorthand.

gentlemen	*where*	*next*
important, importance	*company*	*short*
morning	*manufacture*	

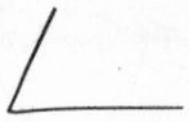

149 Word Beginnings Per-, Pur-

The word beginnings *per-, pur-* are represented by *p-r*.

Spell: pur-s-n, person; pur-chay-a-s, purchase

Per-

person	*perhaps*	*perfect*
personal	*permanent*	*permit*

Pur-

purchase	*purpose*	*purple*

150 Word Beginnings De-, Di-

The word beginnings *de-, di-* are represented by *d*.

Spell: de-s-ī-d, decide; de-r-e-k-t, direct

De-

decide *depend* *deliver*

decision *deposit* *desire*

Di-

direct *direction* *director*

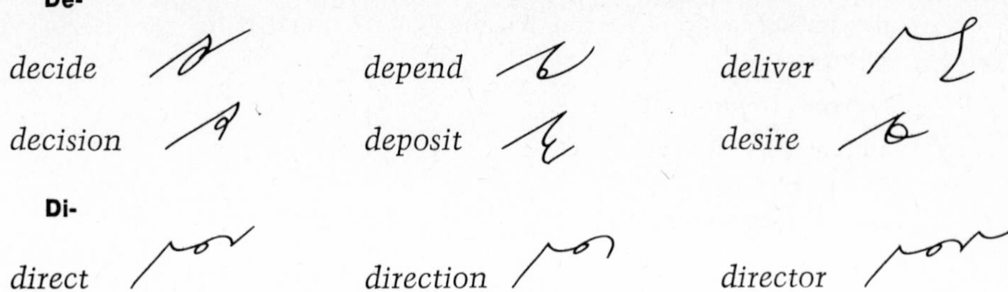

Building Transcription Skills

151 SIMILAR-WORDS DRILL

The English language contains many groups of words that sound or look alike, but each member of the group may be spelled differently and have its own meaning.

Example: **sent** (dispatched); **scent** (a smell); **cent** (a coin).

In addition, there are many groups of words that sound or look *almost* alike.

Example: **area** (space); **aria** (a melody).

The stenographer or secretary who is not alert may, while transcribing, select the wrong member of the group, with the result that the transcript makes no sense.

In this lesson and in a number of others that follow, you will find a Similar-Words Drill that will call to your attention common groups of similar words on which a careless stenographer might stumble.

Study each definition carefully and read the illustrative examples. These similar words are used in the letters of the Reading and Writing Practice exercises.

SIMILAR-WORDS DRILL personal, personnel

personal Individual; private; pertaining to the person or body.

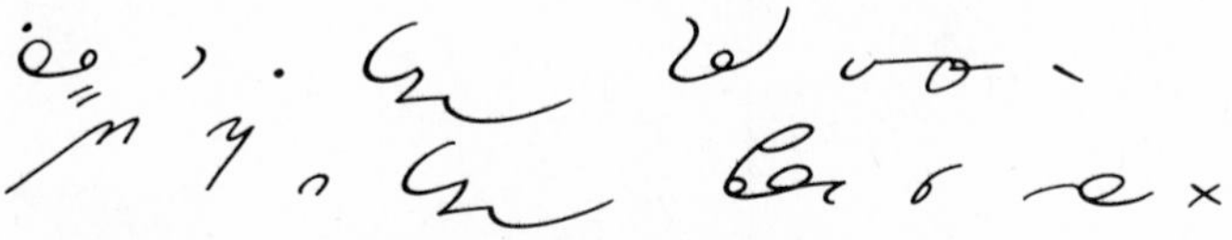

Harry is a personal *friend of mine.*
Do you watch your personal *appearance with care?*

personnel The people who work for a firm; the staff.

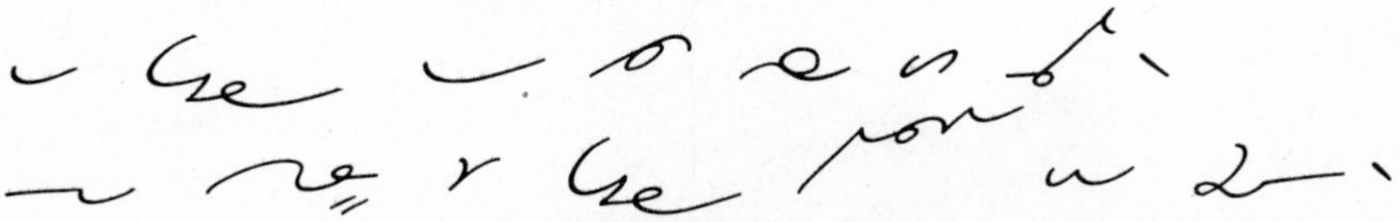

Our personnel *will take care of your needs.*
Mr. Green is the personnel *director of our firm.*

152 Business Vocabulary Builder

purchasing agent A person responsible for purchasing goods or supplies for a company.

proceed To move ahead.

anticipated Expected.

Reading and Writing Practice

153 Brief-Form Letter

116-1117

[153]

154

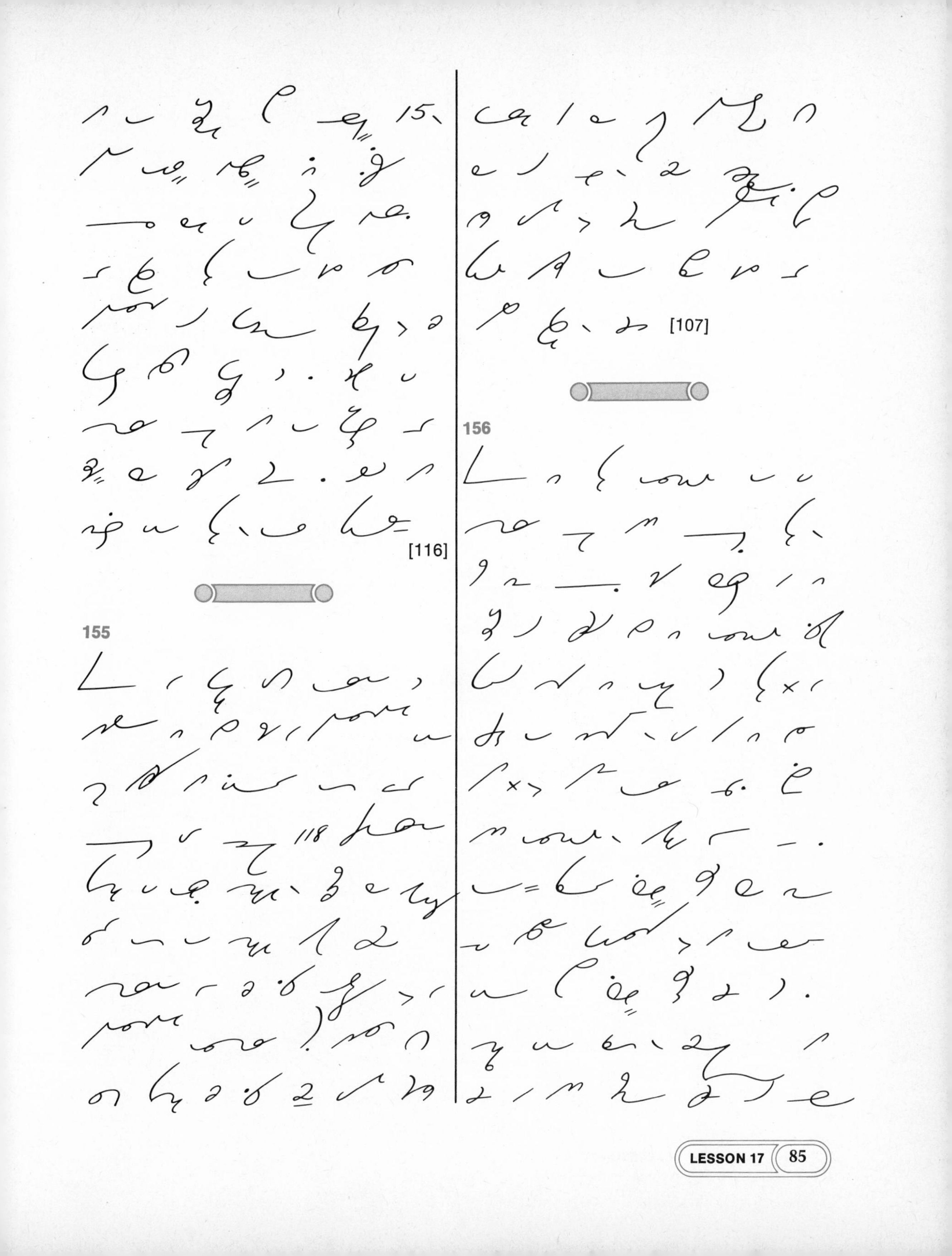

[116]

155

[107]

156

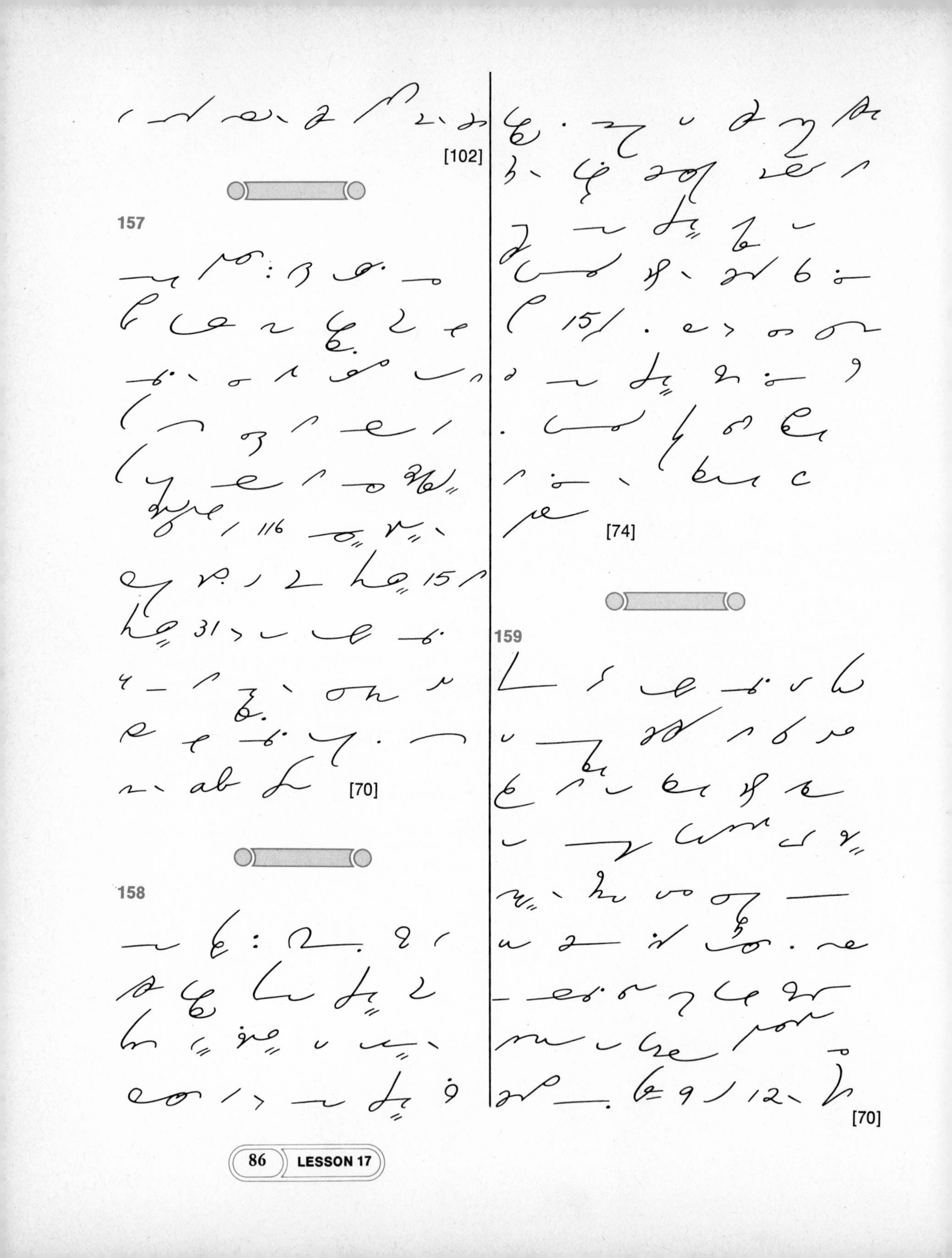

[102]

157

[70]

158

[74]

159

[70]

RECALL

Lesson 18 contains no new shorthand devices for you to learn. In this lesson you will find: (1) a number of additional principles of joining, (2) a Recall Chart, and (3) a Reading and Writing Practice that you will find not only interesting but informative as well.

Principles of Joining

160 At the beginning of a word and after *k*, *g*, or a downstroke, the combination *oo-s* is written without an angle.

husky 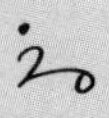 *gust*  *just*

but

does  *loose*  *rust*

161 The word beginning *re-* is represented by *r* before a downstroke or a vowel.

revised  *reference* 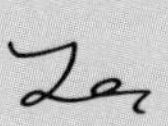 *reopen*

but

retake  *remake*  *relate*

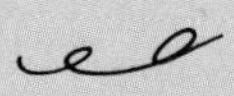

162 The word beginnings *de-*, *di-* are represented by *d* except before *k* or *g*.

deserving 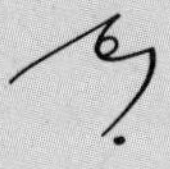 *depressed*  *direct*

but

declare  *decay*  *degrade*

163 As you have perhaps already noticed from your study of Lessons 1 through 17, the past tense of a verb is formed by adding the stroke for the sound that is heard in the past tense. In some words, the past tense will have the sound of *t,* as in *baked;* in others, it will have the sound of *d,* as in *saved.*

baked	*missed*	*faced*
saved	*changed*	*showed*

164 Recall Chart

The following chart reviews the brief forms of Chapter 3 as well as the shorthand principles you studied in Chapters 1, 2, and 3. The chart contains 96 outlines. Can you read it in 9 minutes or less?

BRIEF FORMS

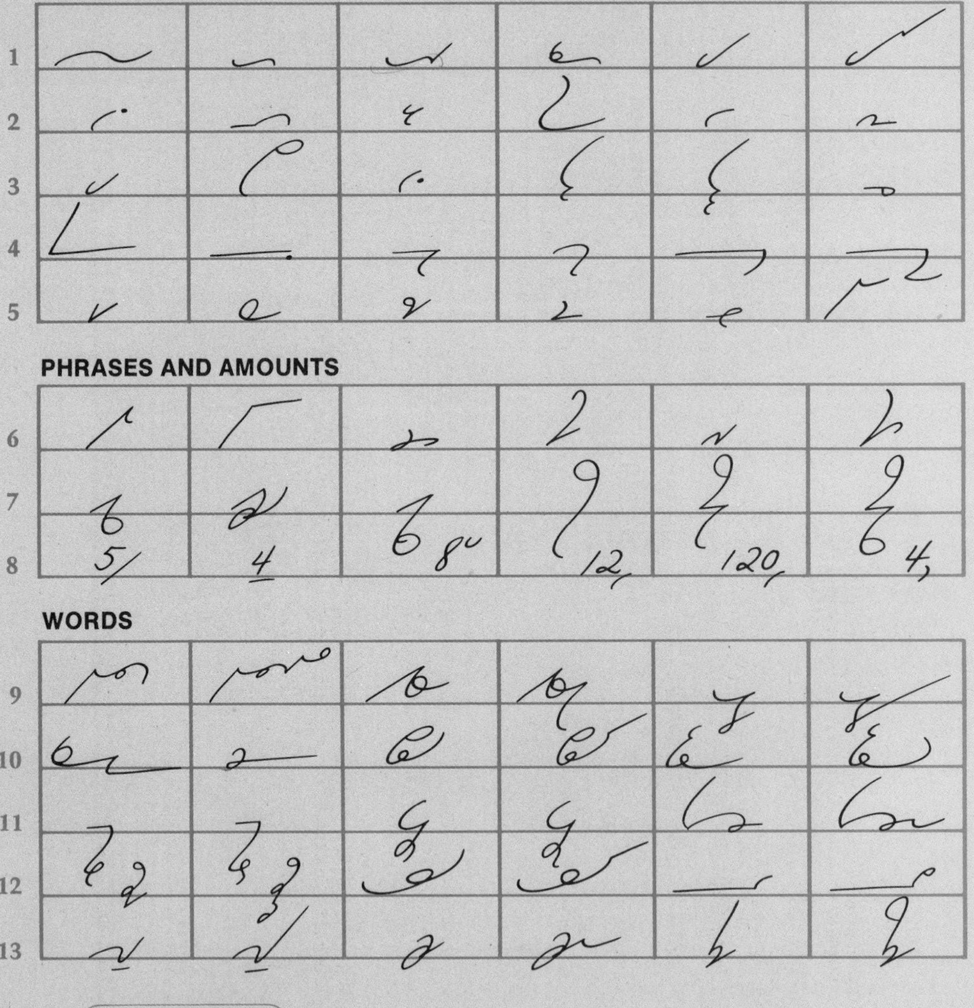

14

15

16

Building Transcription Skills

165 Business Vocabulary Builder

adjacent Nearby; close to.

primary Of first importance.

routine Ordinary.

Reading and Writing Practice

Reading Scoreboard One of the factors in measuring shorthand growth is the rate at which you can read shorthand. Here is an opportunity for you to measure your reading speed on the *first reading* of the material in Lesson 18. The following table will help you determine how rapidly you can read shorthand.

Lesson 18 contains 447 words

If you read Lesson 18 in **17 minutes** your reading rate is **26 words a minute**
If you read Lesson 18 in **19 minutes** your reading rate is **24 words a minute**
If you read Lesson 18 in **21 minutes** your reading rate is **21 words a minute**
If you read Lesson 18 in **25 minutes** your reading rate is **18 words a minute**
If you read Lesson 18 in **29 minutes** your reading rate is **16 words a minute**
If you read Lesson 18 in **33 minutes** your reading rate is **14 words a minute**

If you can read Lesson 18 through the first time in less than 17 minutes, you are doing well indeed. If you take considerably longer than 33 minutes, here are some questions you should ask yourself.

- 1 Am I spelling each outline I cannot read immediately?
- 2 Am I spending too much time deciphering an outline that I cannot read even after spelling it?
- 3 Should I perhaps reread the directions for reading shorthand on page 10?

After you have determined your reading rate, make a record of it in some convenient place. You can then watch your reading rate grow as you time yourself on the Reading Scoreboards in later lessons.

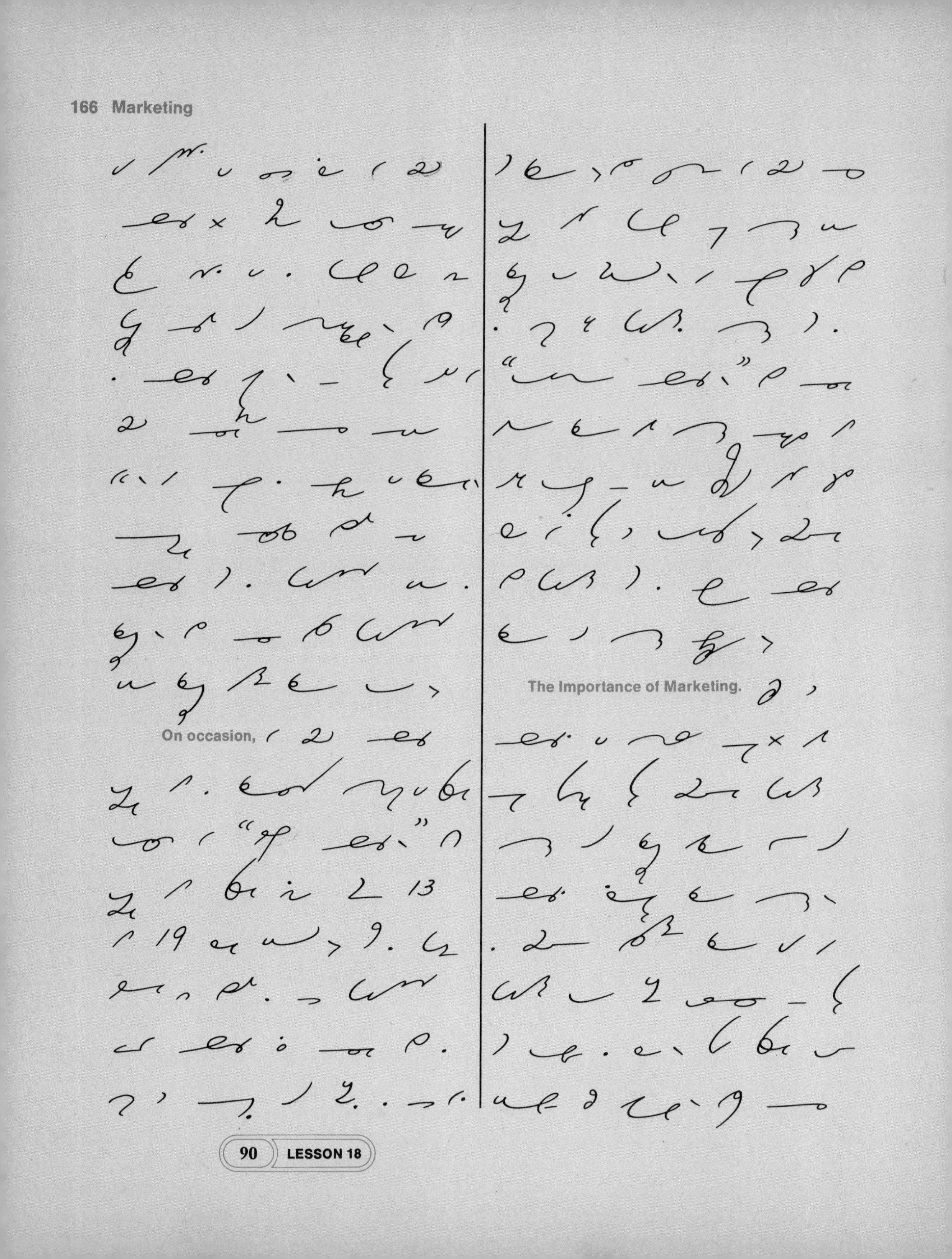

On occasion,

The Importance of Marketing.

Selling goods

[347]

167 A Worker's Creed

[100]

CHAPTER

What Does the Secretary Do?

A secretary is an administrative assistant who has a mastery of office skills, who assumes responsibility, who works without direct supervision, and who exercises initiative and judgment.

The specific duties of the secretary depend largely upon the nature of the employer's business and the amount of responsibility delegated by the immediate superior.

Usually the secretary handles a variety of business details independently, in addition to stenographic duties. One important aspect of the secretary's job is to represent the employer to the public and to other business people. And it is the secretary who relieves the boss of routine duties, supervises clerical workers, handles correspondence, and records confidential material.

The secretary receives, sorts, and opens mail directed to the employer. Letters marked "Personal" may or may not be opened, depending upon the employer's instructions. The secretary, being the one most familiar with the employer's business practices, may answer much of the mail without supervision. Mail that requires the employer's personal attention is classified for convenience. The boss may either dictate replies or ask the secretary to answer the correspondence according to instructions.

In many instances, the secretary answers inquiries, obtains information, and refers calls to other departments or personnel without disturbing the employer. Many secretaries act as "buffers" by screening all visitors and callers before scheduling appointments. The secretary may take notes at meetings, office conferences, or large meetings. The secretary may also transcribe the reports of the meeting and handle the distribution of copies. In some offices, the secretary supervises other office personnel and assigns work to typists and other clerical workers.

The secretary must be thoroughly familiar with the filing system in order to retrieve information at a moment's notice. The secretary must be able to make travel arrangements and reservations for the employer's business trips and schedule luncheon or dinner dates with clients or customers. The secretary may also be required to take care of the employer's personal business files, business bank account, and business income tax records.

Other duties depend upon the secretary's specialization. A social secretary, for example, would be responsible for arranging social functions, sending invitations, keeping the employer informed of social activities, and answering personal correspondence. A legal secretary should know and be able to use legal terminology. A technical secretary employed by engineers, chemists, or biologists should understand scientific terms and be able to transcribe highly technical dictation.

Although a secretary's duties vary widely from position to position, the mark of every superior secretary is the ability to assume responsibility and do high-quality work without direct supervision.

Principles

168 Brief Forms

Here is another group of brief forms—only six this time.

present		*advertise*		*immediate*	
part		*Ms.*		*opportunity*	

169 U

The sound of *u*, as in *use*, is represented by .

Spell: u-s, use

use		*review*		*united*	
few		*unit*		*unique*	

170 Word Ending -ment

The word ending *-ment* is represented by *m*.

Spell: p-a-ment, payment

payment		*appointment*		*advertisement*	
management		*refreshment*		*department*	
arrangement		*shipment*		*assignment*	

▶ Notice that in *assignment, m* for *ment* is joined to the *n* with a jog.

171 Word Ending -tial (-cial)

The word ending *-tial* is represented by *ish*.

Spell: e-n-e-shul, initial

initial		*social*		*especially*	
initialed		*special*		*financial*	
initially		*partial*		*official*	

Building Transcription Skills

172 SPELLING When you look at the letter on page 96, you get a favorable impression. The letter is nicely placed; the right-hand margin is even; the date, inside address, and closing are all in their proper places. When you read the letter casually, it makes good sense and apparently represents what the dictator said.

But that favorable impression vanishes when you read the letter carefully. In fact, the dictator will never sign it because it contains several misspelled words. No executive will knowingly sign a letter that contains a misspelled word!

If you are to succeed as a stenographer or secretary, your letters must not only be accurate transcripts of what your employer dictated but they must also be free of spelling errors. A stenographer or secretary who regularly submits letters for signature that contain spelling errors will not long be welcome in a business office.

To make sure that you will be able to spell correctly when you have completed your shorthand course, you will from this point on give special attention to spelling in each Reading and Writing Practice.

As you read the Reading and Writing Practice, you will occasionally find shorthand outlines printed in a second color. These outlines represent words that transcribers often misspell. When you encounter such an outline, finish reading the sentence in which it occurs; then glance at the margin, where you will find the word in type, properly syllabicated.

Spell the word aloud if possible, pausing slightly after each word division. (The word divisions indicated are those given in *Webster's New Collegiate Dictionary*.)

---

173 Business Vocabulary Builder

board of trustees A group of people who direct a company's work.

unique Unusual; one of a kind.

prospective Likely to become.

LUNN

LUNN INCORPORATED

245 PARK AVENUE

NEW YORK, NEW YORK 10035

CHARLOTTE
COLUMBUS
DENVER
DUBUQUE
ELGIN
FLINT
FT. WAYNE
FT. WORTH
HUNTINGTON
LEXINGTON
MADISON
MEMPHIS
NASHVILLE
NORFOLK
PORTLAND
ST. LOUIS
ST. PAUL
SANTA FE
SAVANNAH
SEATTLE
TEXARKANA
TUCSON
TULSA
WICHITA

September 22, 19--

Mr. John Case
2001 Huron Street
Seattle, Washington 98117

Dear Mr. Case:

It is a comfortible feeling to know that the heating system in your home does not have to depend on the elements. Snow and ice cannot leave you shiverring when you heat with gas. It travels under ground.

The dependability of gas is only one of its many virtues. A gas heating system costs less to instal and less to operate. It needs lots less serviceing, and it lasts longer. It has no odor and makes no filmy deposits that cause extra work.

No wonder more than 400,000 users of other feuls changed to gas last year.

Why not let us show you how easy it is to instal gas heat in your home.

Yours truely,

Thomas A. Frost
Sales Manager

TAF:re

Can you find all the errors in this letter?

Reading and Writing Practice

174 Brief-Form Letter

ap·pli·cants

di·rec·tor

as·sign·ment

de·sir·able

[152]

175

im·me·di·ate·ly

valu·able

through

[148]

176

re·fer·ring

va·can·cies

be·gin·ning

[101]

177

pur·chase

than

per·son·al·ly

[81]

178

men's

suf·fi·cient

[50]

Principles

179 Ow

The sound *ow,* as in *now,* is written [shorthand].

Spell: n-ow, now

now	[shorthand]	*how*	[shorthand]	*announce*	[shorthand]
found	[shorthand]	*house*	[shorthand]	*south*	[shorthand]
account	[shorthand]	*amount*	[shorthand]	*crowd*	[shorthand]

180 Word Ending -ther

The word ending *-ther* is represented by *ith.*

Spell: oo-ther, other

other	[shorthand]	*mother*	[shorthand]	*either*	[shorthand]
another	[shorthand]	*gather*	[shorthand]	*leather*	[shorthand]
whether	[shorthand]	*gathered*	[shorthand]	*bothered*	[shorthand]

181 Word Beginning Con-

The word beginning *con-* is represented by *k.*

Spell: con-s-e-r-n, concern

concern	[shorthand]	*considerable*	[shorthand]	*consisted*	[shorthand]
concrete	[shorthand]	*control*	[shorthand]	*contract*	[shorthand]

182 Word Beginning Com-

The word beginning *com-* is also represented by *k*.

Spell: com-p-l-e-t, complete

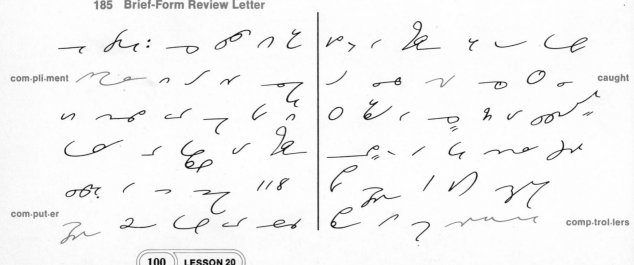

complete *compare* *complain*

computer *combine* *compliment*

183 Con-, Com- Followed by a Vowel

When con-, com- are followed by a vowel, these word beginnings are represented by *kn* or *km*.

connect *committee* *commercial*

Building Transcription Skills

184 Business Vocabulary Builder

compliment *(verb)* To express a favorable comment.

comptrollers Persons who supervise the financial affairs of a business.

utilized Made use of.

comprehensive Covering completely or broadly.

Reading and Writing Practice

185 Brief-Form Review Letter

com·pli·ment

com·put·er

caught

comp·trol·lers

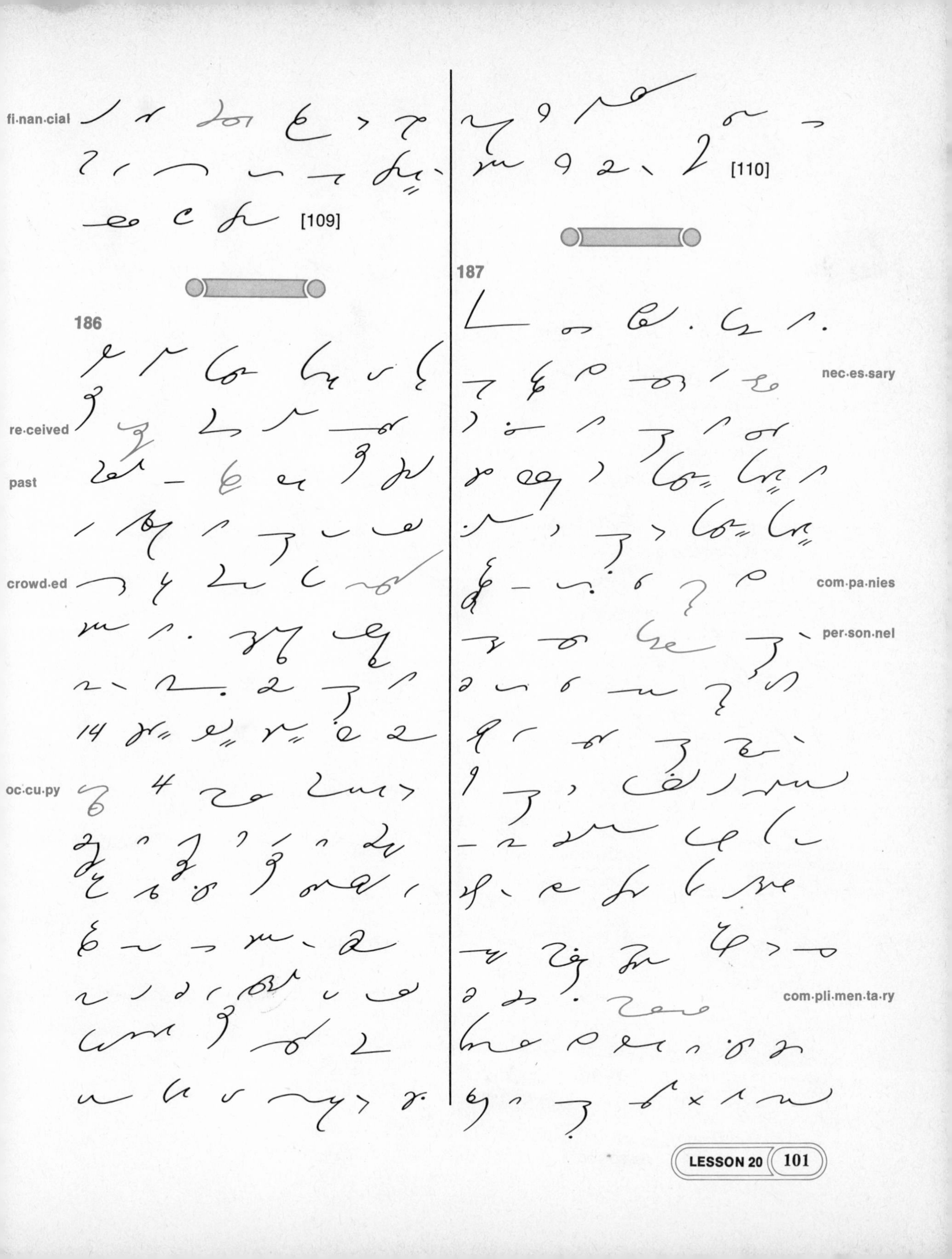

fi·nan·cial

[109]

186

re·ceived

past

crowd·ed

oc·cu·py

[110]

187

nec·es·sary

com·pa·nies

per·son·nel

com·pli·men·ta·ry

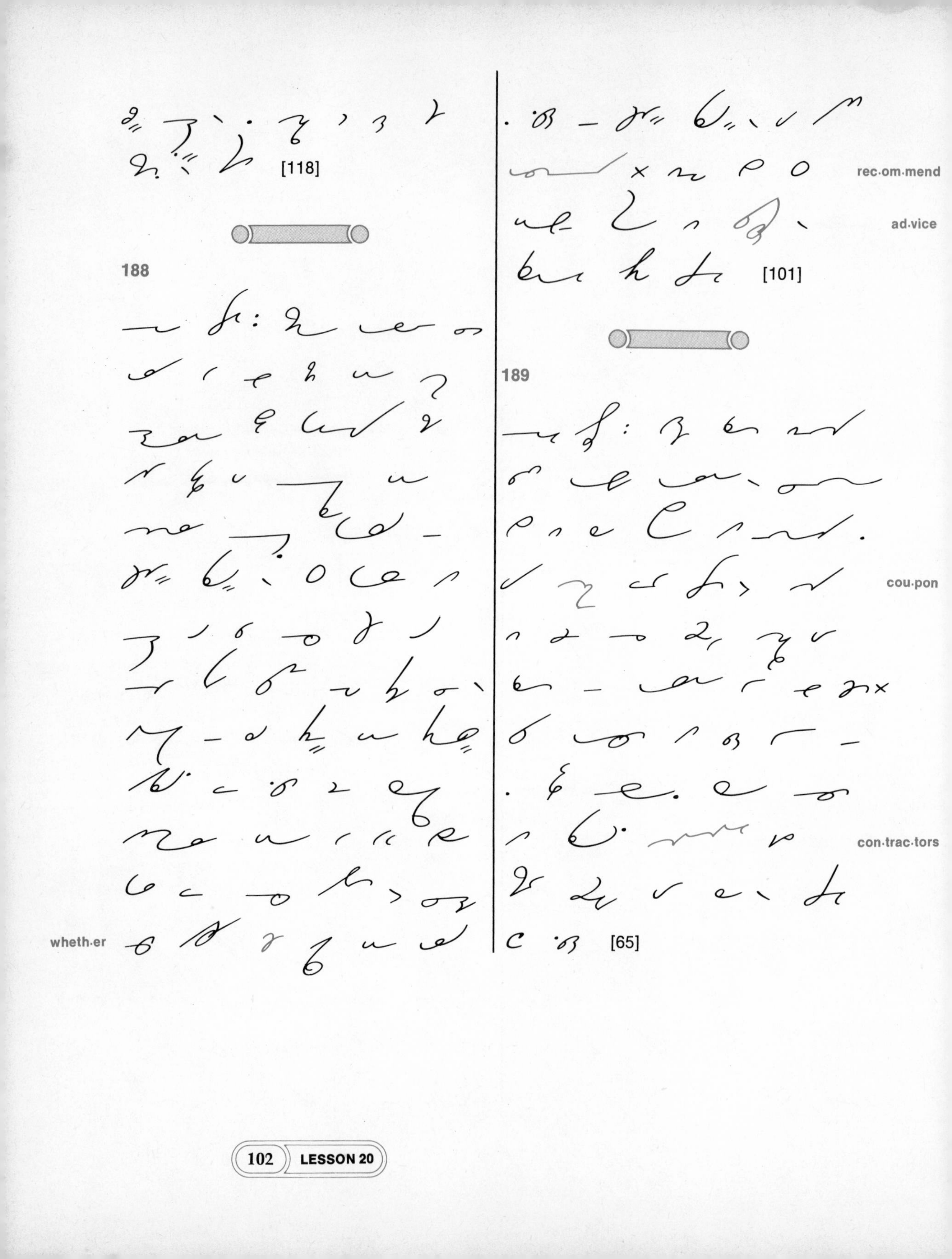

[118]

188

wheth·er

[101]

rec·om·mend

ad·vice

189

cou·pon

con·trac·tors

[65]

Principles

190 Brief Forms

advantage	*several*	*ever, every*
suggest	*out*	*very*

191 Ten

By rounding off the angle between *t-n,* we obtain the fluent *ten* blend.

Ten

Spell: a-ten-d, attend; k-o-ten, cotton

attend	*remittance*	*bulletin*
attention	*stand*	*cotton*
written	*standard*	*button*
tennis	*assistance*	*tonight*

192 Den

The stroke that represents *ten* also represents *d-n.*

Spell: e-v-den-t, evident

evident	*president*	*dentist*
student	*deny*	*danger*
confident	*sudden*	*dinner*

193 Tain

The stroke that represents *t-n, d-n* also represents *-tain.*

Spell: o-b-tain, obtain

obtain		*certain*		*obtainable*	
maintain		*attain*		*container*	

Building Transcription Skills

194 Business Vocabulary Builder

remittance Money sent to someone.

creditors Persons to whom money is owed.

browse To look over casually.

reproduced Made a copy of.

Reading and Writing Practice

195 Brief-Form Letter

re·mit·tance

es·caped

ad·van·tage

los·ing

[125]

196

cat·a·log

browse

wom·en's

equip·ment

con·fi·dent

[147]

197

50

cop·ies

as·sis·tance

ap·prov·al

[130]

198

10

15

as·sis·tant

sal·a·ry

than

[89]

199

ac·cept·ed

[62]

STUDY-HABIT CHECKLIST *No doubt as a conscientious student you do your home assignments faithfully. Do you, however, derive the greatest benefit from the time you devote to practice?*

- *You do* if you practice in a quiet place that enables you to concentrate.
- *You don't* if you practice with one eye on the television and the other on your practice work!
- *You do* if once you have started your assignment, you do not leave your desk or table until you have completed it.
- *You don't* if you interrupt your practice from time to time to call a friend or raid the refrigerator!

Principles

200 Tem

By rounding off the angle between *t-m,* we obtain the fluent *tem* blend.

Tem

Compare: ten *tem*

Spell: tem-p-l, temple

temple	*attempt*	*estimate*
temporary	*item*	*customer*
system	*tomorrow*	*automobile*

201 Dem

The stroke that represents *tem* also represents *d-m.*

Spell: dem-a-end, demand

demand	*damage*	*seldom*
demonstrate	*domestic*	*medium*

202 Business Abbreviations

Here are additional salutations and closings frequently used in business.

Dear Mr.	*Dear Ms.*	*Yours sincerely*
Dear Mrs.	*Dear Miss*	*Cordially yours*

203 Useful Phrases

With the *ten* and *tem* blends, we form these useful phrases:

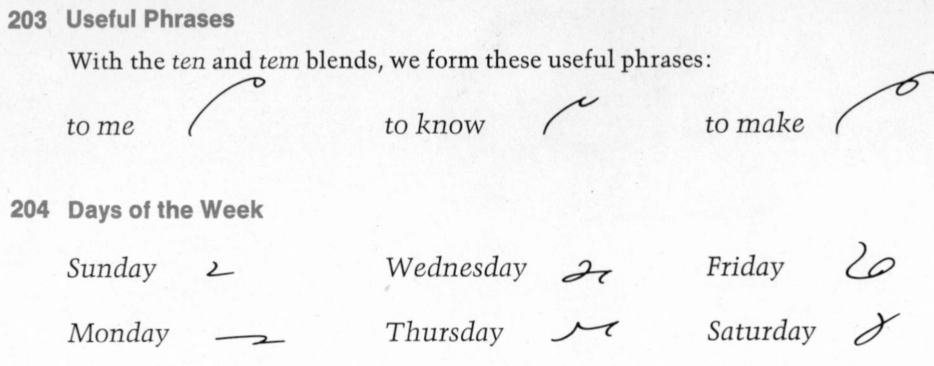

204 Days of the Week

205 Months of the Year

You are already familiar with the outlines for several of the months, as they are written in full.

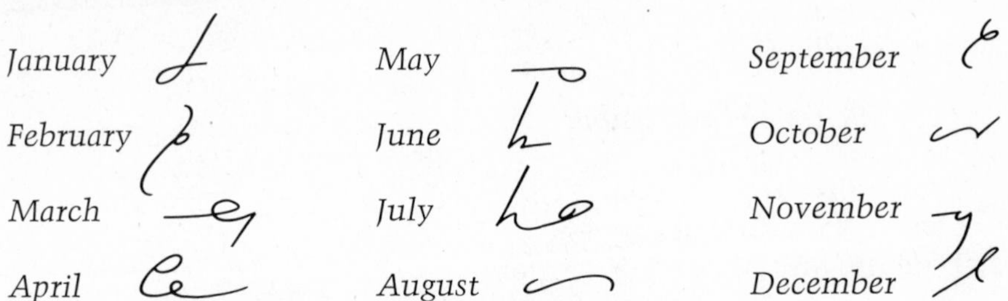

Building Transcription Skills

206 Business Vocabulary Builder

potential Possible but not yet realized.

commencing Beginning.

personable Attractive.

● Reading and Writing Practice

207 Brief-Form Review Letter

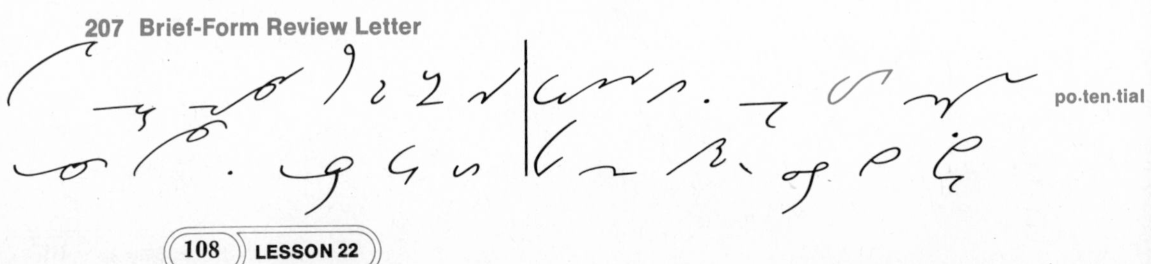

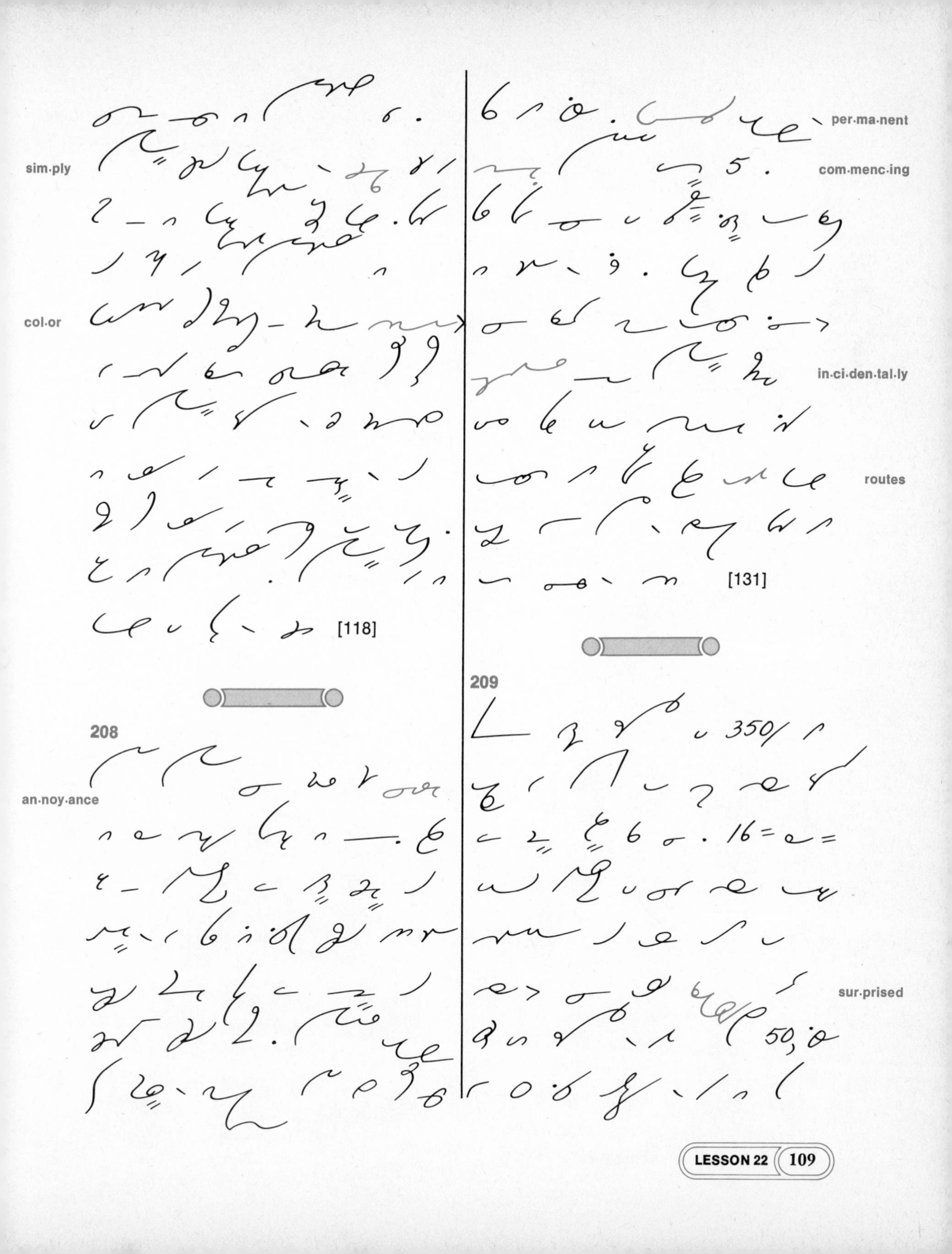

sim·ply

col·or

[118]

per·ma·nent

com·menc·ing

in·ci·den·tal·ly

routes

[131]

208

an·noy·ance

209

sur·prised

enough

pro·ceed

[120]

launched

sim·i·lar

[104]

210

Feb·ru·ary
too

211

sup·plies

shipped

[67]

Principles

212 Brief Forms

After this group, you have only four more groups to learn.

time · *general* · *organize*

acknowledge · *question* · *over**

*The outline for *over* is written above the following character. It is also used as a prefix form, as in:

overdue · *overcame* · *oversee*

213 Def, Dif

By rounding off the angle between *d-f*, we obtain the fluent *def, dif* blend.

Def, Dif

Spell: def-n-e-t, definite

definite · *defeat* · *different*

definitely · *defend* · *differences*

214 Div, Dev

The stroke that represents *def, dif* also represents *div* and *dev*.

Spell: div-ī-d, divide

divide · *develop* · *devote*

division · *devised* · *devoted*

215 Ea, Ia

The sound of *ea,* as in *create* and *piano,* is represented by a large circle with a dot placed within it.

Spell: *k-r-eah-t, create*

create — *appreciate* — *brilliant*

piano — *appropriate* — *area*

Building Transcription Skills

216 SIMILAR-WORDS DRILL to, too, two

to *(preposition)* In the direction of. (*To* is also used as the sign of the infinitive.)

I would like to *talk* to *you about this matter.*

too Also; more than enough.

I, too, *am free on that day.*

Harry has too *many irons in the fire.*

two One plus one.

James bought two *new suits.*

The word in this group on which many stenographers stumble is *too.* They carelessly transcribe *to.* Don't make that mistake.

---

217 Business Vocabulary Builder

media (*plural of* medium) Channels of communication.

contemplate Consider.

associate *(noun)* Partner; colleague.

merge To combine into one.

Reading and Writing Practice

218 Brief-Form Letter

ac·knowl·edge

re·ferred

me·dia

rev·e·nue

re·cent·ly

[200]

219

ac·knowl·edged

mod·el

bril·liant

every day

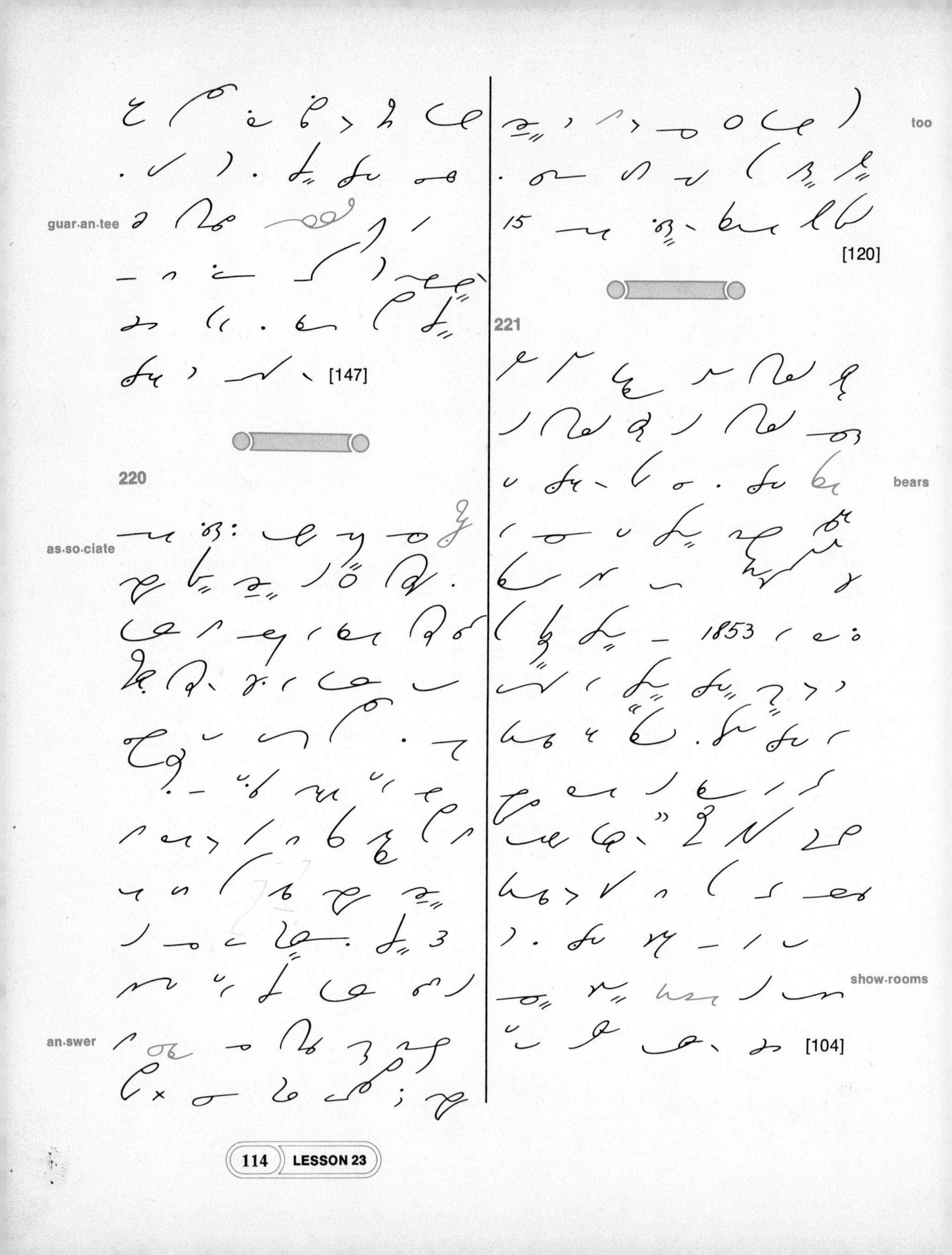

guar·an·tee

[147]

220

as·so·ciate

3

an·swer

too

15

[120]

221

bears

1853

show·rooms

[104]

RECALL

In Lesson 24 you will have no new shorthand devices to learn; you will have a little time to "digest" the devices that you have studied in previous lessons. In Lesson 24 you will find a new feature—Accuracy Practice—that will help you improve your shorthand writing style.

Accuracy Practice

The speed and accuracy with which you will be able to transcribe your shorthand notes will depend on how well you write them. If you follow the suggestions given in this lesson when you work with each Accuracy Practice, you will soon find that you can read your own notes with greater ease and facility.

So that you may have a clear picture of the proper shapes of the shorthand strokes that you are studying, enlarged models of the alphabetic characters and of the typical joinings are given, together with a short explanation of the things that you should keep in mind as you practice.

To get the most out of each Accuracy Practice, follow this simple procedure:

- a *Read the explanations carefully.*
- b *Study the model to see the application of each explanation.*
- c *Write the first outline in the Practice Drill.*
- d *Compare what you have written with the enlarged model.*
- e *Write three or four more copies of the outline, trying to improve your outline with each writing.*
- f *Repeat this procedure with the remaining outlines in the Practice Drill.*

222

To write these strokes accurately:

- a *Start and finish each one on the same level of writing.*

- b *Make the* beginning *of the curve in* r *and* l *deep. Make the* end *of the curve in* k *and* gay *deep.*
- c *Make the* l *and* gay *considerably longer than* r *and* k.

practice drill

Are-our-hour; will-well; can, good.
Air, lay, ache, gay.

223 **K-r** **R-k** **Gay-l**

To write these combinations accurately:

- a *Make the curves rather flat.*
- b *Make the combinations* k-r *and* r-k *somewhat shorter than the combined length of* r *and* k *when written by themselves.*
- c *Make the combinations* gay-l *somewhat shorter than the combined length of* gay *and* l *when written by themselves.*

practice drill

Cream, crate, maker, mark, dark.
Gleam, glean, glare, legal.

224 Recall Chart

This chart contains all the brief forms in Chapter 4 and an illustration of many of the shorthand devices you studied in Chapters 1 through 4.

The chart contains 90 outlines. Can you read the entire chart in 7 minutes or less?

BRIEF FORMS

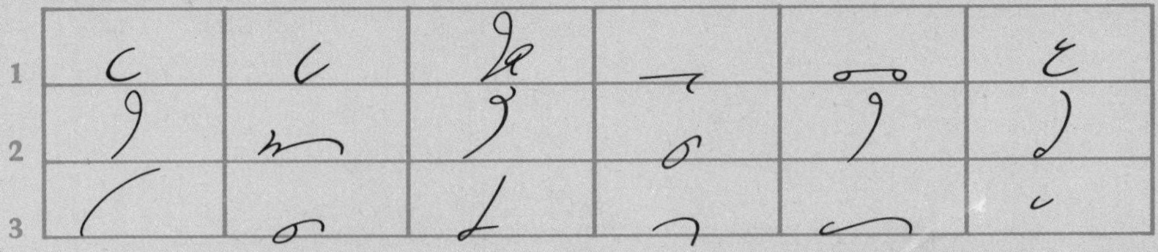

PHRASES

WORDS

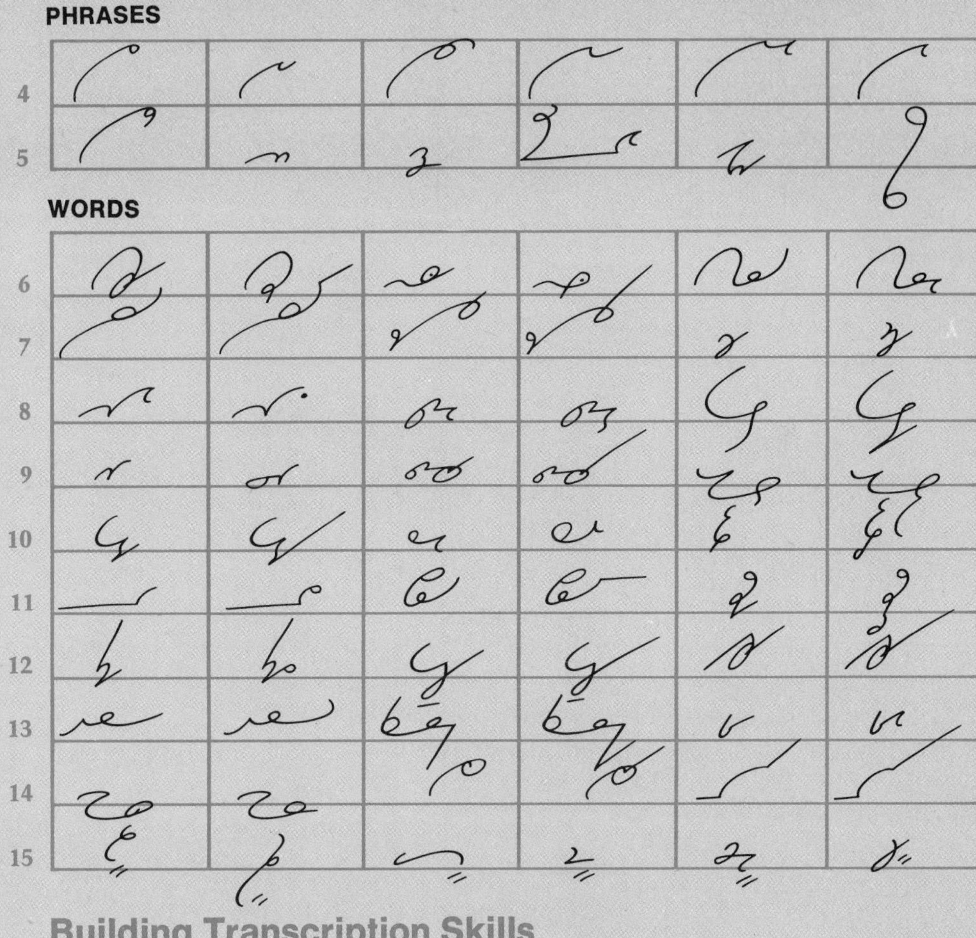

Building Transcription Skills

225 Business Vocabulary Builder

commercials Advertisements broadcast on radio or television.

rejects Refuses to accept.

derive Receive.

sponsor One who pays the cost of a radio or television program in return for limited advertising time.

Reading and Writing Practice

226 Safe Driving

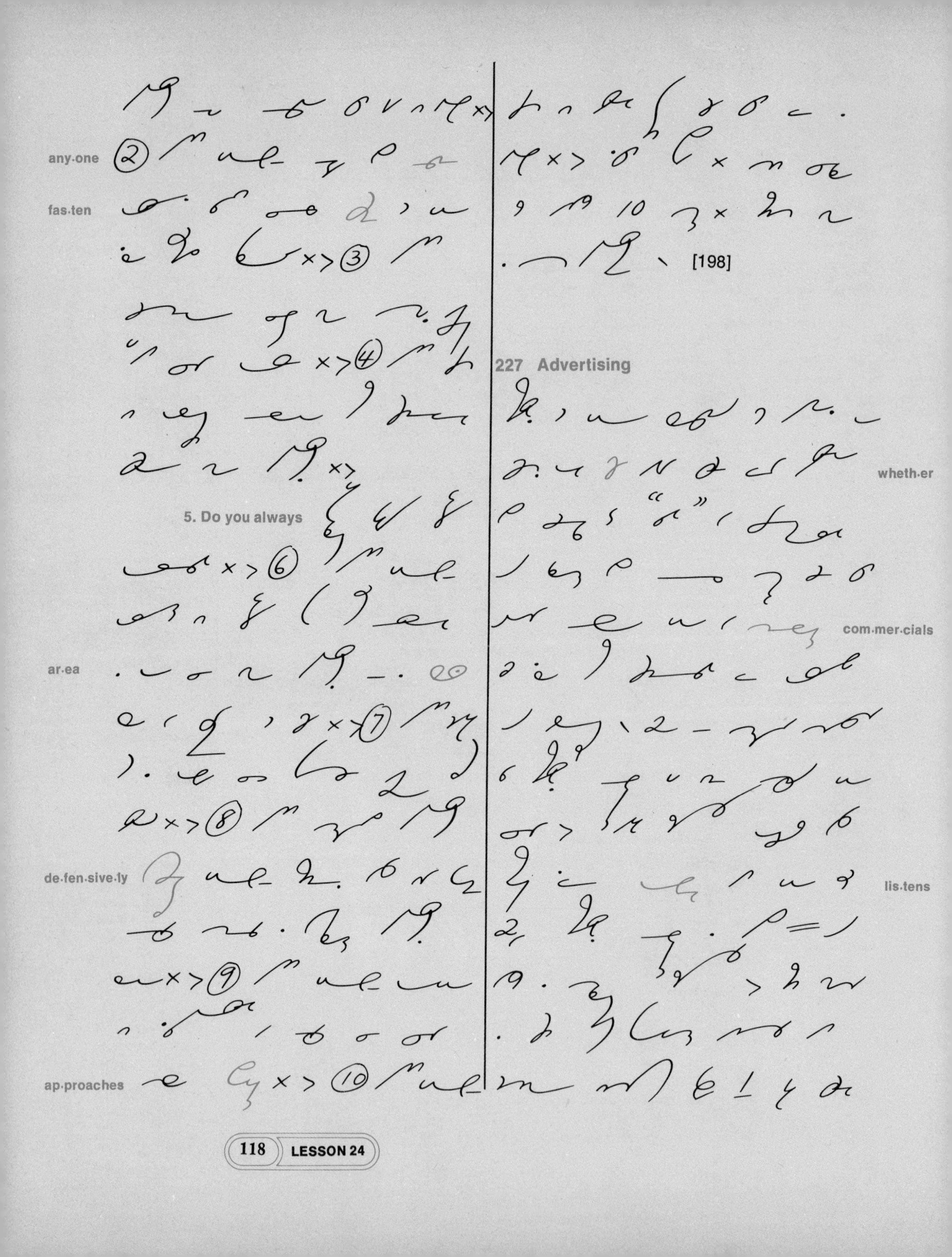

any·one

fas·ten

5. Do you always

ar·ea

de·fen·sive·ly

ap·proaches

[198]

227 Advertising

wheth·er

com·mer·cials

lis·tens

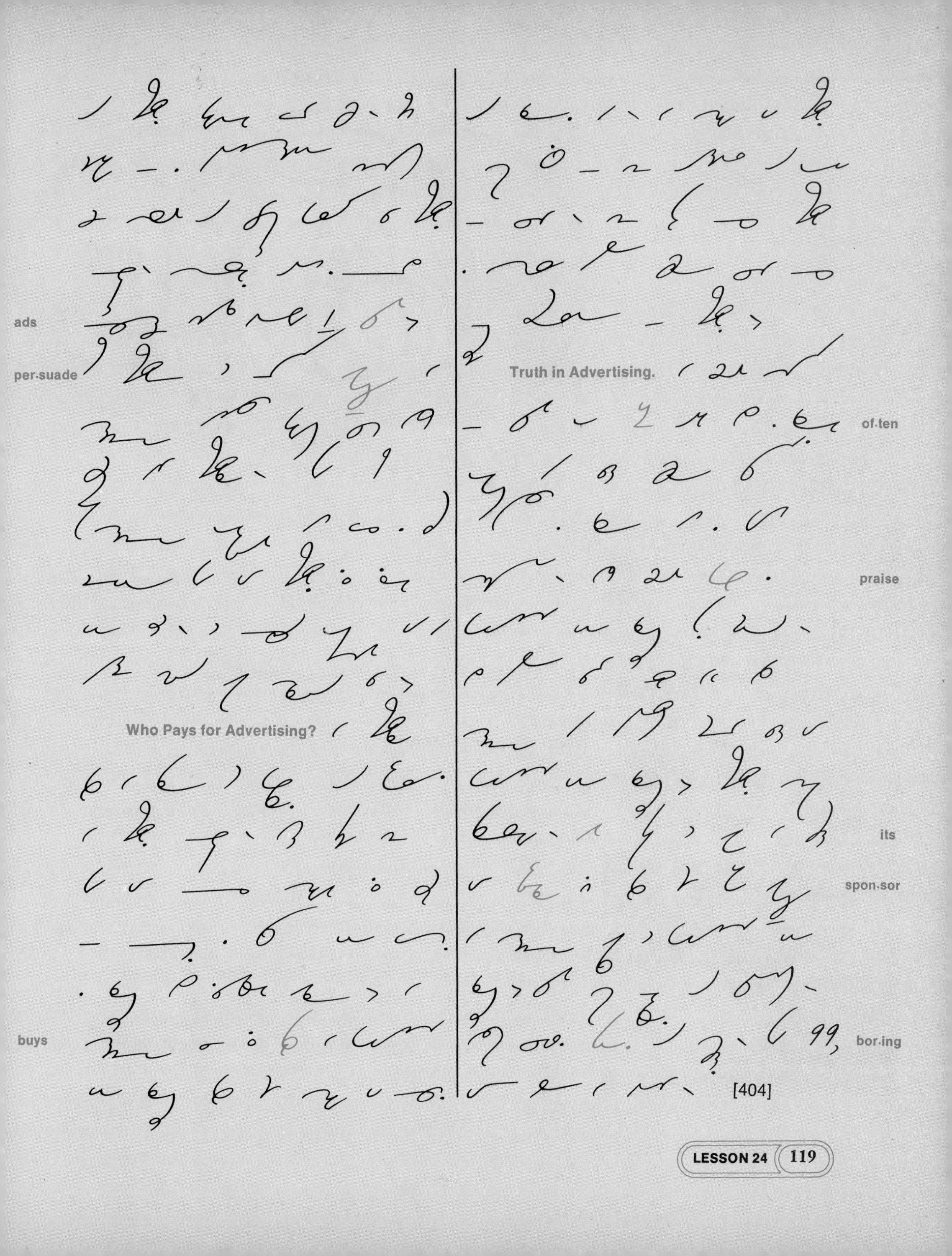

ads

per·suade

buys

Who Pays for Advertising?

Truth in Advertising.

of·ten

praise

its

spon·sor

bor·ing

[404]

CHAPTER

Secretarial Jobs
A Wide Range

Today's secretary can choose a job from many different fields. The positions range from those of a general secretarial nature to the highly specialized jobs in the legal, medical, or technical professions. The secretary's job options span a variety of private businesses and numerous public service fields. Positions are available in all geographical areas of the United States and in many other countries as well.

There are many fine opportunities for secretaries who are interested in developing their skills and increasing their knowledge in special areas. Let's take a look at just three of the many fascinating fields in which a secretary can become an active and indispensable participant.

Advertising and Public Relations

In the closely related fields of advertising and public relations, qualified secretaries are offered many challenging opportunities. In either field, the secretary must not only be able to work well under pressure but must also be able to communicate well with other people. The secretary must be people-oriented because employers in these fields deal constantly with clients, editors, account executives, freelance writers, artists, photographers, models, actors, and printers. The secretary must be able to work with details and be able to synchronize countless dates, facts,

figures, faces, names, and sources. In addition, the secretary must be able to both organize and follow through on many complicated, long-range campaigns and projects.
Creativity is contagious, and the secretary in advertising and public relations has an enviable opportunity to cultivate special talents.

Government Service

The range of opportunities for the secretary in government is very wide. A civil service job may take the secretary to Washington, D.C. or to a number of other cities in the United States and other countries. The secretary may work for a senator, a representative, or a member of the President's staff. Or a position may be available with the Bureau of Indian Affairs, the Department of Housing and Urban Development, the Federal Bureau of Investigation, or with any number of other fascinating departments or agencies. The list is almost endless—and so is the challenge.

The Legal Field

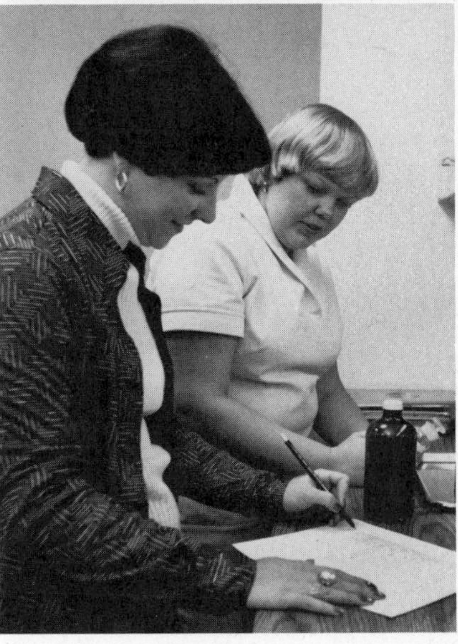

The legal secretary may work for one attorney, for a large law firm, or for a corporation. The position may involve all types of legal work, or it may involve only one area, such as criminal, tax, or corporate law. The job may involve working for a judge whose court work is on the city, state, or national level. Regardless of the type of law office, the secretary must understand thoroughly the legal terminology and must be extremely accurate in all communication. The secretary may serve as receptionist, make appointments for clients, and notarize papers. Many times the job involves considerable responsibility in management of the business portion of the law practice. Of particular importance in every situation is the ability to keep close control of the employer's court calendar and the vital dates connected with each client's legal proceedings.

This is only a sampling of three of the many fields in which a secretary may work. Choose an area that matches your interests, and you are well on your way to an interesting, rewarding job in a secretarial field that fits you personally.

Principles

228 Brief Forms

difficult	*success*	*request*
envelope	*satisfy, satisfactory*	*wish*
progress	*state*	*under**

*The outline for *under* is written above the following shorthand character. It is also used as a prefix form, as in:

underneath *understudy* *undertake*

229 Cities and States

In your work as a stenographer and secretary, you will frequently have occasion to write geographical expressions. Here are a few important cities and states.

Cities

New York	*Boston*	*Los Angeles*
Chicago	*Philadelphia*	*St. Louis*

States

Michigan	*Massachusetts*	*Missouri*
Illinois	*Pennsylvania*	*California*

230 Useful Business Phrases

The following phrases are used so frequently in business that special forms have been provided for them. Study these phrases as you would study brief forms.

as soon as · *of course* · *let us*

as soon as possible · *to do* · *I hope*

Building Transcription Skills

231 Business Vocabulary Builder

competitors Rivals.

reverse *(adjective)* Opposite.

invaluable Priceless.

Reading and Writing Practice

232 Brief-Form Letter

ap·proach·ing

sat·is·fy·ing

com·pet·i·tors

[144]

233

15

ap·pre·ci·ate

cus·tom·ers

co·op·er·a·tion

war·ran·ty

[173]

234

ad·van·tage

be·lieve

con·fi·dent

im·me·di·ate·ly

5 6

[153]

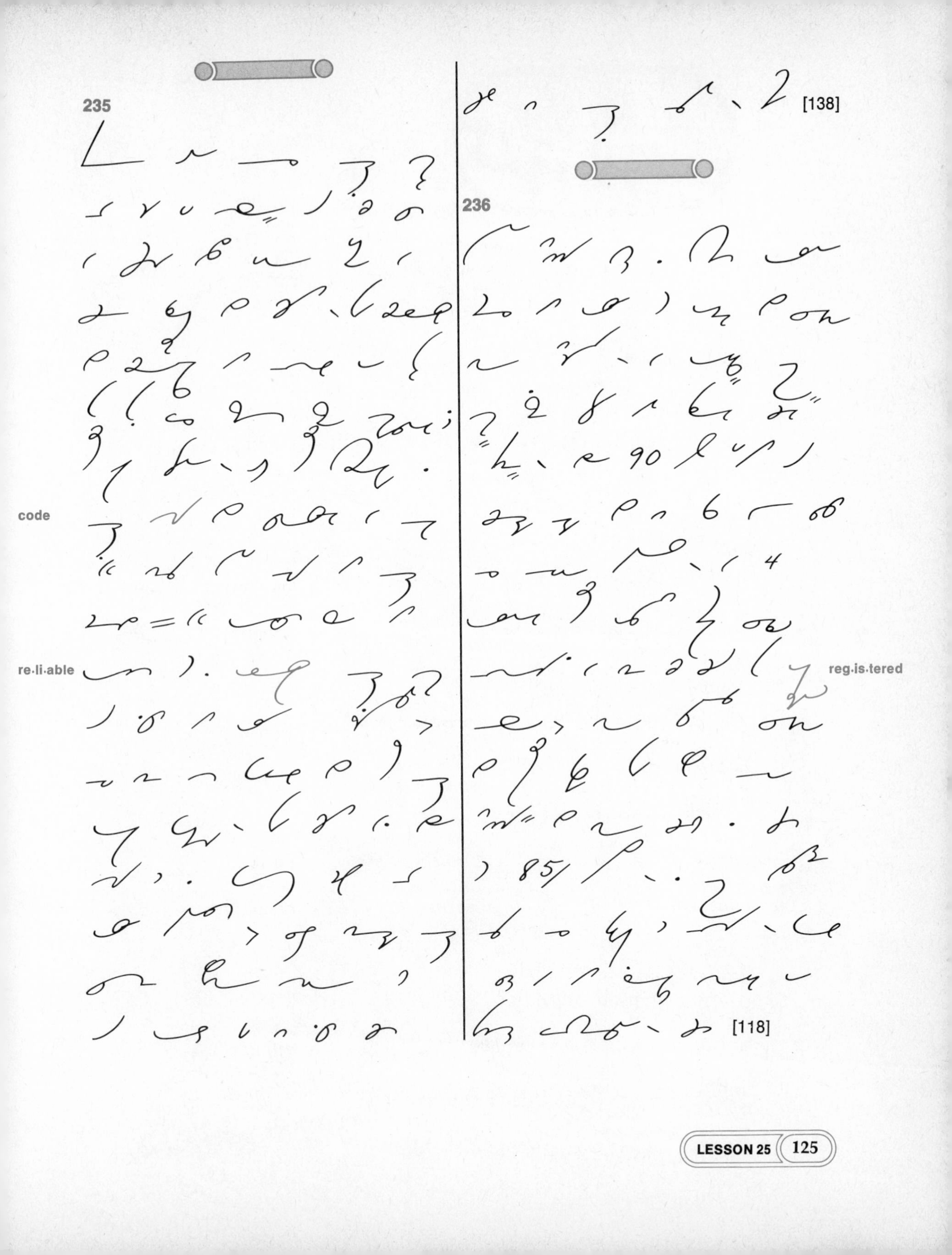

235

code

re·li·able

[138]

236

reg·is·tered

[118]

Principles

237 Long ī and a Following Vowel

Any vowel following long *ī* is represented by a small circle within a large circle.

Compare: *signs* *science*

Spell: *s-īah-n-s, science*

trial *drier* *appliance*
client *prior* *reliance*

238 Word Beginnings En-, Un-

The word beginnings *en-*, *un-* are represented by *n*.

En-

Spell: *en-j-oi, enjoy*

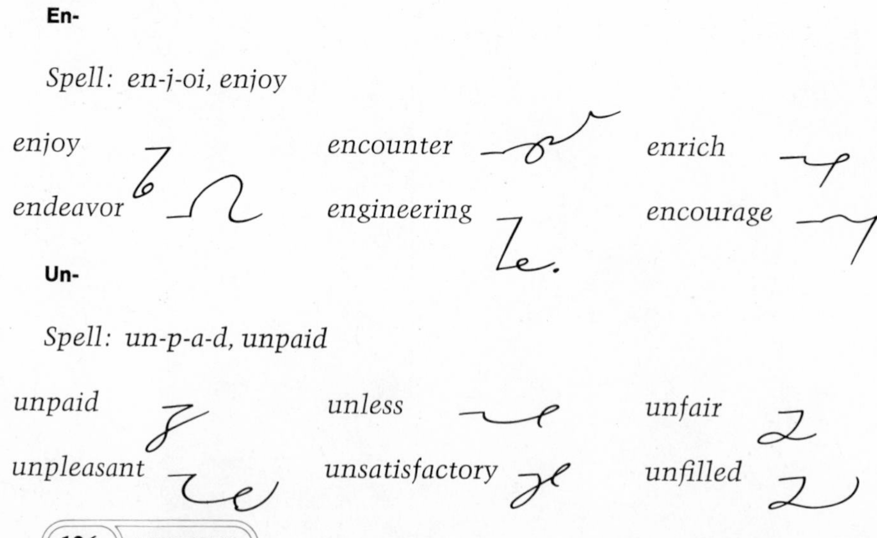

enjoy *encounter* *enrich*
endeavor *engineering* *encourage*

Un-

Spell: *un-p-a-d, unpaid*

unpaid *unless* *unfair*
unpleasant *unsatisfactory* *unfilled*

239 In-, En-, Un- Followed by a Vowel

When *in-*, *en-*, or *un-* is followed by a vowel, the word beginning is written in full.

innovation *enact* *unable*

240 Useful Business Phrases

Here are additional frequently used phrases for which special forms have been provided. Study them as you would study brief forms.

more than *to us* *your order*

we hope *let me* *you ordered*

Building Transcription Skills

241 Business Vocabulary Builder

office appliances Calculators, typewriters, duplicators, etc.

laymen Persons who are not expert in a particular field.

unbiased Fair.

precision Exactness.

Reading and Writing Practice

242 Brief-Form Review Letter

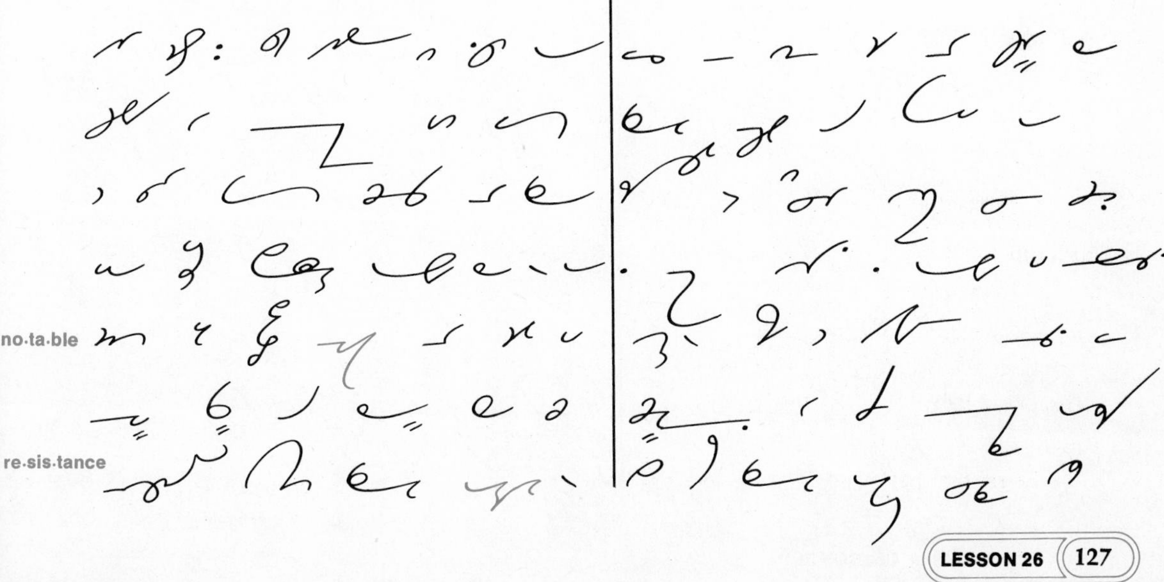

co·op·er·a·tion

[155]

243

com·plete·ly

too

lay·men

un·bi·ased

cou·pon

[163]

244

un·pleas·ant

ac·knowl·edg·ment

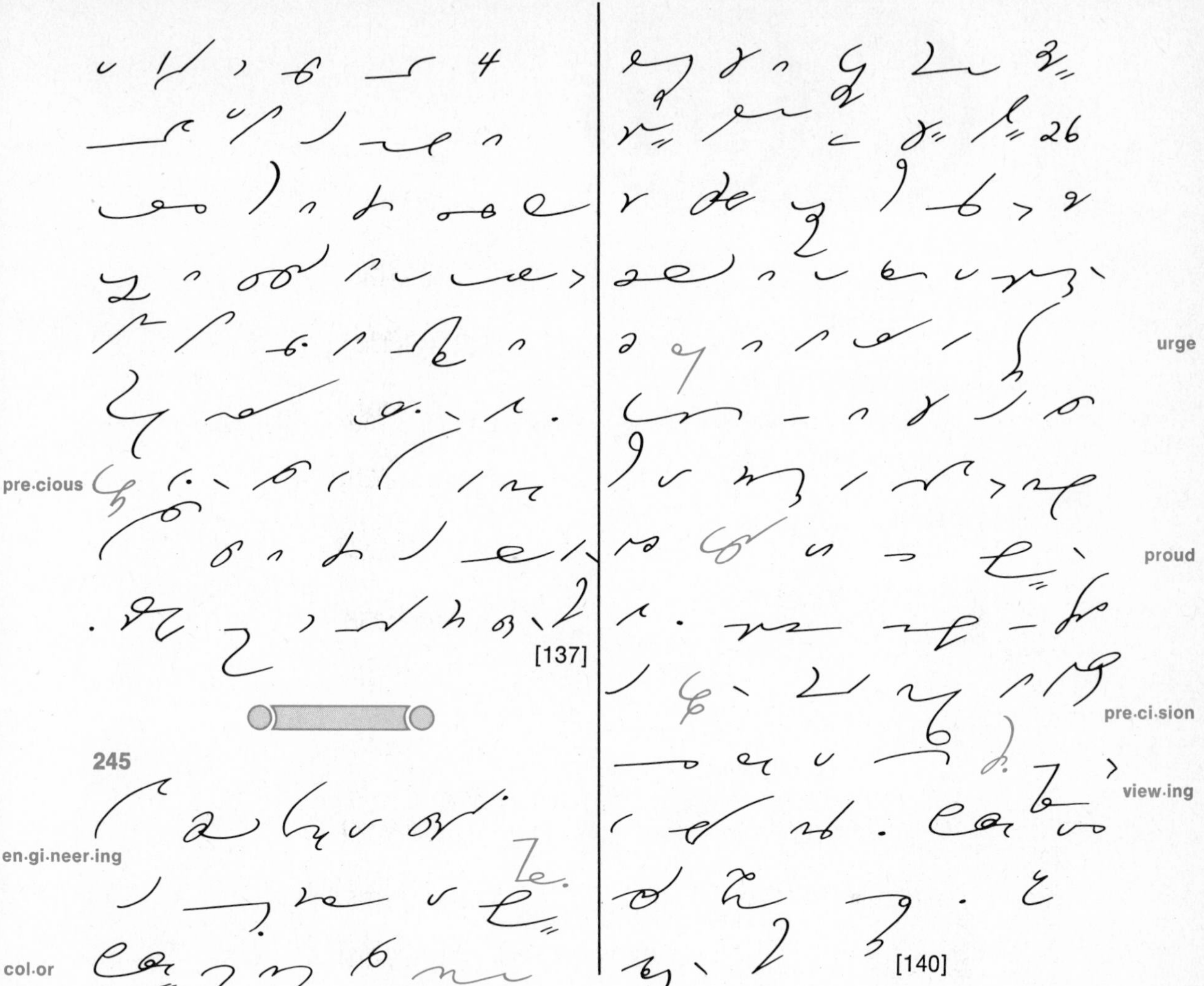

PROPORTION CHECKLIST *The writer who can read his shorthand notes fluently is the one who is careful of his proportions. In your shorthand writing, do you:*

- 1 Make the large *a* circle huge; the small *e* circle tiny?
- 2 Make the straight strokes very straight and the curves very deep?
- 3 Make the *o* and *oo* hooks deep and narrow?
- 4 Make short strokes, such as *t* and *n*, very short and long strokes, such as *ted* and *men*, very long?

Principles

246 Brief Forms

After you have learned the following group of nine brief forms, you will have only two more groups to go!

particular *speak* *regard*
probable *idea* *newspaper*
regular *subject* *opinion*

247 Ng

The sound of *ng*, as in *sing*, is written .

Compare: *seen* *sing*

Spell: *s-e-ing, sing*

sing *long* *bring*
sang *spring* *single*
song *strong* *young*

248 Ngk

The sound of *ngk*, as in *sink*, is written .

Compare: *seem* *sink*

Spell: *s-e-ink, sink; oo-ink-l, uncle*

rank *bank* *anxious*

frank	*banquet*	*uncle*
ink	*link*	*blank*

249 Omission of Vowel Preceding -tion

When *t, d, n,* or *m* is followed by *-ition, -ation,* the circle is omitted.

edition	*reputation*	*donation*
addition	*invitation*	*station*
condition	*permission*	*stationed*

Building Transcription Skills

250 Business Vocabulary Builder

enlightening Instructional.

medium A means of conveying information.

automation The state of being operated automatically.

Reading and Writing Practice

251 Brief-Form Letter

ac·cept·ed

pi·o·neer

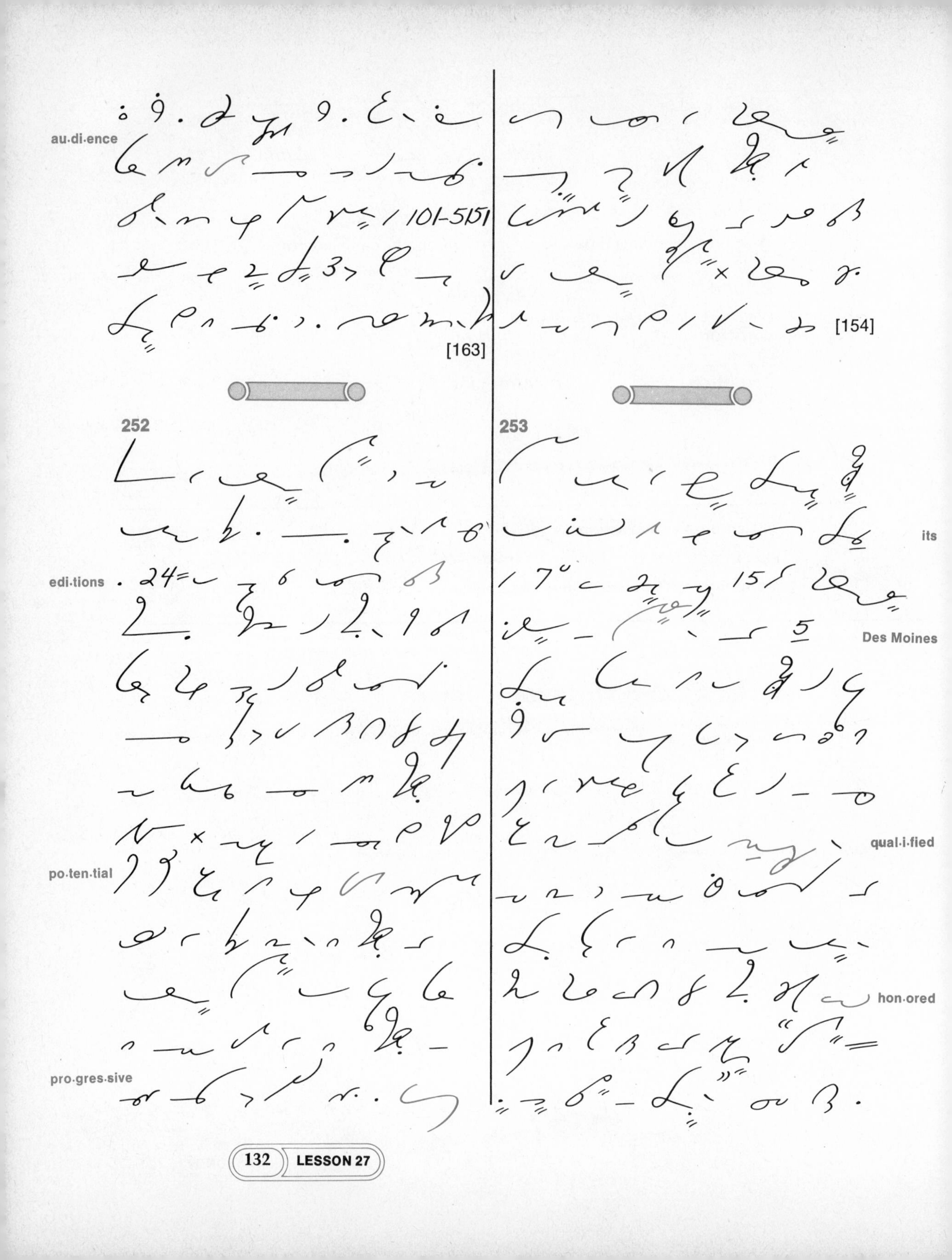

au·di·ence

[163]

[154]

252

edi·tions

po·ten·tial

pro·gres·sive

253

its

Des Moines

qual·i·fied

hon·ored

350 [171]

254

new·ly mar·ried

40

pre·mi·um

[130]

ques·tion·naire

255

May·or

5

15

pre·vails

mi·nor

ma·jor

[111]

Principles

256 Ah, Aw

A dot is used for *a* in words beginning *ah* and *aw.*

Spell: a-h-e-d, ahead; a-oo-a, away

ahead *await* *aware*

away *awake* *award*

257 X

The letter x is usually represented by an *s* written with a slight backward slant.

Compare: miss *mix*

fees *fix*

Spell: m-e-x, mix

box *tax* *fix*

index *taxes* *fixes*

258 Omission of Short U

In the body of a word the sound of short *u*, as in *done,* is omitted:

Before N

done *luncheon* *begun*

fun *run* *refund*

Before M

sum		*come*		*welcome*	
summer		*become*		*lumber*	

Before a Straight Downstroke

rush		*touch*		*judge*	
such		*much*		*budget*	

Building Transcription Skills

259 Business Vocabulary Builder

peruse Examine; study.

budget The amount of money set aside for a particular purpose.

talents Abilities.

Reading and Writing Practice

260 Brief-Form Review Letter

your

han·dling

suf·fered

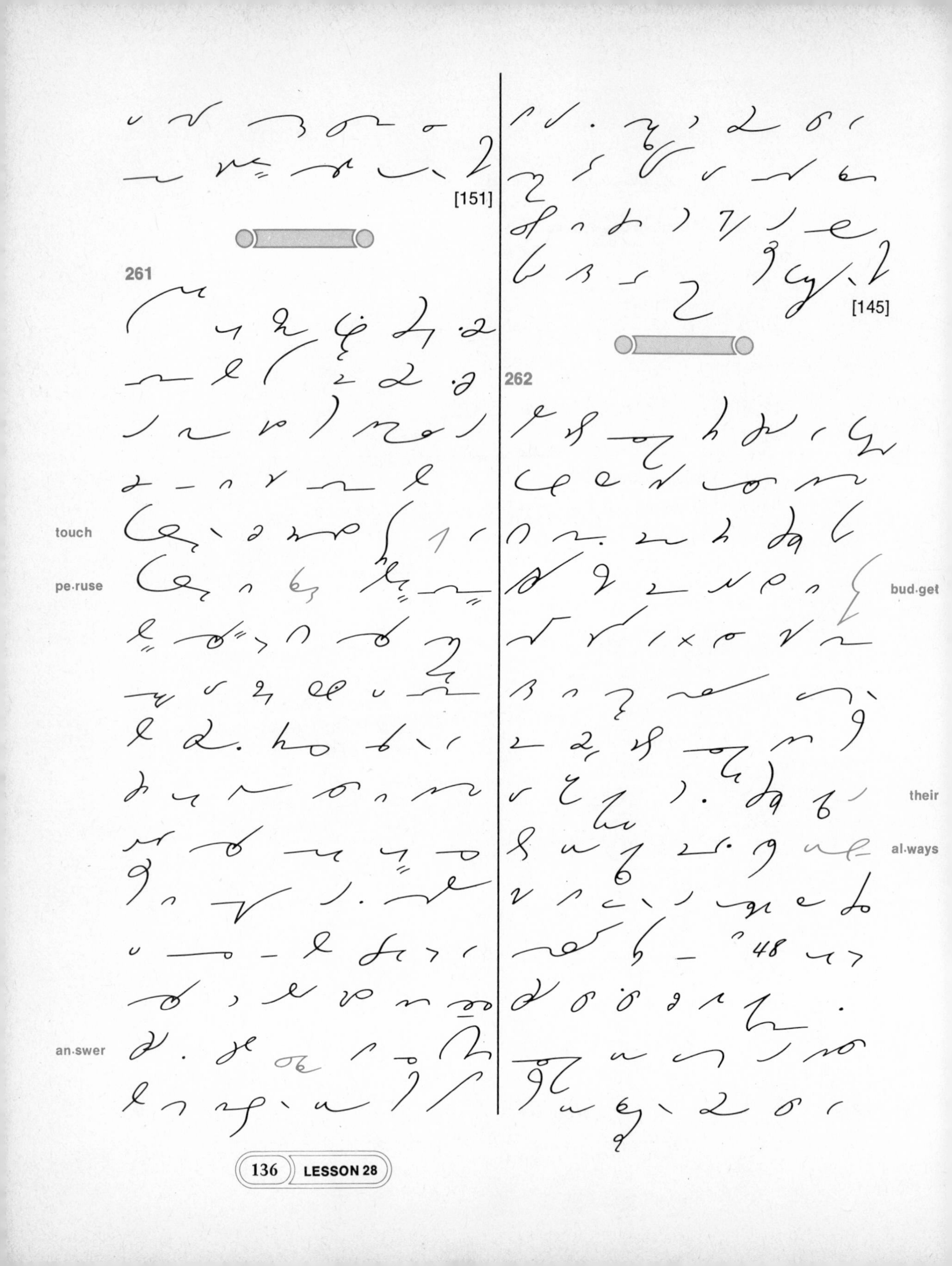

[151]

261

touch

pe·ruse

an·swer

[145]

262

bud·get

their

al·ways

48

41

wel·come

[151]

263

re·ceipt

suc·cess

ap·pli·cants

[104]

264

de·ci·sions

sim·ply

[99]

Principles

265 Brief Forms

You have only one more group to learn after this one.

responsible	*publish, publication*	*usual*
worth	*ordinary*	*world*
public	*experience*	*recognize*

266 Word Beginning Ex-

The word beginning *ex-* is represented by *e-s.*

Spell: ex-p-n-sez, expenses

expenses	*extremely*	*extent*
expert	*exactly*	*expiration*
expectation	*exceeded*	*extra*

267 Word Ending -ful

The word ending *-ful* is represented by *f.*

Spell: k-a-r-ful, careful

careful	*useful*	*helpful*
delightful	*successful*	*helpfully*
thoughtful	*doubtful*	*helpfulness*

268 Word Endings -cal, -cle

Word endings *-cal* and *-cle* (and the preceding vowel) are represented by a disjoined *k*.

Spell: t-e-k-n-ical, technical; a-r-t-ical, article

technical *practical* *articles*

medical *typical* *physical*

logical *economical* *physically*

Building Transcription Skills

269 SIMILAR-WORDS DRILL it's, its

it's Contraction for *it is.*

It's *his day to wash the dishes.*

its Possessive form of *it.*

Its *operating efficiency makes cooking on our stove a delight.*

270 Business Vocabulary Builder

maximum The most.

exceeded Went beyond.

franchises Rights granted to market a company's goods in a particular territory.

Reading and Writing Practice

271 Brief-Form Letter

it's

state's

ex·pe·ri·enced

an·a·lyzes

mon·ey's

their

its

[140]

272

copies

[183]

per·son·nel

273

en·joy·able

au·di·ence

com·plete·ly

speak·er's

[198]

274

own·ing

fran·chises

quite

ev·ery day

[147]

RECALL

After studying the new shorthand devices in Lessons 25 through 29, you have earned another breathing spell! Therefore, you will find no new shorthand strokes or principles in Lesson 30.

In this lesson you will find an Accuracy Practice devoted to the curved strokes of Gregg Shorthand, a Recall Chart, and a Reading and Writing Practice that offers you some interesting suggestions on how to be a good conversationalist.

Accuracy Practice

To get the most benefit from this Accuracy Practice, be sure to follow the procedures suggested on page 115.

275

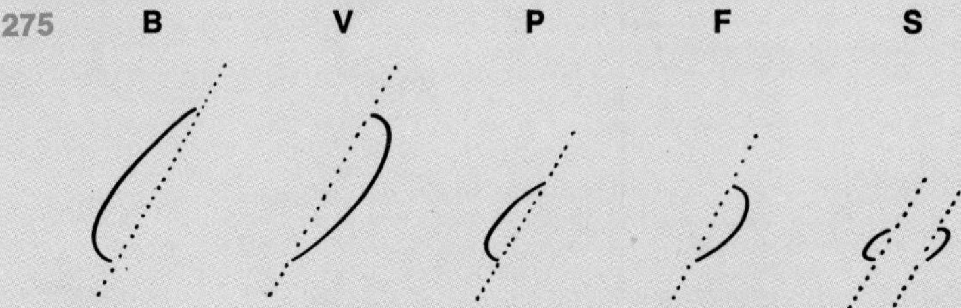

To write these strokes accurately:

- a *Give them approximately the slant indicated by the dotted lines.*
- b *Make the curve deep at the* beginning *of* v, f, *comma* s; *make the curve deep at the* end *of* b, p, *left* s.

practice drill

Puts, spare, business, bears, stairs, sphere, leaves, briefs.

276 **P-r** **P-l** **B-r** **B-l**

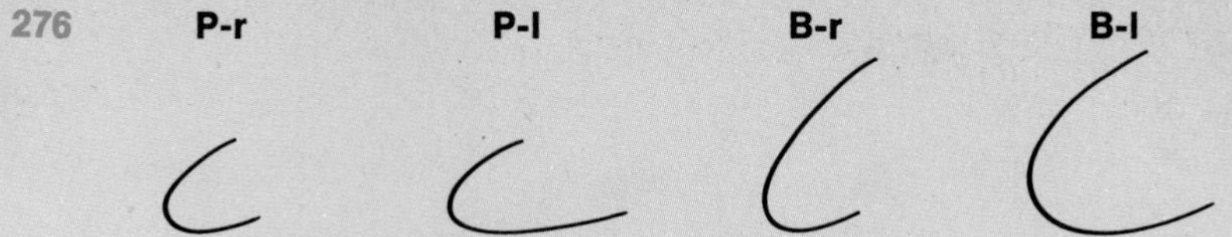

To write these combinations accurately:

- a *Write each without a pause between the first and second letter of each combination.*
- b *Watch your proportions carefully.*

practice drill

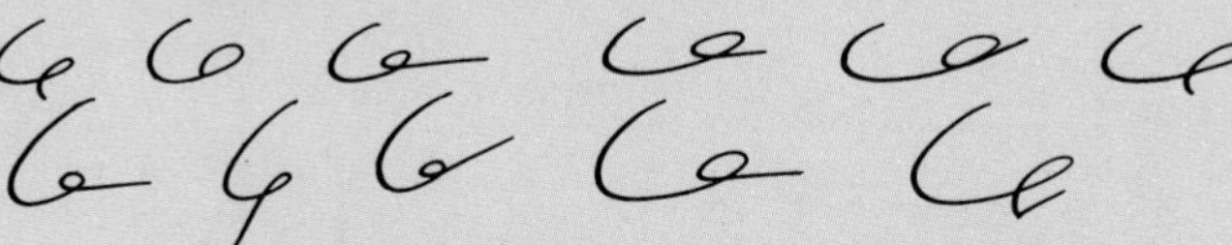

Press, pray, prim, plan, plate, place.
Brim, bridge, bread, blame, blast.

277 **F-r** **F-l**

To write these combinations accurately:

- *Write them with one sweep of the pen, with no stop between the* f *and the* r *or* l.

practice drill

Free, freeze, frame, flee, flame, flap.

278 **Recall Chart**

The following chart contains brief forms, phrasing principles, and word-building principles you studied in Chapter 5.

Can you read the entire chart in 6 minutes or less?

BRIEF FORMS AND DERIVATIVES

1
2

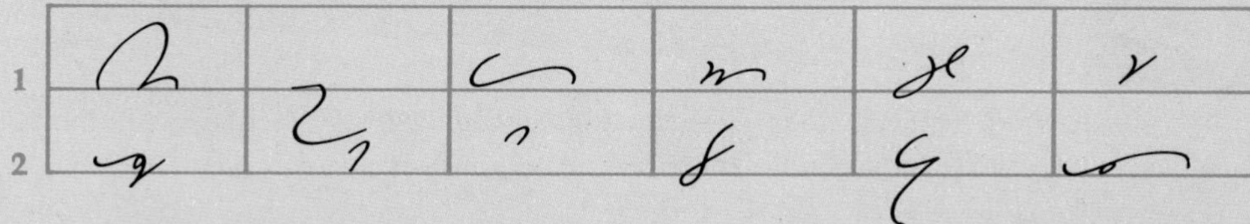

3

4

5

PHRASES

6

7

WORDS

8

9

10

11

12

13

14

15

Building Transcription Skills

279 Business Vocabulary Builder

pastimes Things that amuse.

decipher To make out the meaning of.

facial Of or relating to the face.

Reading and Writing Practice

Reading Scoreboard If you have been studying each Reading and Writing Practice faithfully, your reading speed has no doubt increased since you last measured it in Lesson 18. Let us measure that increase on the first reading of the material in Lesson 30. The following table will help you:

Lesson 30 contains 715 words

If you read Lesson 30 in	20 minutes	your reading rate is	36 words a minute
If you read Lesson 30 in	23 minutes	your reading rate is	31 words a minute
If you read Lesson 30 in	26 minutes	your reading rate is	28 words a minute
If you read Lesson 30 in	29 minutes	your reading rate is	25 words a minute
If you read Lesson 30 in	31 minutes	your reading rate is	23 words a minute
If you read Lesson 30 in	34 minutes	your reading rate is	21 words a minute

If you can read Lesson 30 in 20 minutes or less, you are doing well. If you take considerably longer than 34 minutes, perhaps you should review your homework procedures. For example, are you:

- 1 Practicing in a quiet place at home?
- 2 Practicing without the radio or television set on?
- 3 Spelling aloud any words that you cannot read immediately?

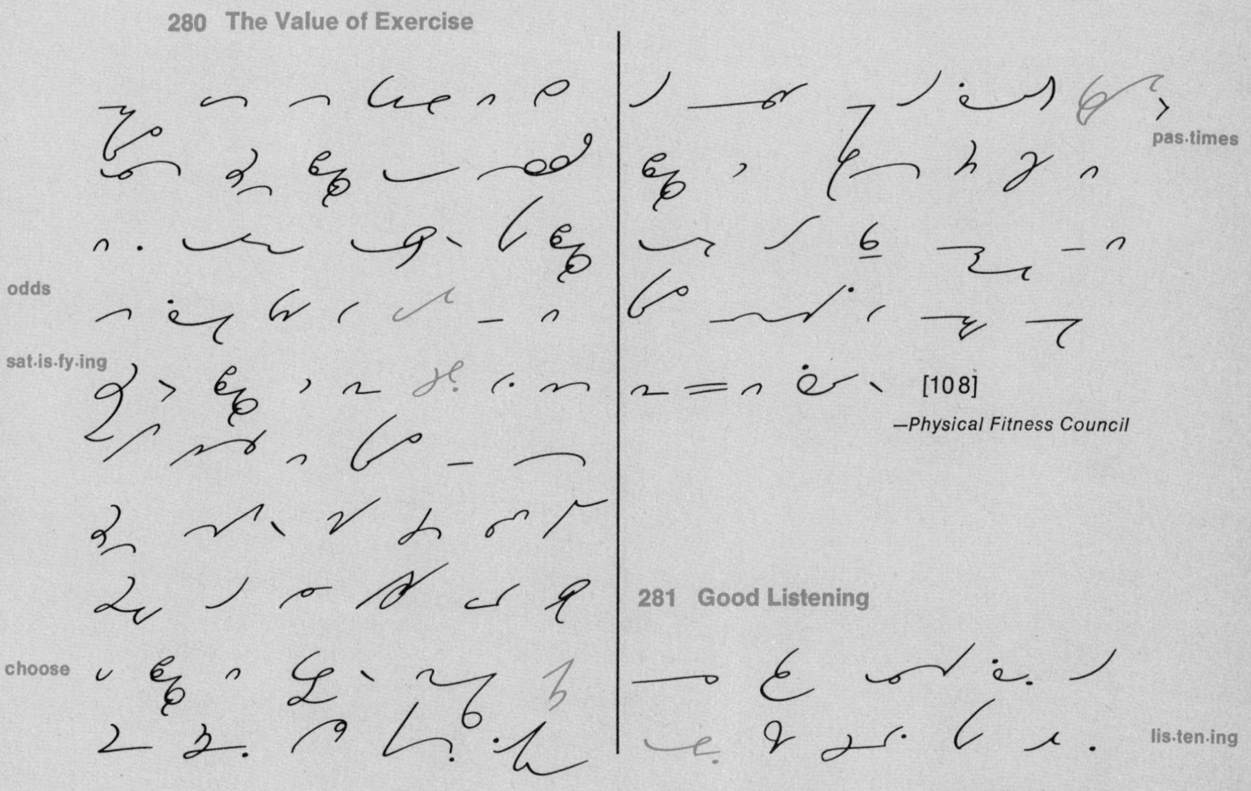

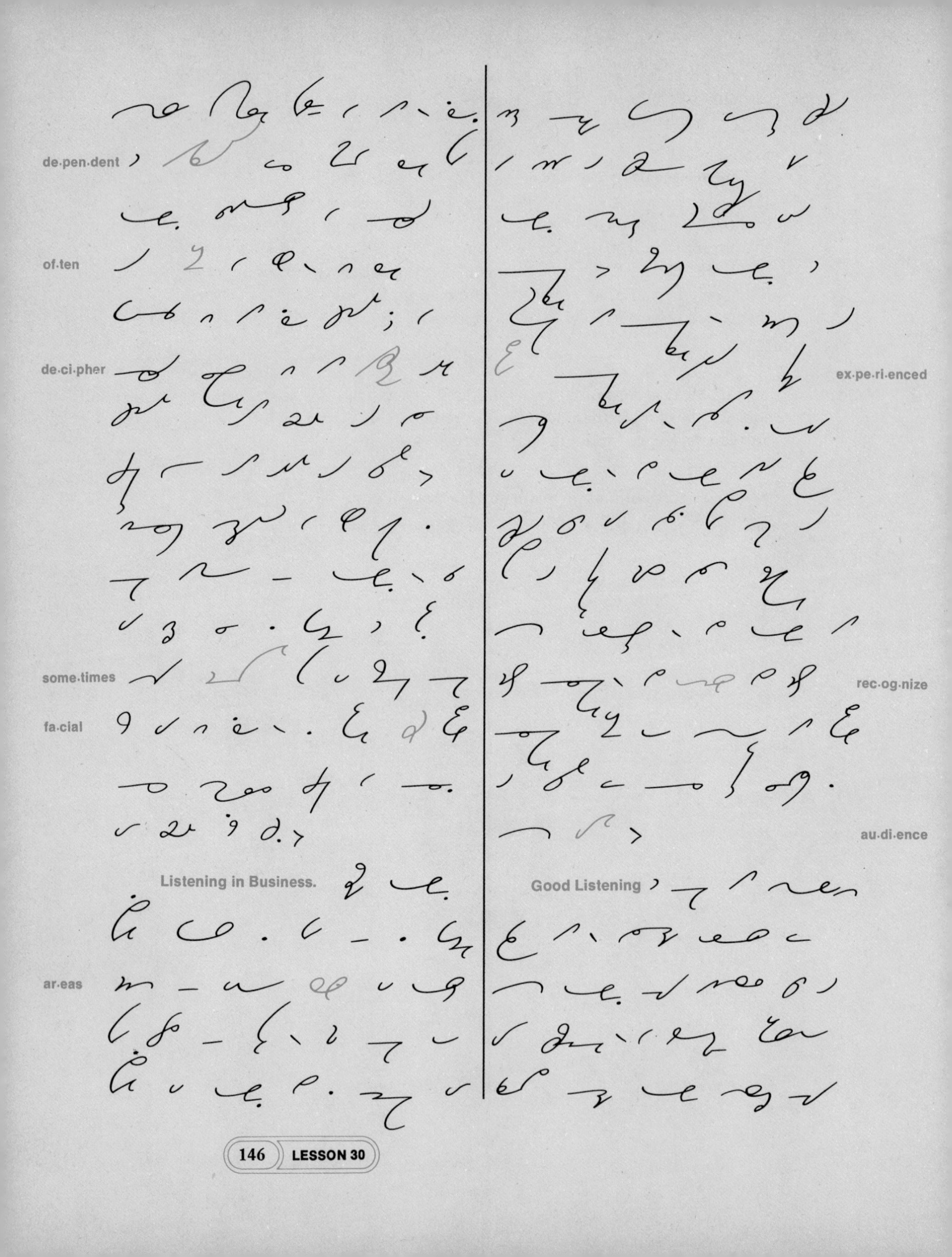

de·pen·dent

of·ten

de·ci·pher

some·times

fa·cial

Listening in Business.

ar·eas

ex·pe·ri·enced

rec·og·nize

au·di·ence

Good Listening

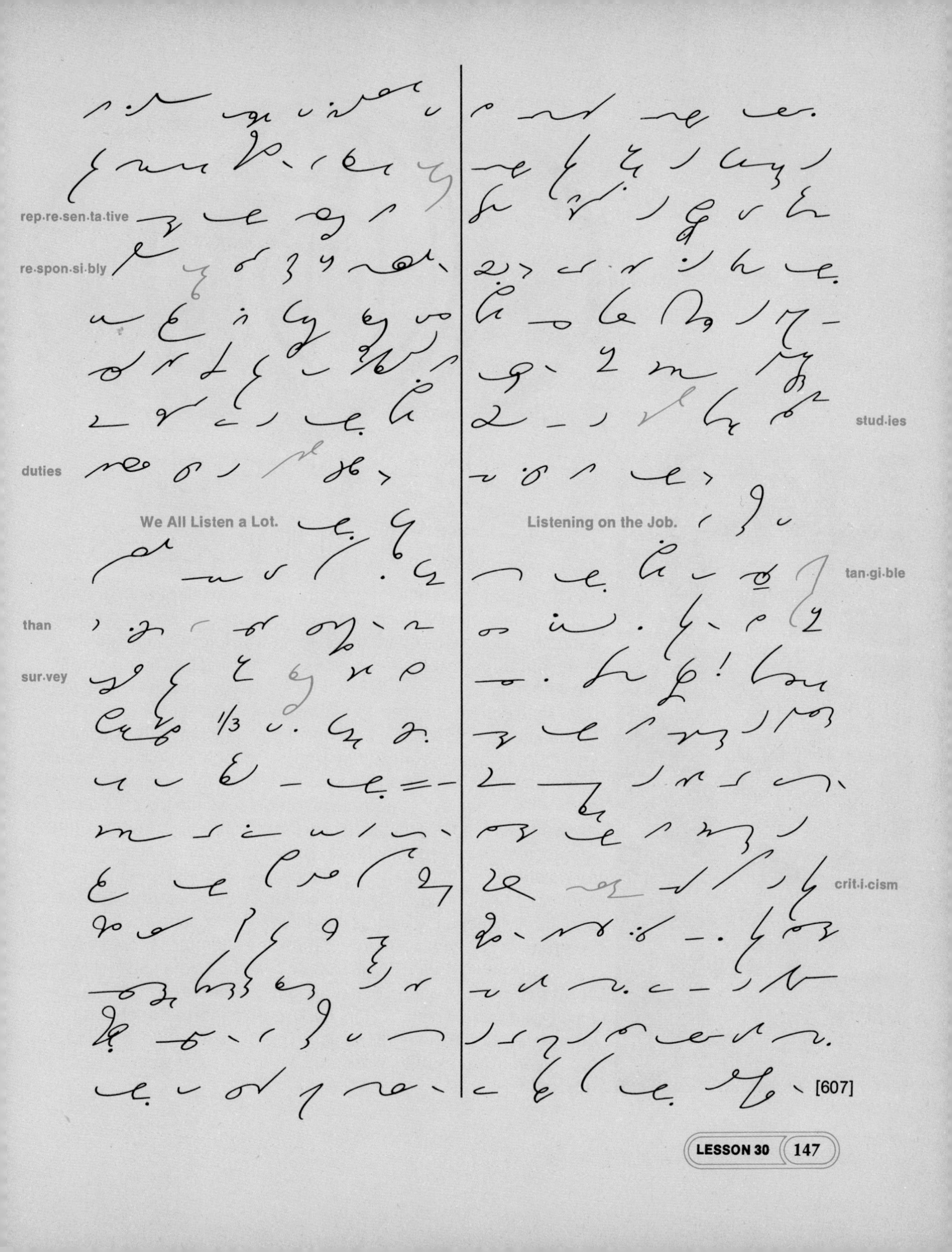

rep·re·sen·ta·tive

re·spon·si·bly

duties

We All Listen a Lot.

than

sur·vey

stud·ies

Listening on the Job.

tan·gi·ble

crit·i·cism

[607]

CHAPTER

The Secretary Communicates

Taking dictation, writing letters, answering the telephone, greeting visitors, interacting with co-workers or clients—all are part of the secretary's job and all depend on the ability to communicate.

In the office, *communications* refers to anything having to do with the written or spoken word. Therefore, most of what the secretary does in the office involves communicating.

Written communications are a vital part of any business. It is the secretary who is responsible for preparing most, if not all, of such communications. An effective business letter, for example, promotes goodwill and elicits the reader's favorable reaction toward both the writer and the organization represented. In all correspondence, the secretary is responsible for accuracy, appearance, and completeness. This means that no less than perfect grammar, spelling, punctuation, and typing will do. It also means that all facts and figures, including addresses and dates, must be accurate.

To produce superior correspondence, the secretary should have a thorough knowledge of English. Grammatical errors may not always be noticed during dictation, but they show up immediately on a typed page. The secretary must learn to correct such errors before they reach the printed page. There is little value in typing at top speed if the resulting work must be redone because of misspelled words.

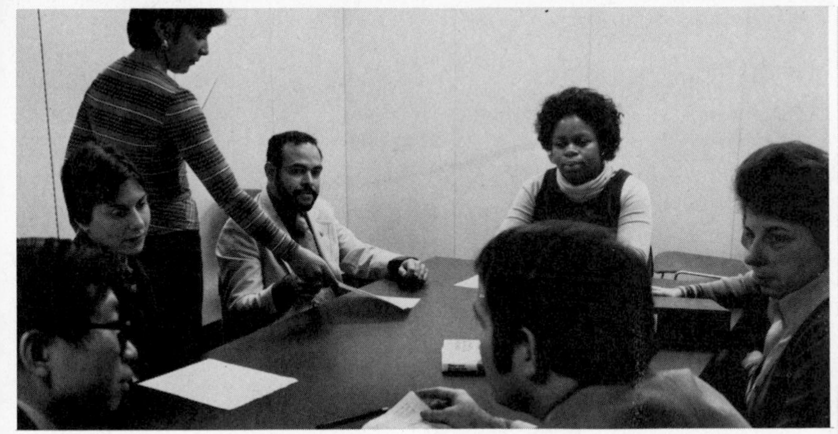

Employers expect their secretaries to spell correctly words which are in general use and to learn to spell technical words that are part of the language of the particular business or profession. Punctuation, too, must be correct. If punctuation does not clarify the writing, the reader may misinterpret the ideas. Incorrect punctuation can easily lead to misunderstanding.

Other important ways of communicating are speaking and listening. The good secretary can handle visitors and telephone callers intelligently and courteously by speaking in a well-modulated voice, enunciating distinctly, choosing words that convey thoughts clearly, and expressing sincere interest.

Studies have shown that executives may spend one-half to two-thirds of their time listening to others. Secretaries must listen nearly as much. Misunderstandings are avoided and work production is increased when the secretary listens intelligently.

Writing, speaking, and listening are skills every secretary needs in order to fulfill one of the most important aspects of the secretarial job—communication.

Principles

282 Brief Forms

This is the last group of brief forms you will have to learn.

never	*throughout*	*govern*
quantity	*object*	*correspond, correspondence*
executive	*character*	

283 Word Ending -ure

The word ending *-ure* is represented by *r*.

Spell: f-u-t-r, future

future	*venture*	*nature*
picture	*miniature*	*natural*

284 Word Ending -ual

The word ending *-ual* is represented by *l*.

Spell: gay-r-a-d-l, gradual

gradual	*individual*	*annual*
eventually	*actual*	*equal*

Building Transcription Skills

285 PUNCTUATION PRACTICE Another skill you must possess if you are to be a successful stenographer or secretary is the ability to punctuate correctly. Some executives dictate punctuation, but most of them rely on their stenographers or secretaries to supply the proper punctuation when they transcribe.

To sharpen your punctuation skill, you will hereafter give special attention to punctuation in each Reading and Writing Practice. In the lessons ahead you will review nine of the most common uses of the comma. Each time one of these uses of the comma occurs in the Reading and Writing Practice, it will be encircled in the shorthand, thus forcefully calling it to your attention.

Practice Suggestions If you follow these suggestions in your homework practice hereafter, your ability to punctuate should improve noticeably.

■ 1 Read carefully the explanation of each comma usage (for example, the explanation of the parenthetical comma given below) to be sure that you understand it. You will encounter many illustrations of each comma usage in the Reading and Writing Practice exercises, so that eventually you will acquire the knack of applying it correctly.

■ 2 Continue to read and copy each Reading and Writing Practice as you have done before. However, add these two important steps:

■ a Each time you see an encircled comma in the Reading and Writing Practice, note the reason for its use, which is indicated directly above the encircled comma.

■ b As you copy the Reading and Writing Practice in your shorthand notebook, insert the commas in your shorthand notes, encircling them as in the textbook.

PUNCTUATION PRACTICE , parenthetical A word or a phrase that is used parenthetically (that is, one not necessary to the grammatical completeness of the sentence) should be set off by commas.

If the parenthetical expression occurs at the end of the sentence, only one comma is used.

There is, of course, *no charge for our services.*

Please let us know, Mr. Strong, *if we can help you.*

We actually print your picture on the card, Ms. Green.

Each time a parenthetical expression occurs in the Reading and Writing Practice, it will be indicated thus in the shorthand: par (,)

---

286 Business Vocabulary Builder

miniature A copy which has been reduced in size.

ventures Business matters involving risk.

exhausted Used up.

Reading and Writing Practice

287 Brief-Form Letter

gov·ern·ment

cor·re·spon·dence

sym·pa·thy

sta·tio·nery

crit·i·cal·ly

par

par

par

par

par

[178]

288

ap·ply·ing

amazed

re·spon·si·ble

par

par

1978

par

rec·om·mend

[167]

289

its

1785

Phil·a·del·phia

pri·ma·ry

suc·cess·ful

par

achieved

par ex·cel·lence

par

bright

[173]

290

Man·u·al

par

opin·ion

par

cop·ies

par

ac·knowl·edge

[131]

291

ac·cept

par

[101]

292

par

man·u·al

com·pli·ments

par

suc·cess

[102]

Principles

293 Word Ending -ily

The word ending *-ily* is represented by a narrow loop.

Compare: *ready* *readily*

Spell: *r-e-d-ily, readily*

easily	*speedily*	*family*
steadily	*temporarily*	*families*

Note the special joining of *s* used in *families.* The special joining enables us to form an outline that is easily read.

294 Word Beginning Al-

The word beginning *al-* is expressed by *o.*

Spell: *all-m-o-s-t, almost*

almost	*altogether*	*although*
also	*already*	*alter*

295 Word Beginnings Dis-, Des-

The word beginnings *dis-, des-* are represented by *d-s.*

Spell: *dis-k-oo-s, discuss; dis-k-r-ī-b, describe*

Dis-

discuss	*disturb*	*disposal*
discussion	*discover*	*discourage*

Des-

describe	*destination*	*destroy*

Building Transcription Skills

296 PUNCTUATION PRACTICE , apposition An expression in apposition (that is, a word or a phrase or a clause that identifies or explains other terms) should be set off by commas. When an expression in apposition occurs at the end of a sentence, only one comma is necessary.

My employer, Mr. Frank Smith, *is on a business trip.*

I will see him on Friday, June 15, *at 3 o'clock.*

His book, Principles of Accounting, *is out of stock.*

For more information call Mr. Brown, our production manager.

▶ Note: When the clarifying term is very closely connected with the principal noun so that the sense would not be complete without the added term, no commas are required.

My brother Fred *arrived yesterday.*

The word embarrassed *is often misspelled.*

Each time an expression in apposition occurs in the Reading and Writing Practice, it will be indicated thus in the shorthand: ap

297 Business Vocabulary Builder

fumes Irritating smoke or gas.

sturdily Strongly; substantially.

apathy Lack of interest or concern; indifference.

endorsement Approval.

Reading and Writing Practice

298 Brief-Form Review Letter

ap

or·ga·ni·za·tion

ap

pol·lu·tion

de·stroy

al·ter

cor·re·spon·dence

ap

de·scrip·tive

par

[162]

299

ac·com·plish

ap

stur·di·ly

than

ap

de·scribes

ad·van·tages

par

al·ready

[158]

300

ap·a·thy

be·lieve

sen·a·tor

en·dorse·ment

enough

ev·ery·body's

[153]

as·sis·tant

com·plete·ly

im·me·di·ate·ly

[151]

301

302

re·ceived

par

[116]

303

ap

15

dis·turb·ing

ap

in·ject

[87]

DICTATION CHECKLIST *When you take dictation, do you—*

- 1 Make every effort to keep up with the dictator?
- 2 Refer to your textbook whenever you are in doubt about the outline for a word or phrase?
- 3 Insert periods and question marks in your shorthand notes?
- 4 Make a real effort to observe good proportion as you write—making large circles large, small circles small, etc.?
- 5 Do you write down the first column of your notebook and then down the second column?

Principles

304 Word Beginnings For-, Fore-

The word beginnings *for-*, *fore-* are represented by *f*.

Spell: *for-gay-e-v, forgive*

forgive *inform* *foreclose*
forget *information* *afford*
form *force* *comfortable*

The *f* is joined with an angle to *r* or *l* to indicate that it represents a word beginning. The *f* is disjoined if the following character is a vowel.

forerunner *forlorn* *forever*

305 Word Beginning Fur-

The word beginning *fur-* is also represented by *f*.

Spell: *fur-n-a-s, furnace*

furnace *furthermore* *refurnish*
further *furnish* *furniture*

306 Ago in Phrases

In expressions of time, *ago* is represented by *gay*.

weeks ago *several days ago* *months ago*
years ago *long time ago* *minutes ago*

Building Transcription Skills

307 PUNCTUATION PRACTICE , series

When the last member of a series of three or more items is preceded by *and* or *or*, place a comma before the conjunction as well as between the other items.

For his birthday he received a tie, a shirt, and a wallet.

I need a person to take dictation, to answer the phone, and to greet callers.

I can see her on July 18, on July 19, or on July 30.

▶ Note: Some authorities prefer to omit the comma before the conjunction. In your shorthand textbooks, however, the comma will always be inserted before the conjunction.

Each time a series occurs in the Reading and Writing Practice, it will be indicated thus in the shorthand: ser (,)

---

308 Business Vocabulary Builder

suites *(of furniture)* Sets of matched furniture for a room.

refurnish To equip with new furniture.

canceled check A check which has been processed by a bank.

Reading and Writing Practice

309 Brief-Form Review Letter

par (,) ef·fect suites 15 30 40 re·fur·nish par (,) (,) [133] char·ac·ter ser (,) (,)

310

15

show·room

cor·re·spon·dence

ser

10

re·spon·si·ble

ser

fur·ther·more

par

ours

[166]

311

ap

15

ap

Fac·to·ry

12

can·celed

is·sues

ser

par

re·ceipt

[119]

312

40

For·ty

ap

rec·og·nized

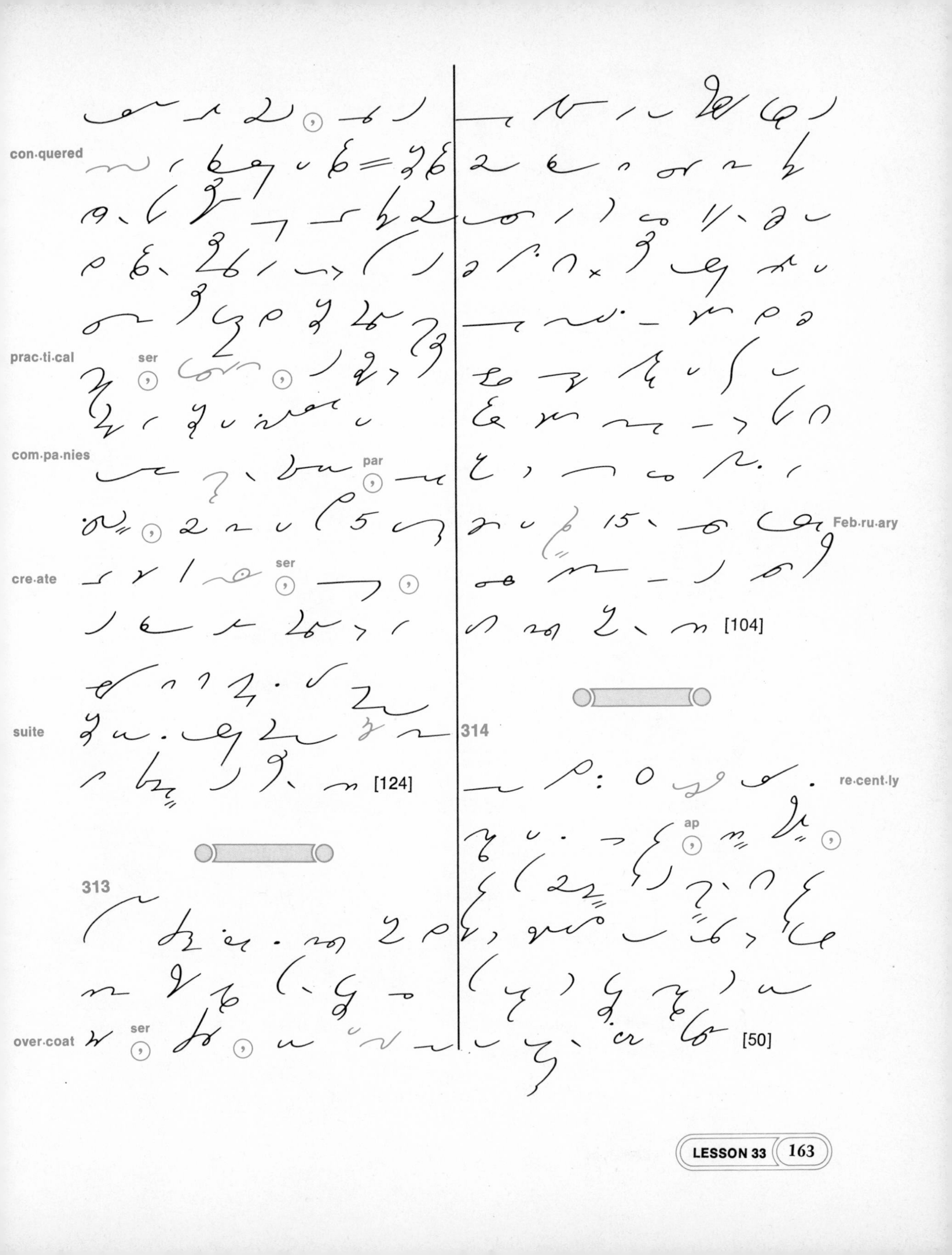

con·quered

prac·ti·cal

ser

com·pa·nies

par

cre·ate

ser

suite

[124]

313

over·coat

ser

Feb·ru·ary

[104]

314

re·cent·ly

ap

[50]

Principles

315 Want in Phrases

In phrases, *want* is represented by the *nt* blend.

you want — *I wanted* — *do you want*

if you want — *we want* — *he wants*

316 Ort

The *r* is omitted in the combination *ort*.

Spell: re-p-o-t, report

report — *airport* — *quarterly*

support — *export* — *mortal*

317 R Omitted in -ern, -erm

The *r* is omitted in the combinations *tern, term, thern, therm, dern.*

Spell: t-e-n, turn

turn — *term* — *southern*

return — *termination* — *thermometer*

eastern — *determine* — *modern*

318 Md, Mt

By rounding off the angle between *m-d,* we obtain the fluent *md* blend. The same stroke also represents *mt.*

Md, Mt

Compare: seem — seemed

Spell: s-e-emd, seemed; emt-e, empty

named	informed	termed
framed	confirmed	empty
claimed	welcomed	prompt

Building Transcription Skills

319 SIMILAR-WORDS DRILL addition, edition

addition Anything added.

This picture is a fine addition *to our collection.*

edition All the copies of a book published at one time.

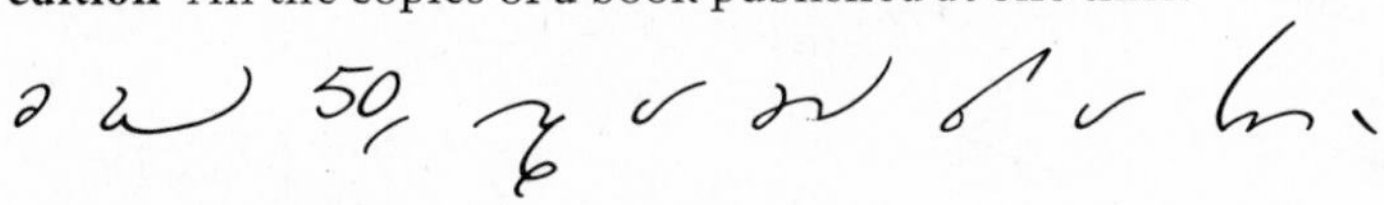

We sold 50,000 copies of the second edition *of the book.*

---

320 Business Vocabulary Builder

undependable Unreliable.

quarterly Every three months.

confirmed Acknowledged.

Reading and Writing Practice

321 Brief-Form Review Letter

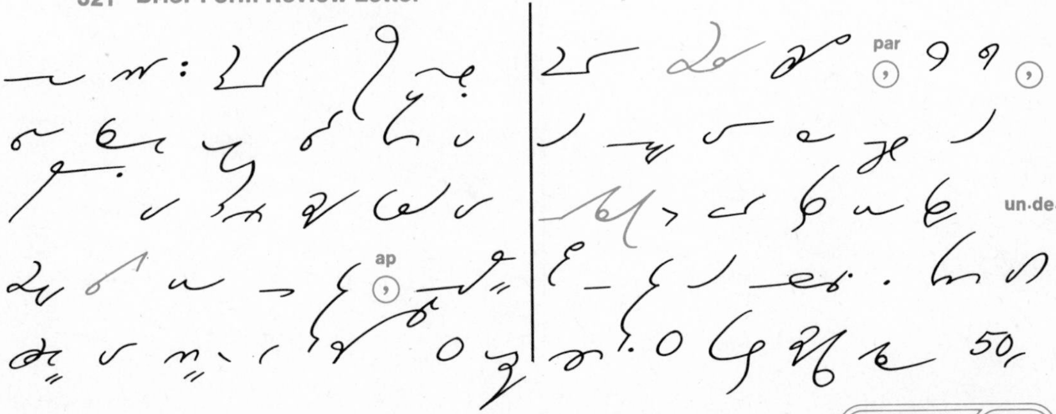

var.ied

un.de.pend.able

edi.tion

par

re·spon·si·ble

ad·di·tion

ap

ad·ver·tis·ing

[178]

322

par

fam·i·ly

year's

ap

ser

Jan·u·ary

mod·ern

Phil·a·del·phia

[196]

323

dif·fer·ence

ser

ser

wor·ry

eco·nom·i·cal

ser

dis·tance

[135]

324

ap

re·ceived

passed

ac·cept

par

[110]

325

ex·pe·ri·enc·ing

ser

par

Mas·sa·chu·setts

[82]

Principles

326 Word Beginnings Inter-, Intr-, Enter-, Entr-

The similar sounding word beginnings *inter-, intr-, enter-, entr-* (and the word *enter*) are represented by a disjoined *n*. This disjoined word beginning, as well as other disjoined word beginnings that you will study in later lessons, is placed above the line of writing close to the remainder of the word.

Inter-

Spell: inter-s-t, interest

interest *international* *interfere*
interview *interrupted* *interval*

Intr-

Spell: intro-d-oo-s, introduce

introduce *introduced* *introduction*

Enter-, Entr-

Spell: enter-ing, entering

entering *enterprises* *entrance*
entered *entertain* *entrances*

327 Word Ending -ings

The word ending *-ings* is represented by a disjoined left *s*.

Spell: o-p-n-ings, openings

openings *meetings* *earnings*
evenings *dealings* *proceedings*

328 Omission of Words in Phrases

It is often possible to omit one or more unimportant words in a shorthand phrase to gain writing speed. In the phrase *one of the,* for example, the word *of* is omitted; we write *one the.* When transcribing, the stenographer will insert *of,* as the phrase would make no sense without that word.

one of the	*some of them*	*many of these*
one of these	*men and women*	*up to date*
one or two	*in the world*	*in the future*

Building Transcription Skills

329 Business Vocabulary Builder

turnover The number of persons hired within a period to replace those leaving a work force.

perplexing Puzzling.

eligible Qualified.

limousine A large chauffeur-driven sedan.

Reading and Writing Practice

330 Brief-Form and Phrase Letter

This letter contains many brief forms and derivatives as well as several illustrations of the phrasing principle you studied in this lesson.

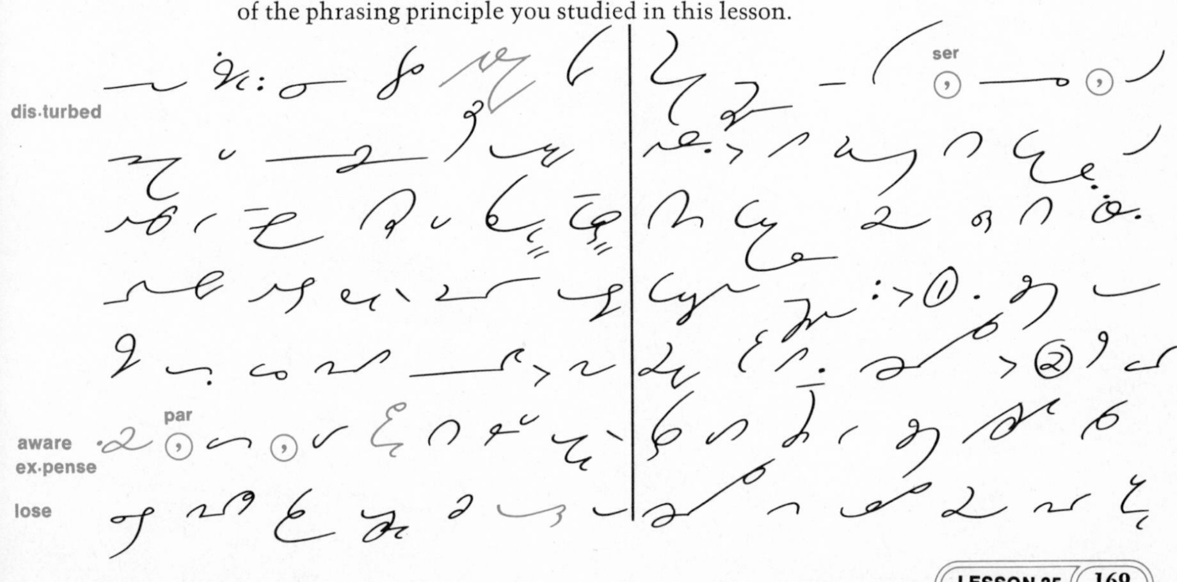

el·i·gi·ble

par

suc·cess·ful·ly

crit·i·cal

[187]

331

morn·ing's

ap

par

sym·pa·thies

ap

ser

prin·ci·ples

[148]

332

crews

ap

ser

un·in·ter·rupt·ed

bored

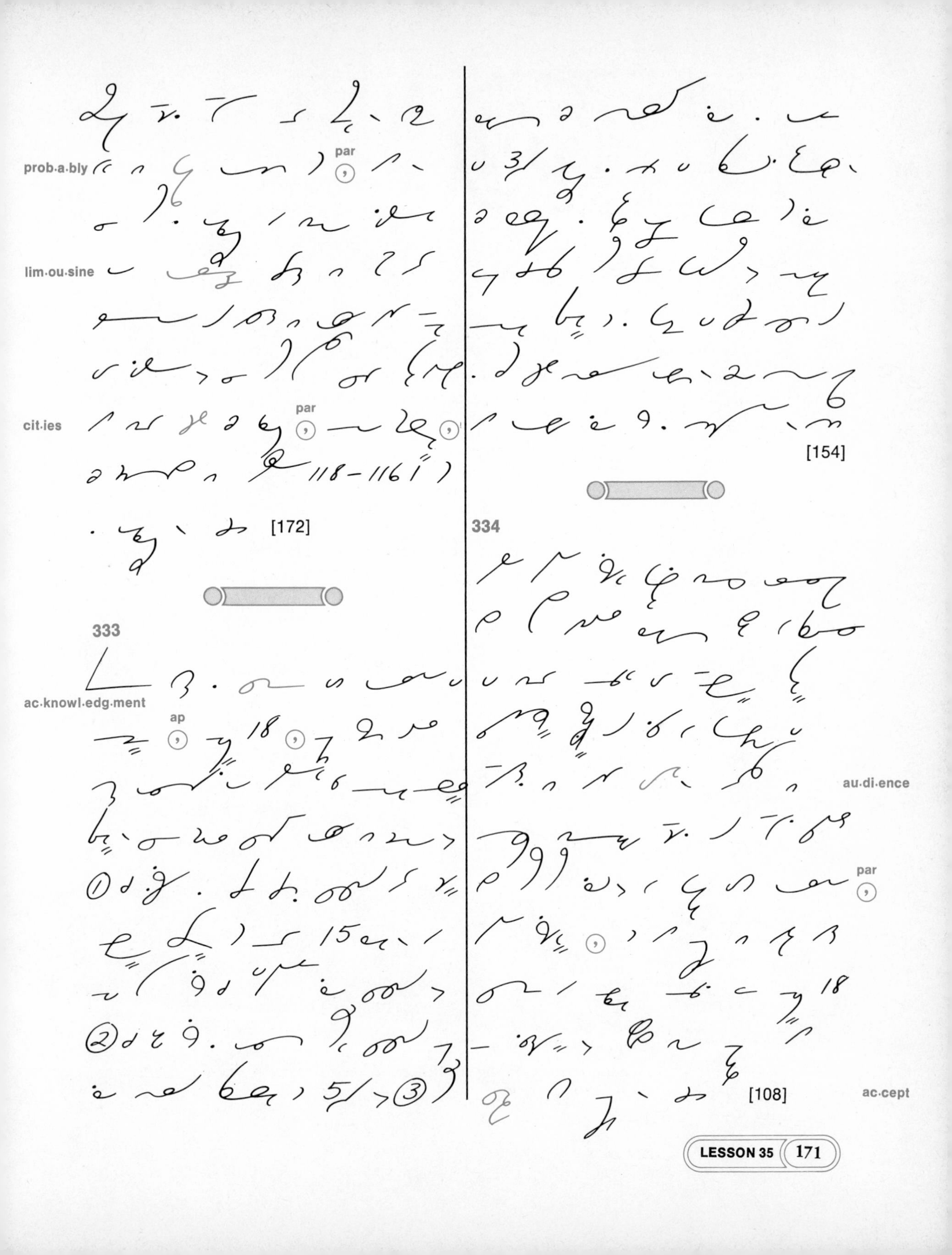

prob·a·bly

lim·ou·sine

cit·ies

[172]

333

ac·knowl·edg·ment

[154]

334

au·di·ence

ac·cept

[108]

RECALL

Lesson 36 is another breather. In Lesson 36 you will find the last principle of joining, a chart that contains a review of shorthand devices you studied in Lessons 1 through 35, and a Reading and Writing Practice that you should find interesting and informative.

Principles of Joining

335 The word endings *-ure* and *-ual* are represented by *r* and *l* except when those endings are preceded by a downstroke.

nature *procedure* *creature*

equal *gradual* *annual*

but

pressure *treasure* *insured*

casual *visual* *visually*

Accuracy Practice

336 **O** **On** **Sho** **Non**

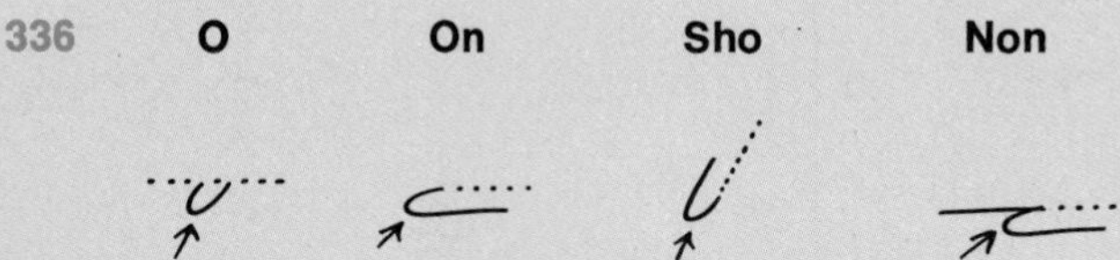

To write these combinations accurately:

■ a *Keep the* o *hook narrow, being sure that the* **beginning** *and* **end** *are on the same level of writing, as indicated by the dotted line.*

- b *Keep the* **o** *in* **on** *and* **sho** *parallel with the consonant, as indicated by the dotted line.*
- c *Make the* **beginning** *of the* **o** *in* **non** *retrace* **end** *of the first* **n**.
- d *Avoid a point at the* **curved** *parts indicated by the arrows.*

practice drill

Of, know, low, own, home, hot, known, moan, shown.

337 **OO** **Noo** **Noom**

To write these combinations accurately:

- a *Keep the* **oo** *hook narrow and deep.*
- b *Keep the* **beginning** *and* **end** *of the hook on the same level of writing.*
- c *In* **noo** *and* **noom**, *keep the hook parallel with the straight line that precedes it.*
- d *In* **noom**, *retrace the* **beginning** *of the* **m** *on the* **bottom** *of the* **oo** *hook.*
- e *Avoid a point at the places indicated by arrows.*

practice drill

You-your, yours truly, you would, to, do, noon, moon, renewal.

338 **Hard** **Hailed**

To write these combinations accurately:

- a *Give the* **end** *of the* **r** *and of the* **l** *a lift upward.*
- b *Do not lift the* **end** *too soon, or the strokes may resemble the* **nd**, **md** *combinations.*

practice drill

Neared, feared, cheered, dared, hold, sold, bold.

339 Recall Chart

This chart contains illustrations of shorthand principles you studied in previous lessons. There are 12 brief forms and derivatives, 12 phrases, and 66 words in the chart.

Can you read the entire chart in 5 minutes?

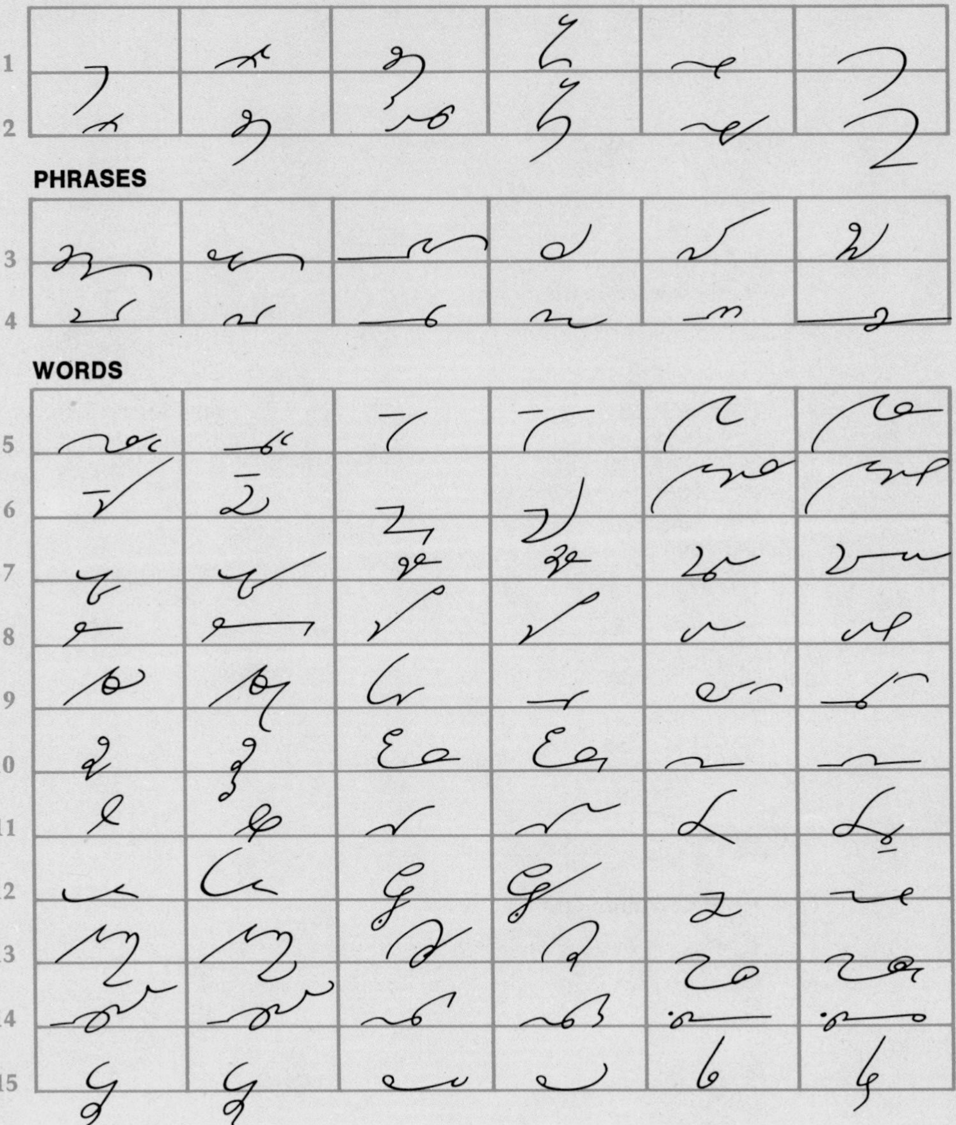

Building Transcription Skills

340 Business Vocabulary Builder

effecting Bringing about; resulting in.

capacity Ability.

accord *(verb)* Give to.

Reading and Writing Practice

341 The Secretary in Business

sci·en·tif·ic

ap

threat

ex·pe·ri·enced

re·spon·si·ble

ser

The Role of the Secretary.

par

role

ad·di·tion

ser

chal·leng·ing

par

cor·re·spon·dence

60, 15

ser

ef·fect·ing

ar·eas

The secretary and

par

Secretarial Positions Differ.

af·fect·ed

or·ga·ni·za·tion

ser

en·ter·prise

pri·mar·i·ly

[486]

342 Courtesy and Success

par

calm

odd

[216]

343 Sleep and Diet

iden·ti·cal

co·op·er·a·tion

ser

Our courtesy

ser

snack

ser

weight

ser

an·swer

cal·o·ries

con·scious

[113]

CHAPTER

7 The Secretary Takes Dictation

The ability to take dictation is the core of the secretary's job, but just being able to write shorthand is not enough. Success in this important part of the secretary's work will depend upon writing good, sensible notes which can be transcribed easily and quickly with accuracy.

Handling dictation may be the secretary's most important task. The secretary must be ready to take dictation whenever the employer wants to give it. When the boss is ready to dictate, all other work must be put aside.

Many secretaries form the good habit of checking—the first thing in the morning—to be sure that their dictation tools are in order. "I wouldn't think of answering my employer's call without a shorthand notebook and my pen," says one secretary. When summoned to the boss's office, the secretary is ready to answer promptly with an open shorthand notebook and a pen.

During the dictation session, the secretary makes it possible for the employer to get the work done as expeditiously as possible. All dictation and instructions are recorded accurately. Nothing is done to divert or annoy the dictator.

The dictating habits of employers vary greatly. For some, dictating is hard work and ideas come slowly. Some employers may pause for long periods during a difficult letter or report, but once they clarify the idea they want to express, they are likely to reel it off very rapidly. Other employers, more gifted at expressing themselves, dictate at a fairly regular or brisk pace.

Employers expect their secretaries to be proficient shorthand writers, able to keep up with the dictation no matter how fast the pace becomes. True, if the dictation speed of an entire letter is average, it may seem fairly slow; yet during every dictation period there are many times when a high shorthand speed is required to keep up.

To maintain your shorthand skill, use it outside the office too. Try using it for all personal notes and instructions. Create opportunities to practice reading and writing shorthand whenever you can.

Following a dictation session, the secretary should get all the instructions and clarifications needed before leaving the boss's office so that it will not be necessary to interrupt later. All instructions should be written so that there is no need to rely on memory alone.

Much of the business conducted today takes the form of letters and other written communications. To expedite communicating information, today's secretary must be able to take and transcribe dictation both quickly and accurately.

Principles

344 Word Ending -ingly

The word ending *-ingly* is represented by a disjoined *e* circle.

Spell: in-k-r-e-s-ingly, increasingly

increasingly *convincingly* *willingly*
exceedingly *amazingly* *interestingly*

345 Word Beginning Im-

The word beginning *im-* is represented by *m*.

Spell: im-p-r-e-s, impress

impress *impartial* *import*
impressive *improvement* *impact*

346 Word Beginning Em-

The word beginning *em-* is also represented by *m*.

Spell: em-p-ī-r, empire

empire *emphatically* *employee*
embarrass *embraced* *employer*

347 Im-, Em- Followed by a Vowel

When *im-, em-* are followed by a vowel, they are written in full.

immodest *immoral* *emotional*

348 Omission of Minor Vowel

When two vowel sounds come together, the minor vowel may be omitted.

various	period	situate
serious	genuine	situated
previous	theory	situation

Building Transcription Skills

349 PUNCTUATION PRACTICE , if clause A subordinate (or introductory) clause followed by a main clause is separated from the main clause by a comma. A subordinate clause is often introduced by subordinating conjunctions including *if, as, when, though, although, because,* and others. In this lesson you will consider only subordinate clauses introduced by *if.*

If you complete the work before 5 o'clock, *you may leave.*

If I cannot come, *I will call you.*

If John is ill, *he should stay home.*

Each time a subordinate clause beginning with *if* occurs in the Reading and Writing Practice, it will be indicated thus in the shorthand: if (,)

350 Business Vocabulary Builder

impartially Fairly.

emphatically Forcefully.

reimbursed Paid back.

Reading and Writing Practice

351 Brief-Form Review Letter

ap (,)

un·usu·al (,)

par

par

ser

pe·ri·od·i·cals

re·quest

if

[181]

352

the·o·ries

ser

par

re·im·bursed

[146]

353

if

ap

em·ploy·ee

el·i·gi·ble

im·pres·sive

ser

par

won

ser

ser

25

ap

15

pre·vi·ous

if

par

sat·is·fac·to·ry

[170]

354

if

1

the·o·ries

ser

2

3

ser

im·par·tial·ly

4

5

amaz·ing·ly

if

par

[157]

Principles

355 Word Ending -ship

The word ending *-ship* is represented by a disjoined *ish.*

Spell: *s-t-e-m-ship, steamship*

steamship *membership* *fellowship*
friendship *relationships* *leadership*

356 Word Beginning Sub-

The word beginning *sub-* is represented by *s.*

Spell: *sub-m-e-t, submit*

submit *subscription* *substantial*
subscribe *subdivision* *suburban*

357 Word Ending -ulate

The word ending *-ulate* is represented by a disjoined *oo* hook.

Spell: *r-e-gay-ulate, regulate*

regulate *congratulate* *tabulator*
stimulate *formulate* *calculated*

358 Word Ending -ulation

The word ending *-ulation* is represented by *oo-shun.*

Spell: r-e-gay-ulation, regulation

regulation *accumulation* *stimulation*

insulation *circulation* *congratulations*

359 Word Ending -rity

The word ending *-rity* (and a preceding vowel) is represented by a disjoined *r.*

Spell: m-a-j-rity, majority

majority *prosperity* *charity*

security *sincerity* *authority*

Building Transcription Skills

360 PUNCTUATION PRACTICE , as clause A subordinate clause introduced by *as* and followed by a main clause is separated from the main clause by a comma.

As you know, *you have not yet paid your June bill.*

As I cannot attend the meeting, *I will send my assistant.*

Each time a subordinate clause beginning with *as* occurs in the Reading and Writing Practice, it will be indicated thus in the shorthand: as (,)

361 Business Vocabulary Builder

prosperity Economic well-being.

subsidiary A company owned by another.

proceeds *(noun)* Income.

Reading and Writing Practice

362 Brief-Form Review Letter

ex.pe.ri.enced

ser

sub·stan·tial·ly

as

sub·sid·iary

ap

Hous·ton

par

prob·a·bly

as

any·thing

if

an·swer

[196]

363

par

as

ap

sub·scrip·tion

ar·ti·cles

ser

[170]

364

char·i·ty

ap

pro·ceeds

par

gen·er·os·i·ty

[118]

365

as

pleas·ant

[104]

Principles

366 Word Ending -lity

The word ending *-lity* (and a preceding vowel) is represented by a disjoined *l*.

Spell: a-b-lity, ability

ability   *dependability*   *utility*
facility   *locality*   *realities*
possibility   *personality*   *qualities*

367 Word Ending -lty

The word ending *lty* (and a preceding vowel) is also represented by a disjoined *l*.

Spell: f-a-k-ulty, faculty

faculty   *penalty*   *royalty*

368 Word Ending -self

The word ending *-self* is represented by *s*.

Spell: h-e-r-self, herself; it-self, itself

herself   *himself*   *myself*
itself   *yourself*   *oneself*

369 Word Ending -selves

The word ending *-selves* is represented by *ses.*

Spell: them-selves, themselves

themselves *ourselves* *yourselves*

Building Transcription Skills

370 PUNCTUATION PRACTICE , when clause A clause introduced by *when* and followed by the main clause is separated from the main clause by a comma.

When I was in Dallas, *I attended three meetings.*

When you do not pay your bills, *you are endangering your credit.*

Each time a subordinate clause beginning with *when* occurs in the Reading and Writing Practice, it will be indicated thus in the shorthand: when

371 Business Vocabulary Builder

individuality Total character distinguishing a person or thing from another.

stability Firmness.

integrity Honesty.

Reading and Writing Practice

372 Brief-Form Review Letter

as ap when re·ceived fac·ul·ty re·spon·si·bil·i·ty

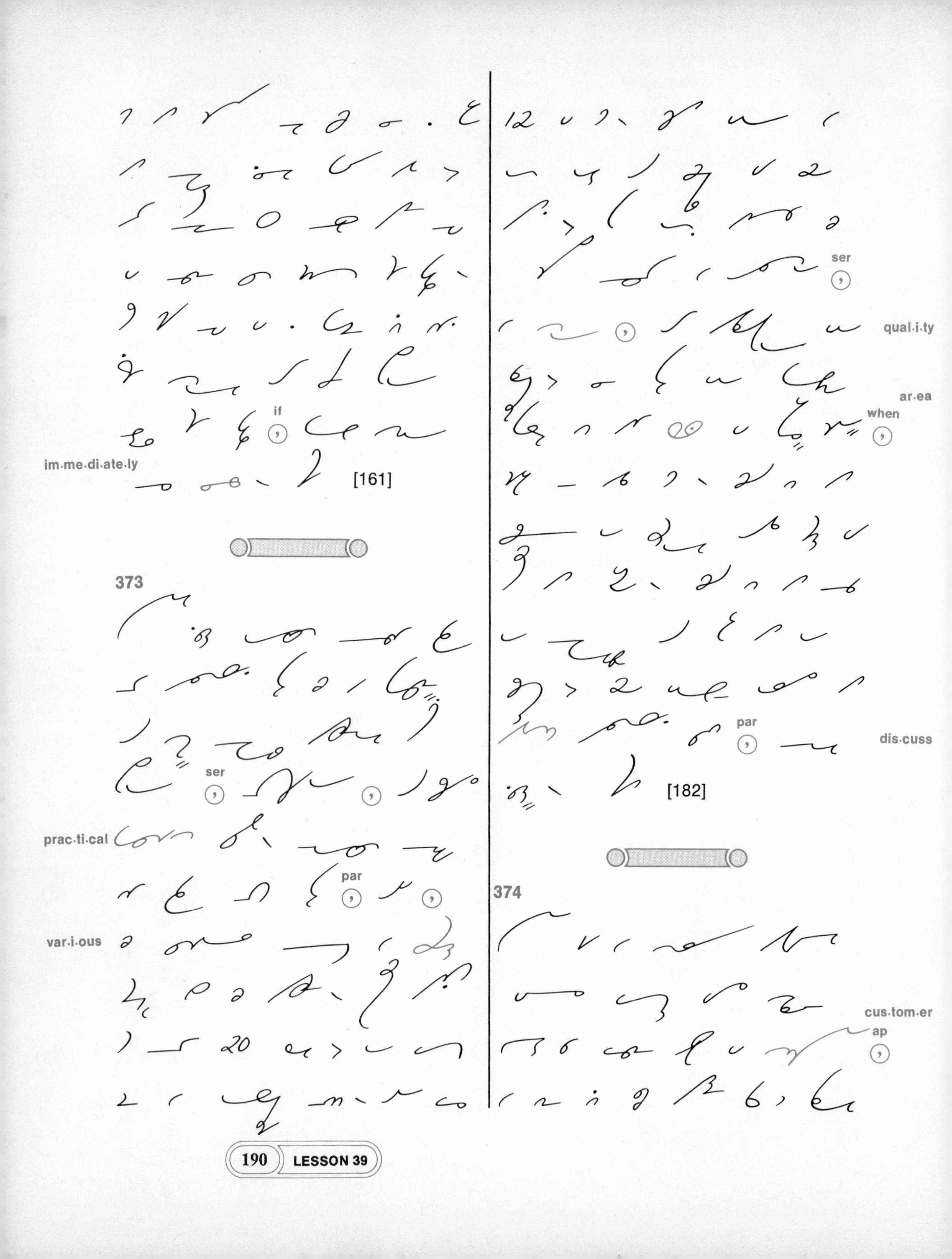

if

im·me·di·ate·ly

[161]

373

ser

prac·ti·cal

par

var·i·ous

ser

qual·i·ty

ar·ea

when

par

dis·cuss

[182]

374

cus·tom·er

ap

due

ap

sub·stan·tial

par

prompt·ly

par

if

re·mit·tances

[135]

375

route

gov·ern·ment

par

as

par·tic·u·lar·ly

text

when

be·lieve

as

pro·ceed

[150]

Principles

376 Abbreviated Words—in Families

Many long words may be abbreviated in shorthand by dropping the endings. This device is, of course, used in longhand, as *Jan.* for *January.* The extent to which you can avail yourself of this device will depend on your familiarity with the words and with the subject matter of the dictation. Whenever you are in doubt as to whether you should abbreviate a word or write it out, write it out!

The ending of a word is not dropped when a special shorthand word-ending form has been provided, such as *-cal* in *practical.*

Notice how many of the words written with this abbreviating device fall naturally into families of similar endings.

-quent

frequent	*consequent, consequence*	*subsequent*
frequently	*consequently*	*eloquent*

-tribute

attribute	*distribute*	*distribution*
contribute	*distributed*	*distributor*

-quire

inquire	*inquired*	*inquiry*
require	*required*	*requirement*

-titute

substitute	*institute*	*constitution*

-titude

aptitude [shorthand] *gratitude* [shorthand] *attitude* [shorthand]

Building Transcription Skills

377 PUNCTUATION PRACTICE , introductory A comma is used to separate a subordinate (or introductory) clause from a following main clause. You have already studied the application of this rule to subordinate clauses introduced by *if, as,* and *when.* Here are additional examples:

While I understand the statement, *I do not agree with it.*

Although it was only 3 o'clock, *he closed the office.*

Before you sign the contract, *discuss it with your lawyer.*

A comma is also used after introductory words or phrases such as *furthermore, on the contrary,* and *for instance.*

Furthermore, *the report was incomplete.*

On the contrary, *you are the one who is responsible.*

For your convenience in sending your check, *I am enclosing an envelope.*

Each time a subordinate word, phrase, or clause other than one beginning with *if, as,* or *when* occurs in the Reading and Writing Practice, it will be indicated thus in the shorthand: intro (,)

Note: If the subordinate clause or other introductory expression follows the main clause, the comma is usually not necessary.

I am enclosing an envelope for your convenience in sending your check.

---

378 Business Vocabulary Builder

atlas A bound collection of maps.

maintenance The upkeep of property or equipment.

endeavor *(noun)* A serious, determined effort.

Reading and Writing Practice

379 Brief-Form Review Letter

con·fer·ence

intro (,)

intro (,)

ex·cel·lent

ban·quet

ap

intro

in·quired

par

oc·ca·sion

intro

ar·ea

[176]

380

lease

when

ser

fu·el

intro

intro

ve·hi·cle

if

if

as

re·al·ize

[138]

381

re·ferred

as

intro

re·quests

par

readi·ly

un·pleas·ant

par

par

en·deav·or

[139]

ap

ur·gent

intro

co·op·er·a·tion

sat·is·fied

par

[138]

382

383

Man·u·al

ap

ap

com·mer·cial

col·ors

piece

intro

in·qui·ries

[132]

384

wom·en

par

com·plete·ly

fur·ther·more

intro

ser

par

[135]

Principles

385 Abbreviated Words—in Families (Continued)

-graph

phonograph	*photograph*	*photographically*
paragraph	*photographic*	*autographed*
telegraph	*photographs*	*stenographer*

386 Abbreviated Words—Not in Families

The ending may be omitted from long words even though they do not fall into a family.

anniversary	*statistic*	*reluctant, reluctance*
convenient, convenience	*statistics*	*privilege*
significant, significance	*statistical*	*privileged*
memorandum	*equivalent*	*privileges*

387 Word Beginning Trans-

The word beginning *trans-* is represented by a disjoined *t.*

Spell: trans-a-k-t, transact

transact	*transmitted*	*transfer*
transaction	*translation*	*transcribe*
transportation	*transistor*	*transplant*

Building Transcription Skills

388 SIMILAR-WORDS DRILL assistance, assistants

assistance Help.

Thank you for the assistance *you gave me with my term paper.*

assistants Helpers.

One of my assistants *will discuss the matter with you.*

---

389 Business Vocabulary Builder

transmitted Forwarded; handed over.

reluctant Unwilling.

autographed Signed by hand.

Reading and Writing Practice

390 Brief-Form Review Letter

par

Gov·er·nor

when

gra·ti·tude

intro

as·sis·tance

per·son·al [129]

391

intro

an·ni·ver·sa·ry

priv·i·lege

par

intro

wouldn't

if ser

en·ve·lope

[173]

392

ap

oc·ca·sion

as

max·i·mum

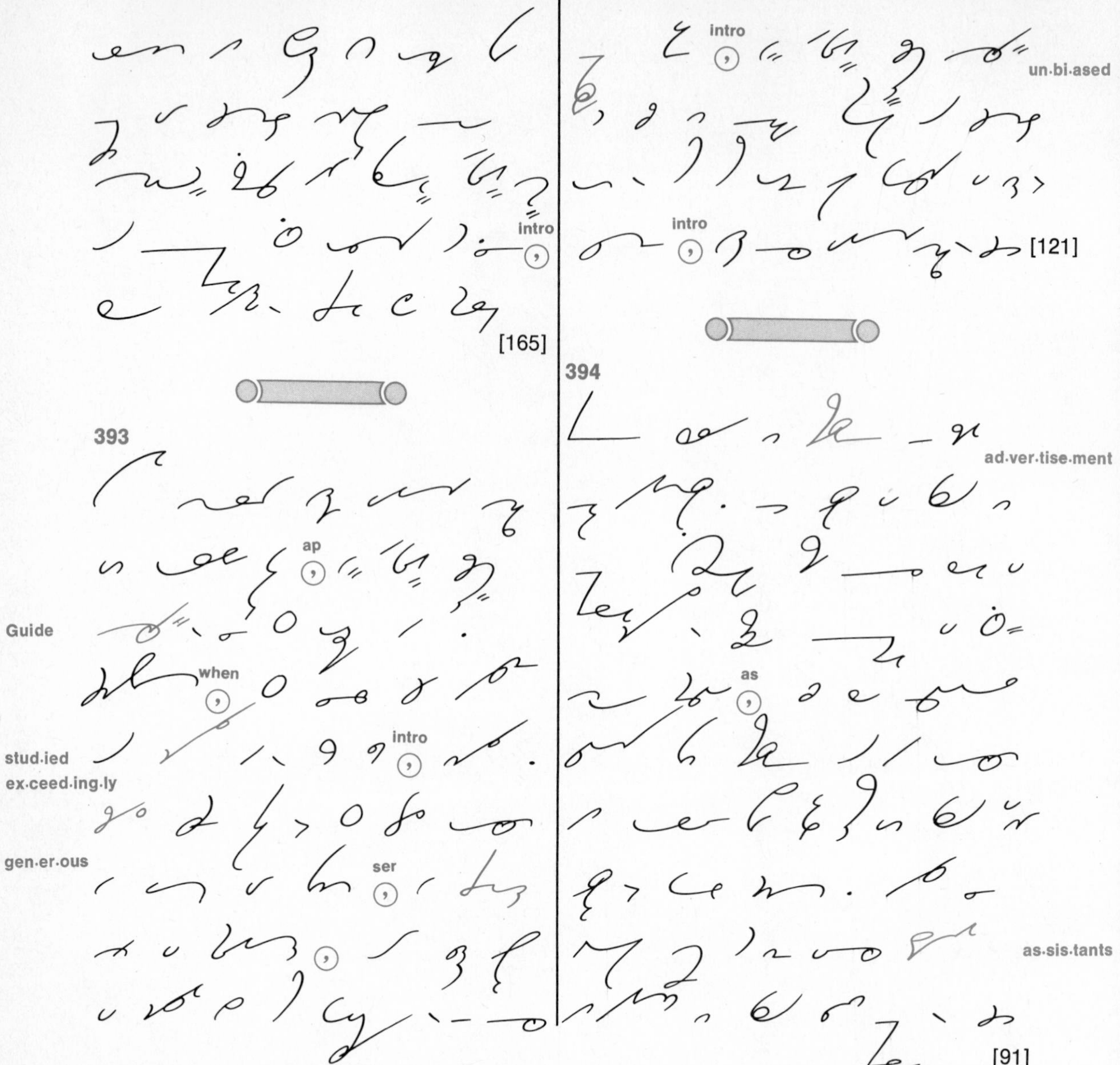

TRANSCRIPTION CHECKLIST *Are you getting the full benefit from the spelling and punctuation helps in the Reading and Writing Practice by—*

- 1 Encircling all punctuation in your notes as you copy each Reading and Writing Practice?
- 2 Noting the reason for the use of each punctuation mark to be sure that you understand why it was used?
- 3 Spelling aloud at least once the words given in the margin of the shorthand?

RECALL

There are no new shorthand devices for you to learn in Lesson 42. However, this lesson does contain an Accuracy Practice and a review of the word beginnings and endings you have studied thus far. The Reading and Writing Practice contains some suggestions that you should heed carefully if you wish to get ahead in business.

Accuracy Practice

395 **My** **Lie** **Fight**

To write these combinations accurately:

- **a** *Join the circle in the same way that you would join an* **a** *circle, but turn the* **end** *inside the circle.*
- **b** *Before turning the* **end** *of the circle inside, be sure that the stroke touches the stroke to which the* **i** *is joined.*
- **c** *Avoid making a point at the places indicated by arrows.*

practice drill

My, night, sight, line, mile.

396 **Ow** **Oi**

To write these combinations accurately:

- a *Keep the hooks deep and narrow.*
- b *Place the circle* **outside** *the hooks as indicated by the dotted lines.*

practice drill

Out, now, doubt, scout, toy, soil, annoy.

397 **Th** **Nt, Nd** **Mt, Md**

To write these combinations accurately:

- a *Slant the strokes as indicated by the dotted lines.*
- b *Start these strokes to the right and upward.*

practice drill

There are, and will, empty, health, lined, ashamed.

Compare:

Hint, heard; tamed, detailed.

398 **Recall Chart**

This chart reviews word beginnings and word endings that you have studied. It has 90 words containing word beginnings and word endings. Can you read the entire chart in 4 minutes or less?

WORD BEGINNINGS AND ENDINGS

1						
2						
3						
4						
5						
6						
7						
8						
9						
10						
11						
12						
13						
14						
15						

Building Transcription Skills

399 Business Vocabulary Builder

tribulations Trying experiences.
comprehend Understand.
similarities Likenesses.
significantly Considerably.

Reading and Writing Practice

Reading Scoreboard The last time you measured your reading speed was in Lesson 30. See how much your reading speed has grown since Lesson 30. The following table will help you measure your reading speed on the *first reading* of Lesson 42.

Lesson 42 contains 454 words

If you read Lesson 42 in **12 minutes** your reading rate is **38 words a minute**
If you read Lesson 42 in **14 minutes** your reading rate is **32 words a minute**
If you read Lesson 42 in **16 minutes** your reading rate is **28 words a minute**
If you read Lesson 42 in **18 minutes** your reading rate is **25 words a minute**
If you read Lesson 42 in **21 minutes** your reading rate is **22 words a minute**
If you read Lesson 42 in **23 minutes** your reading rate is **20 words a minute**

If you can read Lesson 42 through the first time in less than 16 minutes, you are doing well.

400 Evaluate Yourself

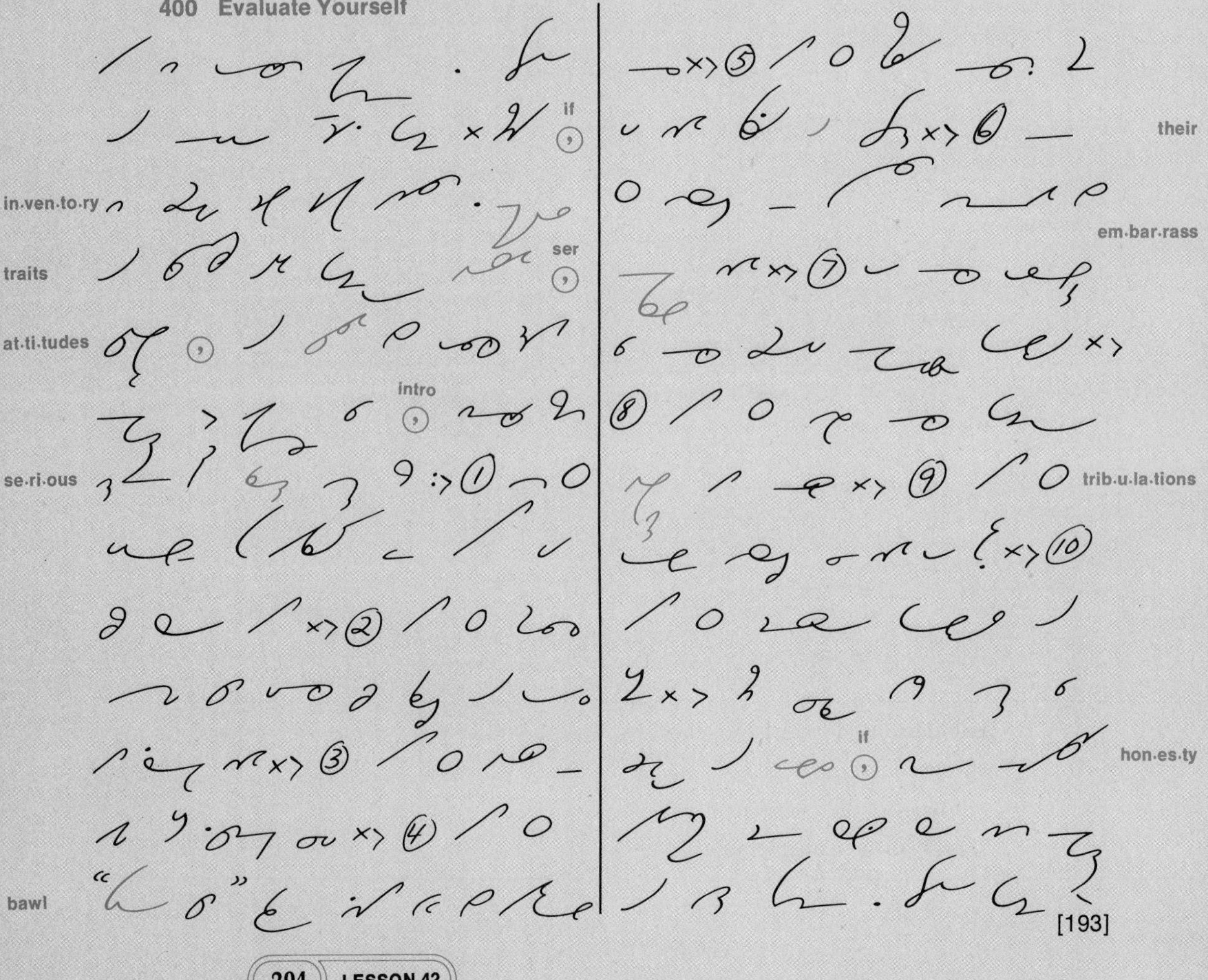

401 Words, Words, Words

as

un·fa·mil·iar

intro

com·pre·hend

achieve

par

of·ten

ap

tech·ni·cal

When you

when

ap

if

piece

sim·i·lar·i·ties

if

[261]

sig·nif·i·cant·ly

CHAPTER

The Secretary Interacts With Others

No one in the business world needs greater skill in both human and public relations than the secretary. From the beginning to the end of the working day, the secretary must deal with people—instructing, asking, requesting, persuading, explaining, reminding, listening, cooperating.

Only when the principles of good human relations are observed in an office, can members of the business team work together successfully. Working well with others involves much more than merely getting along with people. It involves a conscious effort to exercise good judgment and tact, to feel concern for the problems and reactions of others, to show consideration for them and for their viewpoints, and to develop the personal character traits of loyalty, trust, and fairness.

Many situations arise every day in which the secretary will need the cooperation of co-workers. There will be other instances when the secretary will be asked to lend a hand to workers in other departments. These situations may involve working with other secretaries, receptionists, mailroom clerks, messengers, or copy-machine attendants. In addition, good working relationships must be developed with people outside the office. For example, the secretary might deal with a temporary personnel agency, a duplicating service, a machine-maintenance service, or even a florist.

It is necessary to maintain good human relations with all office personnel, but those with the employer are of paramount importance to the secretary. The successful secretary must have an excellent working relationship with the employer. This relationship must be based on mutual respect and understanding of the rights and responsibilities of each person.

Another of the secretary's important functions in human interactions is to maintain good relations with other company executives and, of course, with their secretaries. A secretary can contribute substantially to the employer's success by maintaining good human relationships between company offices.

Although the terms *human relations* and *public relations* are often used interchangeably, they do not mean the same thing. Human relations is based on understanding and responding to an individual or a group. Public relations is the technique of developing and keeping the goodwill of the public and the people with whom the company deals for the company and its employees.

The secretary's role as a public relations representative for the company is vital. It is the secretary to whom most customers and visitors first speak, either in person or by telephone. It is the secretary's voice or typed correspondence that says, "We are pleased to work with you."

Whether the situation involves dealing with another employee, a customer, a supplier, or a visitor, the secretary's skill in dealing with people is very important. The secretary's manner with co-workers, executives, or outside contacts has much to do with the overall success of the business.

Many secretaries consider the opportunities to meet and help others—whether from outside or within the firm—the most important job they do.

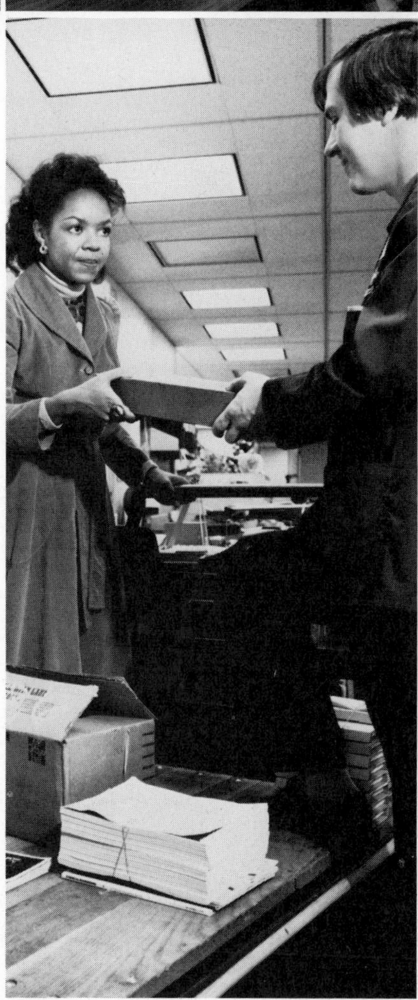

Principles

402 Word Beginning Mis-

The word beginning *mis-* is represented by *m-s*.

Spell: *mis-t-a-k, mistake*

mistake *misapprehension* *misunderstanding*

mistaken *misplaced* *misunderstood*

misprint *mislead* *mystery*

403 Word Beginning Super-

The word beginning *super-* is represented by a disjoined right *s*.

Spell: *super-v-ī-s, supervise*

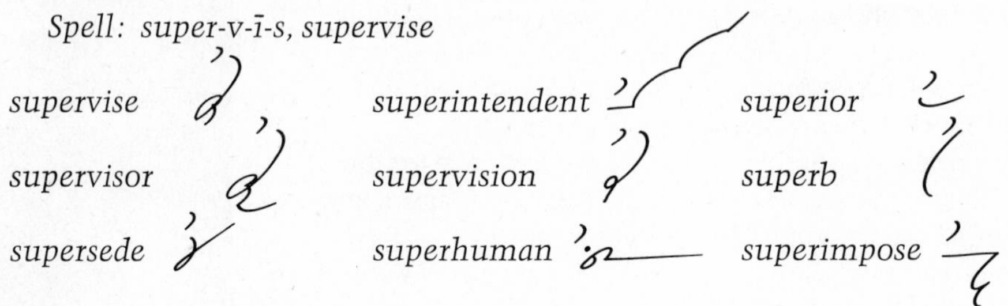

404 U Represented by OO

The *oo* hook may be used after *n* and *m* to represent the sound of *u*, as in *music*.

Spell: *m-oo-s-e-k, music*

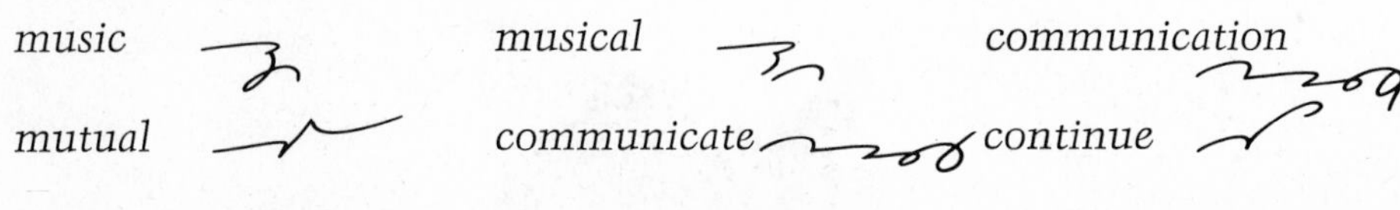

Building Transcription Skills

405 PUNCTUATION PRACTICE , conjunction

A comma is used to separate two independent clauses that are joined by one of these conjunctions: *and, but, or, for, nor.*

An independent clause (sometimes called a main or a principal clause) is one that has a subject and a predicate and that could stand alone as a complete sentence.

There are 15 people in my department, but *only 11 of them are here now.*

The first independent clause is:

There are 15 people in my department.

And the second independent clause is:

Only 11 of them are here now.

Both clauses could stand as separate sentences, with a period after each. Because the thoughts of the two clauses are closely related, however, the clauses were joined to form one sentence. Because the two independent clauses are connected by the conjunction *but,* a comma is used between them and is placed before the conjunction.

Each time this use of the comma occurs in the Reading and Writing Practice, it will be indicated thus in the shorthand: conj (,)

---

406 Business Vocabulary Builder

misapprehension Misunderstanding.

strikingly Impressively.

suitability Fitness.

Reading and Writing Practice

407 Brief-Form Review Letter

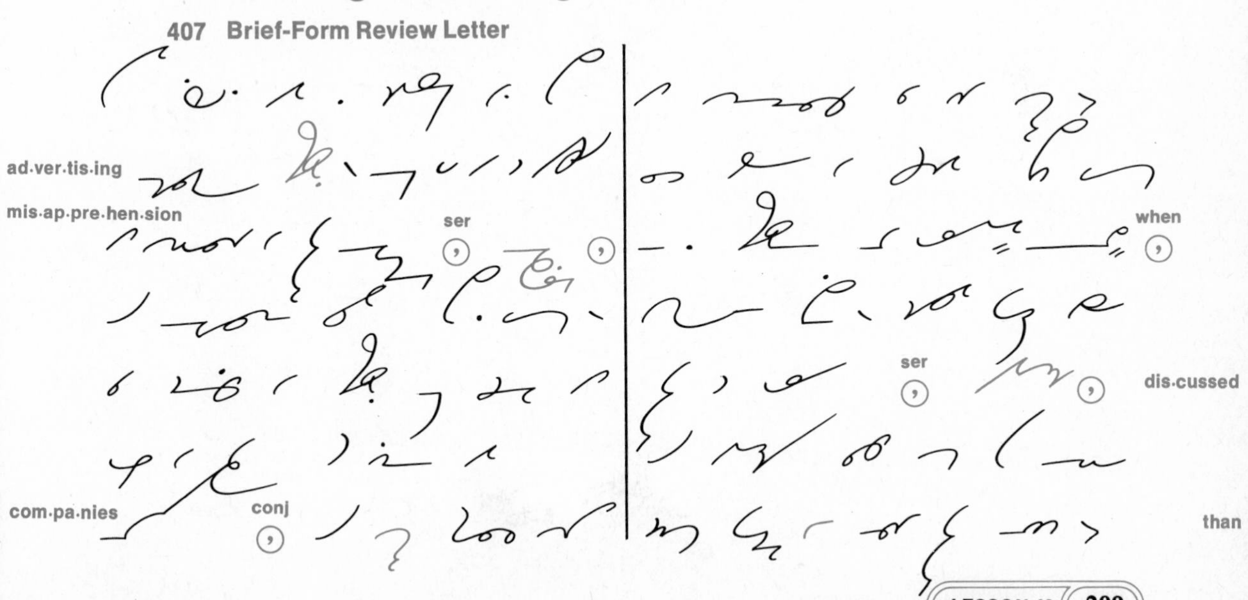

bud·get par [150]

408

su·per·vi·sors

su·perb ap

han·dling ser

conj so·lu·tions

conj

cou·pon

[194]

409

manu·script

conj

su·pe·ri·or

intro ac·cept

if re·view·er's [139]

par prompt·ly [137]

410

Mys·tery conj intro as sci·en·tif·ic yours conj ar·ea

411

as re·spon·si·ble ap conj ac·knowl·edg·ment intro quite any·one if [98]

Principles

412 Word Beginning Self-

The word beginning *self-* is represented by a disjoined left *s*.

Spell: self-m-a-d, self-made

self-made *self-addressed* *selfish*
self-confidence *self-improvement* *selfishness*
self-reliance *self-assurance* *unselfish*

413 Word Beginning Circum-

The word beginning *circum-* is also represented by a disjoined left *s*.

Spell: circum-s-ten-s, circumstance

circumstance *circumstances* *circumstantial*

414 Word Ending -ification

The word ending *-ification* is represented by a disjoined *f*.

Spell: k-l-a-s-ification, classification

classification *notification* *ratification*
specification *gratification* *modifications*
justification *identification* *qualifications*

Building Transcription Skills

415 PUNCTUATION PRACTICE , and omitted

When two or more adjectives modify the same noun, they are separated by commas.

A stamped, addressed *envelope is enclosed.*

However, the comma is not used if the first adjective modifies the combined idea of the second adjective plus the noun.

The book was bound in an attractive brown *cloth.*

Note: You can quickly determine whether to insert a comma between two consecutive adjectives by mentally placing *and* between them. If the sentence makes good sense with *and* inserted between the adjectives, then the comma is used. For example, the first illustration would make good sense if it read:

A stamped and *addressed envelope is enclosed.*

Each time this use of the comma occurs in the Reading and Writing Practice, it will be indicated thus in the shorthand: and o

416 Business Vocabulary Builder

merger The combining of two or more business organizations.

upright Honest; conscientious.

trying *(adjective)* Difficult.

tedious Boring.

Reading and Writing Practice

417 Brief-Form Review Letter

prob.a.bly

as

gov.ern.ment

par

conj

and o

cour.te.ous

priv·i·leges
con·ve·niences

ser

if

[161]

418

stud·ied

when

an·noyed

su·per·in·ten·dent

ap

[111]

419

and o

up·right
cit·i·zens

ser

prin·ci·ples

par

and o

en·ve·lope

[117]

420

para·graph

par

intro

valu·able

intro

poise

ser

for·mal·ly

as

ap·pre·ci·ate

when

ap

con·vinc·ing·ly

and o

conj

te·dious

com·mit·tee

[124]

par

en·roll·ing

if

156-1171 [166]

422

ap

[33]

421

Principles

423 Word Ending -hood

The word ending *-hood* is represented by a disjoined *d.*

Spell: n-a-b-r-hood, neighborhood

neighborhood boyhood parenthood
childhood girlhood likelihood

424 Word Ending -ward

The word ending *-ward* is also represented by a disjoined *d.*

Spell: o-n-ward, onward

onward awkward forward
afterward rewarding forwarded
upward backward downward

425 Ul

Ul is represented by *oo* when it precedes a forward or upward stroke.

Spell: re-s-ul-t, result

result adult multiply
consult ultimately culminate
consulted culture insulted

426 Quantities and Amounts

Here are a few more helpful abbreviations for quantities and amounts.

500		*$5,000,000,000*		*several hundred*	
$500		*a dollar*		*5 pounds*	
$5,000,000		*a million*		*8 feet*	

Notice that the *n* for *hundred* is written *under* the figure as a positive distinction from *million,* in which the *m* is written *beside* the figure.

Building Transcription Skills

427 SPELLING FAMILIES -tion, -sion, -shion An effective device to improve your ability to spell is to study words in related groups, or spelling families, that contain a common problem; for example, words ending in the sound *shun.* This sound is sometimes spelled *tion,* sometimes *sion,* and occasionally *shion.*

Practice each spelling family in this way:

- 1 Spell each word aloud, pausing slightly after each syllable.
- 2 Write each word once in longhand, spelling it aloud as you read it.

You will find many *shun* words in the Reading and Writing Practice.

Words Ending in -tion

ed·u·ca·tion	**no·ti·fi·ca·tion**	**pub·li·ca·tion**
in·for·ma·tion	**cir·cu·la·tion**	**po·si·tion**
or·ga·ni·za·tion	**op·er·a·tions**	**re·la·tions**

Words Ending in -sion

oc·ca·sion	**pro·fes·sion**	**ex·ten·sion**
di·vi·sion	**dis·cus·sion**	**pro·vi·sion**
ses·sion	**de·ci·sion**	**re·vi·sion**

Words Ending in -shion

fash·ion	**cush·ion**

---

428 Business Vocabulary Builder

ultimate Maximum; final.

prone Having a tendency or inclination.

insecure Uncertain.

Reading and Writing Practice

429 Brief-Form Review Letter

ses·sion

ap

com·put·er·iz·ing

ar·ea

conj

and o

prof·it·able

or·ga·ni·za·tion

neigh·bor·hood

par

if

ad·van·tage

[181]

430

phys·i·cal·ly

when

prone

conj

ser

in·se·cure

awk·ward

and o

intro

ex·er·cise

stead

intro

intro

bod·ies

[157] —*Physical Fitness Council*

431

and o

par

as

15

ser

mis·cel·la·neous

due

conj

re·mit·tance

intro

and o

en·ve·lope

prompt·ly

intro

[183]

432

and o

intro

rise

ex·ceed·ing·ly

intro

spe·cial

if

[158]

433

col·ors

conj

pro·fes·sion·al

intro

intro

oc·ca·sion

[113]

BRIEF-FORM CHECKLIST *Are you making good use of the brief-form chart that appears on page 320? Remember, the brief forms represent many of the commonest words in the language; and the better you know them, the more rapid progress you will make in developing your shorthand speed.*

Are you—

- 1 Spending a few minutes reading from the chart each day?
- 2 Timing yourself and trying to cut a few seconds off your reading time with each reading?
- 3 Reading the brief forms in a different order each time—from left to right, from right to left, from top to bottom, from bottom to top?

Principles

434 Word Ending -gram

The word ending *-gram* is represented by a disjoined *gay.*

Spell: t-e-l-gram, telegram

telegram	*cablegram*	*programs*
diagram	*program*	*programmed*

435 Word Beginning Electric-

The word beginning *electric-* (and the word *electric*) is represented by a disjoined *el.*

Spell: electric-l, electrical

electric	*electrically*	*electric wire*
electrical	*electric typewriter*	*electric motor*

436 Word Beginning Electr-

The word beginning *electr-* is also represented by a disjoined *el.*

Spell: electro-n-e-k, electronic

electronic	*electricity*	*electrician*

437 Compounds

Most compound words are formed simply by joining the outlines for the words that make up the compound. In some words, however, it is desirable to modify the outline for one of the words in order to obtain an easier joining.

anyhow	*someone*	*within*
anywhere	*worthwhile*	*withstand*
thereupon	*however**	*notwithstanding*

*The dot may be omitted in *however.*

438 Intersection

Intersection, or the writing of one shorthand character through another, is sometimes useful for special phrases. This principle may be used when constant repetition of certain combinations of words in your dictation makes it clearly worthwhile to form special outlines for them.

a.m.	*vice versa*
p.m.	*Chamber of Commerce*

Building Transcription Skills

439 SIMILAR-WORDS DRILL prominent, permanent

prominent Notable; standing out.

He took lessons from a prominent *musician.*

permanent Not subject to change; lasting.

He was offered a permanent *job with the company.*

440 Business Vocabulary Builder

consultant One who gives professional advice or services; expert.

primarily Chiefly.

priority Something meriting first attention.

Reading and Writing Practice

441 Brief-Form Review Letter

con·sul·tant

ap

plane

for·tu·nate·ly

intro

par

Mu·nic·i·pal

ap

prom·i·nent

if

par

fee

[174]

442

when

some·one

per·ma·nent

elec·tri·cal

ser

neigh·bor·hood

con·ve·nient ap

par

[141]

443

as

Su·pe·ri·or

shelves

man·u·als ser

pri·mar·i·ly par

intro

and o

pro·fes·sion·al

ap

en·joy·able

conj

sou·ve·nir

[176]

444

intro

pro·gram·ming

em·ploy·ees

intro

[106]

Principles

445 Geographical Expressions and Names

In geographical expressions and names, *-burg* is expressed by *b*; *-ingham,* by a disjoined *m*; *-ington,* by a disjoined *ten* blend; *-ville,* by *v*.

-burg

Spell: *h-a-r-e-s-berg, Harrisburg*

Harrisburg *Pittsburgh* *Newburgh*

-ingham

Spell: *b-oo-k-ingham, Buckingham*

Buckingham *Cunningham* *Framingham*

-ington

Spell: *l-e-x-ington, Lexington*

Lexington *Wilmington* *Washington*

-ville

Spell: *n-a-ish-ville, Nashville*

Nashville *Jacksonville* *Evansville*

Building Transcription Skills

446 GRAMMAR CHECKUP Most executives have a good command of the English language. Some rarely make an error in grammar. There are times, though, when even the best dictators will perhaps use a plural verb with a singular noun or use the objective case when they should have used the nominative. They usually know better. In concentrating intently on expressing a thought or idea, however, they occasionally make a grammatical error.

It will be your job as a stenographer to catch these occasional errors and correct them when you transcribe.

From time to time in the lessons ahead you will be given an opportunity to brush up on some of the rules of grammar that are frequently violated.

GRAMMAR CHECKUP comparisons The comparative degree of an adjective or adverb is used when reference is made to two objects; the superlative degree is used when reference is made to more than two objects.

comparative

Of the two girls, Jane is the taller.

Which boy is more *efficient, Jim or Harry?*

Is Mr. Smith or Ms. Green better *qualified to do the job?*

superlative

Of the three boys, John is the tallest.

Which of the girls is the most *efficient, Jane, Mary, or Arlene?*

Is Mr. Smith, Ms. Green, or Mrs. Brown the best *qualified to do the job?*

---

447 Business Vocabulary Builder

fallacy A false idea.

unsurpassed The best; second to none.

extraordinary Remarkable; unusual.

Reading and Writing Practice

448 Brief-Form Review Letter

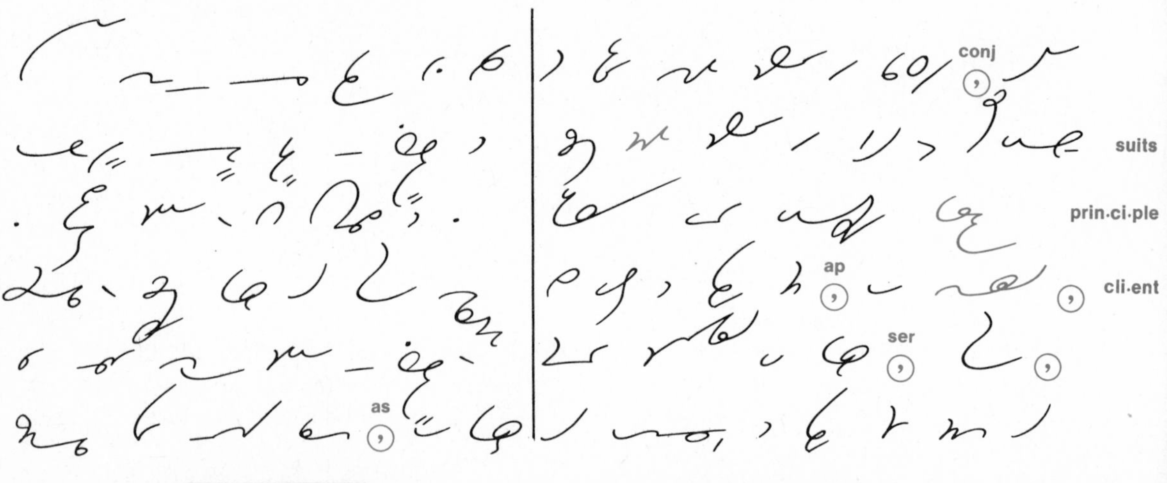

cour·te·ous

and o

pleas·ant

neigh·bor·hood

when

un·sur·passed

and o

par

[187]

449

par

nat·u·ral·ly

intro

intro

ex·ten·sion

par

debts

[138]

450

par

enough

trans·ferred

pass·book

par

[118]

451

intro

ex·traor·di·nary

and o

sim·ple

li·brary

[78]

452

intro

al·ready

intro

ef·fect

ser

and o

en·ve·lopes

par

[167]

RECALL

In Lesson 47 you studied the last of the new shorthand devices of Gregg Shorthand. In this lesson you will find an Accuracy Practice, a Recall Chart that reviews all the word-building principles of Gregg Shorthand, and a Reading and Writing Practice that contains some "food for thought."

Accuracy Practice

453 **Def**

To write this stroke accurately:

- a *Make it large, almost the full height of your notebook line.*
- b *Make it narrow.*
- c *Start and finish the strokes on the same level of writing, as indicated by the dotted line.*

practice drill

Divide, definite, defeat, devote, differ, endeavor.

454 **Th** **Ten** **Tem**

To write these strokes accurately:

- a *Slant the strokes as indicated by the dotted lines.*
- b *Make the* **beginning** *of the curves deep.*

■ c *Make the* **tem** *large, about the full height of the line; the* **th** *small; the* **ten** *about half the size of the* **tem**

practice drill

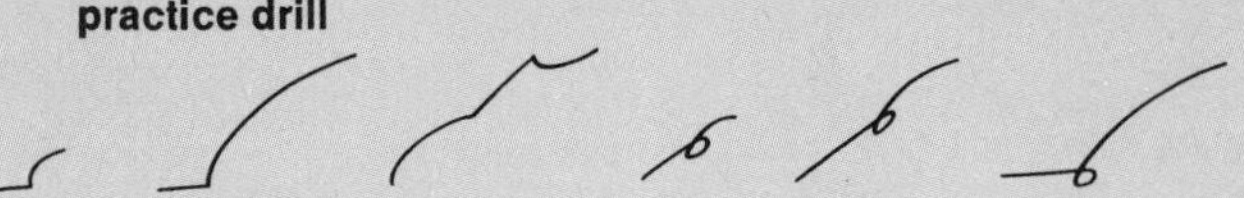

In the, in time, tender, teeth, detain, medium.

455 Recall Chart

This chart contains illustrations of alphabetic characters, word-building principles, and phrasing principles of Gregg Shorthand.

WORDS

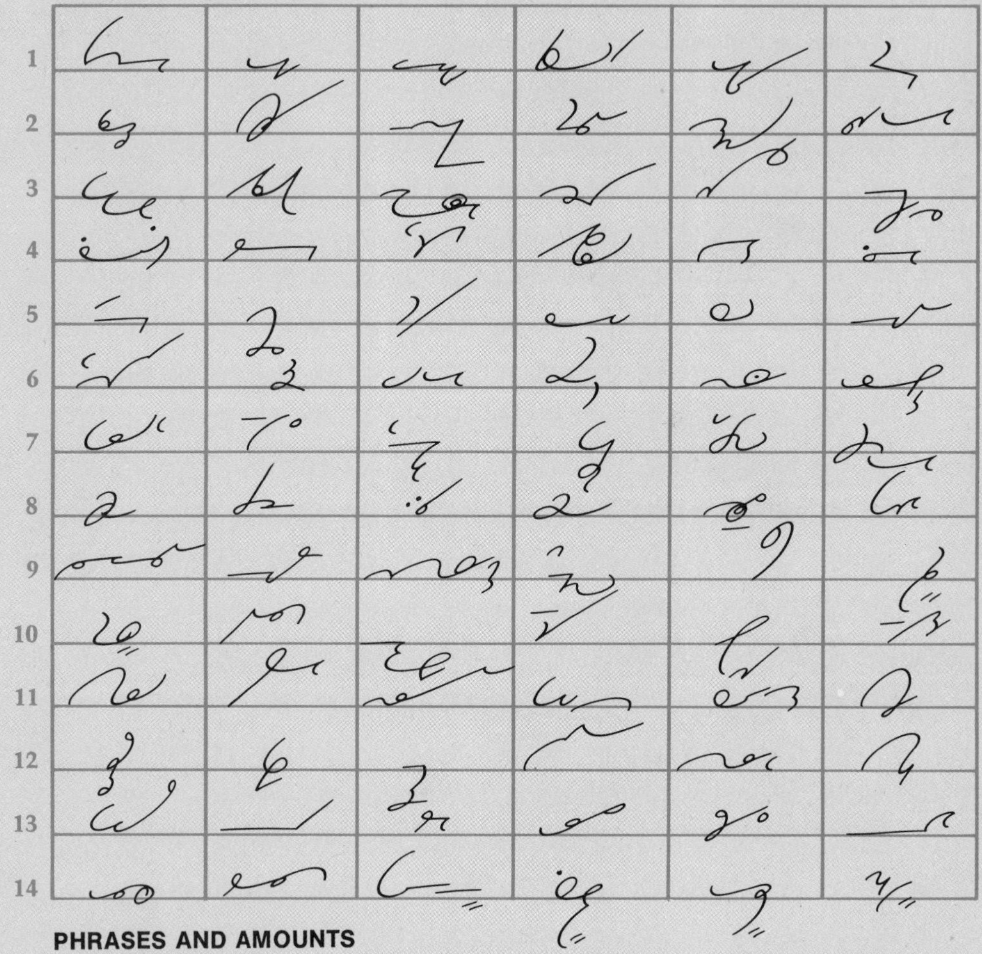

1						
2						
3						
4						
5						
6						
7						
8						
9						
10						
11						
12						
13						
14						

PHRASES AND AMOUNTS

15						

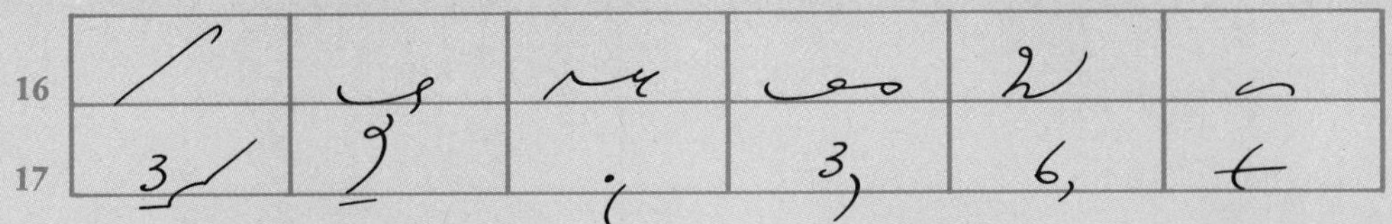

Building Transcription Skills

456 Business Vocabulary Builder

accomplishments Achievements.

phase Aspect; side; part.

extensive Considerable.

Reading and Writing Practice

457 Reading

lev·el

if

conj

intro

Reading for Pleasure.

wheth·er

ser

dai·ly

intro

and o

worth·while

cit·i·zen

conj

well

Reading in School.

as

es·sen·tial

phase

col·lege

if

Reading on the Job.

ser

mis·cel·la·neous

intro

sur·vey

ap

par

ad·di·tion

intro

equip·ment

of·fered

when

sig·nif·i·cant·ly

[488]

PART

Reinforcement

CHAPTER

9 The Secretary's Day

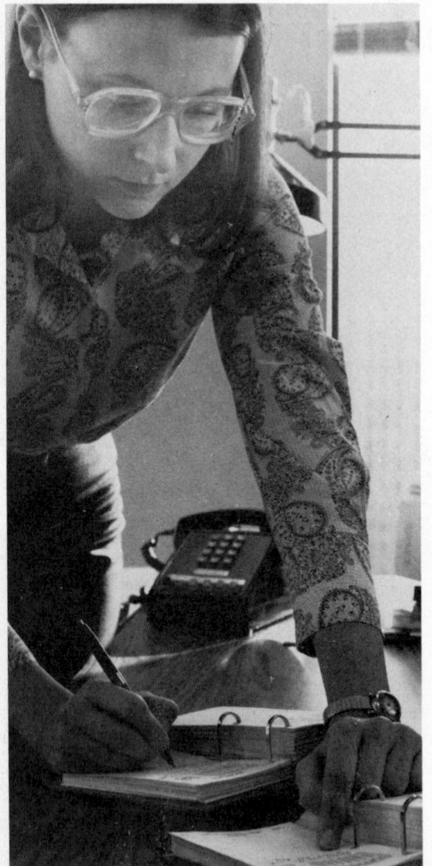

There are as many secretarial job descriptions as there are employer-employee teams, and each job varies considerably from day to day. Although taking dictation and typing are an important part of the day's work, the secretary does many other things as well.

To give you an idea of what a typical day in the life of a secretary is like, imagine that you are secretary to Mrs. Ellen Garcia, marketing manager for a large textile company.

9:00 Arrive at the office. Check Mrs. Garcia's appointment calendar to make sure it agrees with yours. You notice that she has an 11 o'clock staff meeting, a luncheon appointment at 12:30 with Mr. Washington at the Cedar Inn, and a 3 o'clock appointment with Miss Rosen to go over the special department store promotion. A few minutes later, Mrs. Garcia arrives and you remind her of the meetings and appointments for the day. She gives you a corrected draft of a report to type for the staff meeting.

9:15 The morning mail is delivered. You open and sort it and bring it to Mrs. Garcia along with previous correspondence related to the incoming mail. Then you start typing the report.

9:30 Mrs. Garcia calls you in to take dictation.

9:45 You return to your desk to finish typing the report. The telephone rings several times and you provide information to those callers who don't need to speak to Mrs. Garcia personally. Mrs. Garcia asks for some information that must be obtained from the files. The company library calls and asks if Mrs. Garcia is finished with the book she borrowed. Someone else needs it. You check with Mrs. Garcia, and since she no longer needs the book, you take it back to the library.

10:30 You bring the completed report to Mrs. Garcia. While she is reading it, you check to make sure the conference room is ready for the meeting. Mrs. Garcia returns the report with no changes, so you make copies and distribute them for the meeting.

11:00 You make sure that all the materials are ready for the meeting. Then you begin transcribing. And the interruptions begin:

- You answer several telephone calls and take messages.
- Mrs. Garcia calls to ask you to bring a copy of this year's marketing plan to her in the conference room.
- You greet one caller who has come without an appointment. After checking the calendar, you set up a tentative appointment for 10 o'clock tomorrow.

11:45 The meeting is over and Mrs. Garcia stops at your desk to ask you to arrange a two-day trip to the Chicago office Monday and Tuesday of next week. You tell her about the appointment for tomorrow and when she agrees, you call the person and confirm.

12:00 You remind Mrs. Garcia of her luncheon date and then go to lunch yourself, after letting the receptionist know that you are leaving.

1:00 Return from lunch. You make all the necessary arrangements for Mrs. Garcia's trip, including transportation to and from the airports, plane and hotel reservations, and a rental car in Chicago. You type the itinerary and then you return to transcribing.

1:45 Mrs. Garcia returns with Mr. Washington and asks you to give him some papers he needs before he leaves. You get the papers and show him out.

2:00 Mrs. Garcia calls you in so she can start dictating a lengthy report. There are several interruptions; people stop to ask questions and the telephone rings.

2:50 The receptionist calls to say that Miss Rosen has arrived. You go to the reception area and escort her to the office.

3:00 You finish transcribing the morning's dictation.

3:15 Mrs. Garcia buzzes and asks you to bring in the samples of the new line.

3:30 Mrs. Garcia asks you to show Miss Rosen out and then bring your book so that she can continue dictating the report.

4:30 Mrs. Garcia decides to continue the report tomorrow. You prepare the correspondence for her signature. After she has signed the letters, you get them ready for the mail.

5:00 You clear your desk and tell Mrs. Garcia that you are leaving. You go home, knowing that you have worked hard today and that you will work just as hard tomorrow—but that tomorrow's schedule will be entirely different.

The letters in this lesson concentrate on the shorthand principles you studied in Chapter 1. You should have no difficulty reading them.

458 BRIEF FORMS AND DERIVATIVES

1. *I, Mr., have, having, are-hour-our, ours-hours, will-well, willing, a-an, am, at-it, but.*
2. *In-not, increase, invite, indeed, is-his, that, can, cannot, you-your, yours, Mrs., of, with.*

Reading and Writing Practice

459

[57]

460

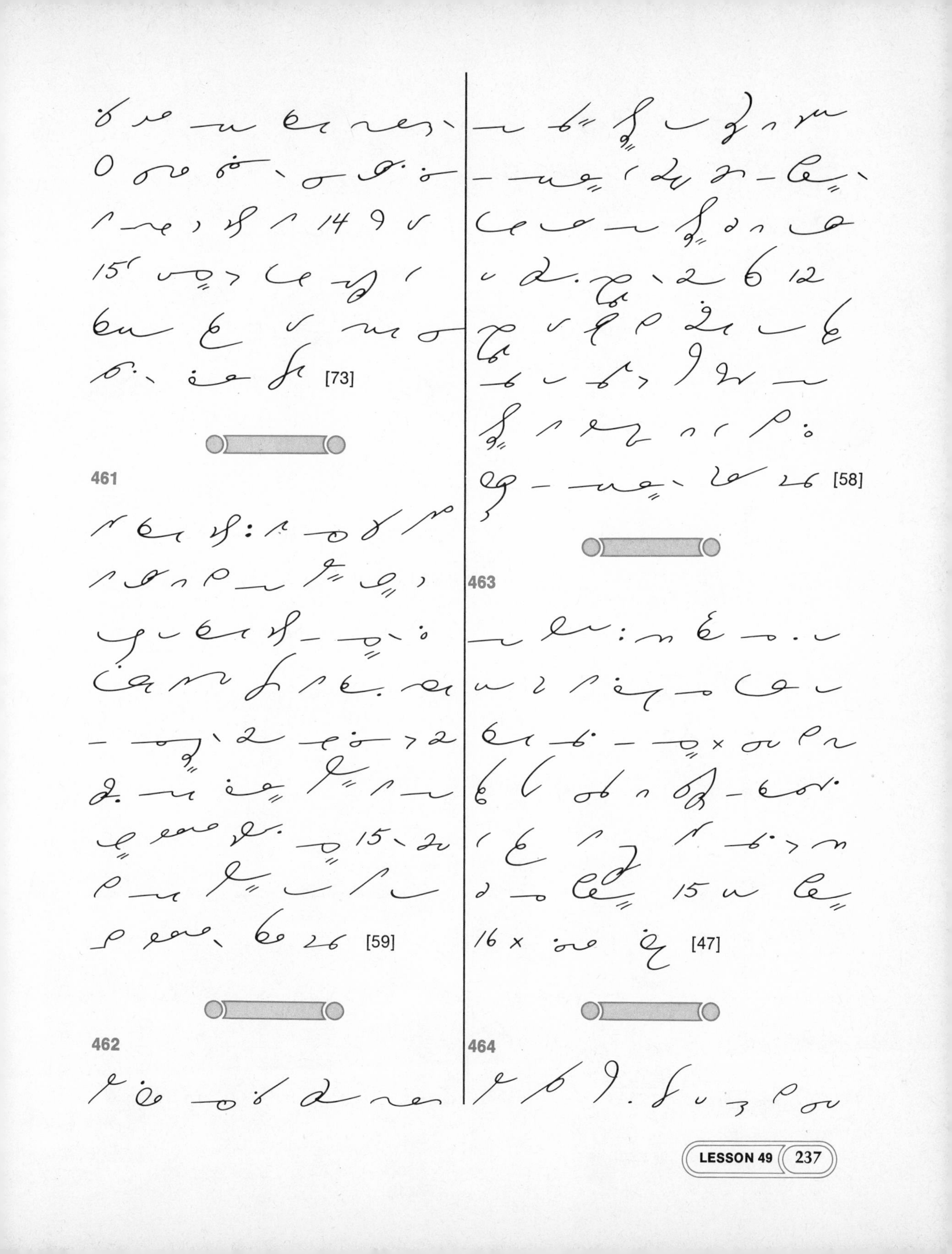

[73]

461

[59]

462

[58]

463

[47]

464

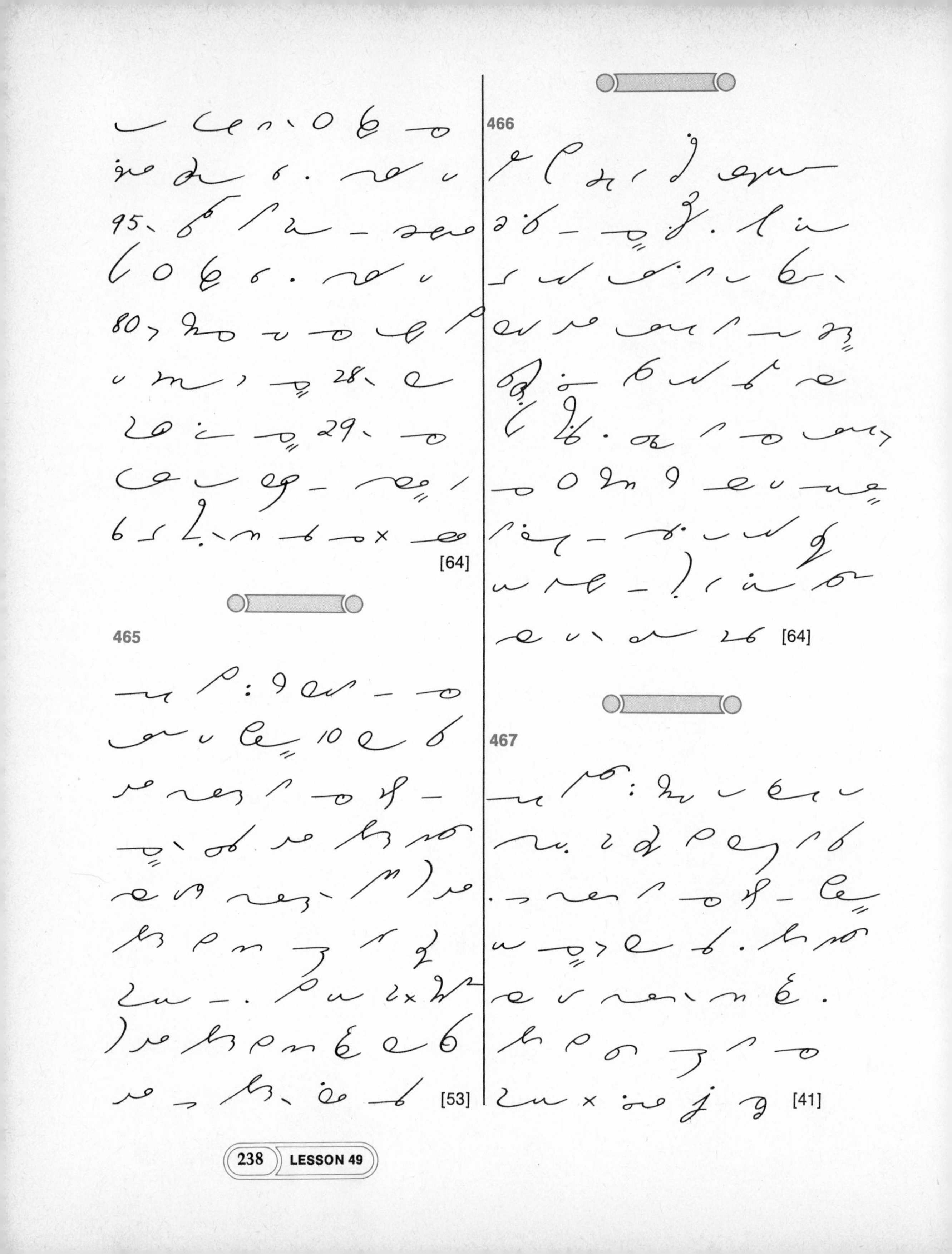

[64]

465

[53]

466

[64]

467

[41]

The practice material in this lesson concentrates on the shorthand principles you studied in Chapter 2.

468 BRIEF FORMS AND DERIVATIVES

1. Be-by, before, began, believe, because, for, would, there (their), theirs, this.
2. Good, goods, they, which, them, and, when, from.
3. Could, send, sending, after, afternoon, street, streets, were, should.

Building Transcription Skills

469 Business Vocabulary Builder

inspired Motivated.

fatal Causing death.

role Part.

Reading and Writing Practice

470

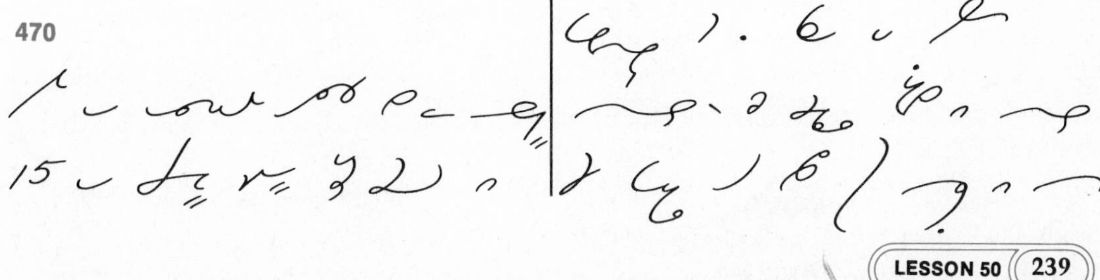

[75]

471

[95]

472

[81]

473

[87]

474

475

[94]

[109]

Lesson 51 concentrates on the shorthand principles you studied in Chapter 3.

476 BRIEF FORMS AND DERIVATIVES

1. *Gladly, worked, yesterday, circular, ordered, sooner, thank, enclosed, was.*
2. *Valuable, one (won), once, than, what, about, thing-think, thinks, businesses, doctor, anything.*
3. *Gentlemen, morning, important-importance, where, company, manufacturer, next, shortly.*

Building Transcription Skills

477 Business Vocabulary Builder

suitable Adapted to a use or purpose.

launching Originating or setting in motion.

Reading and Writing Practice

478

[98]

479

116-1181 12 [100]

480

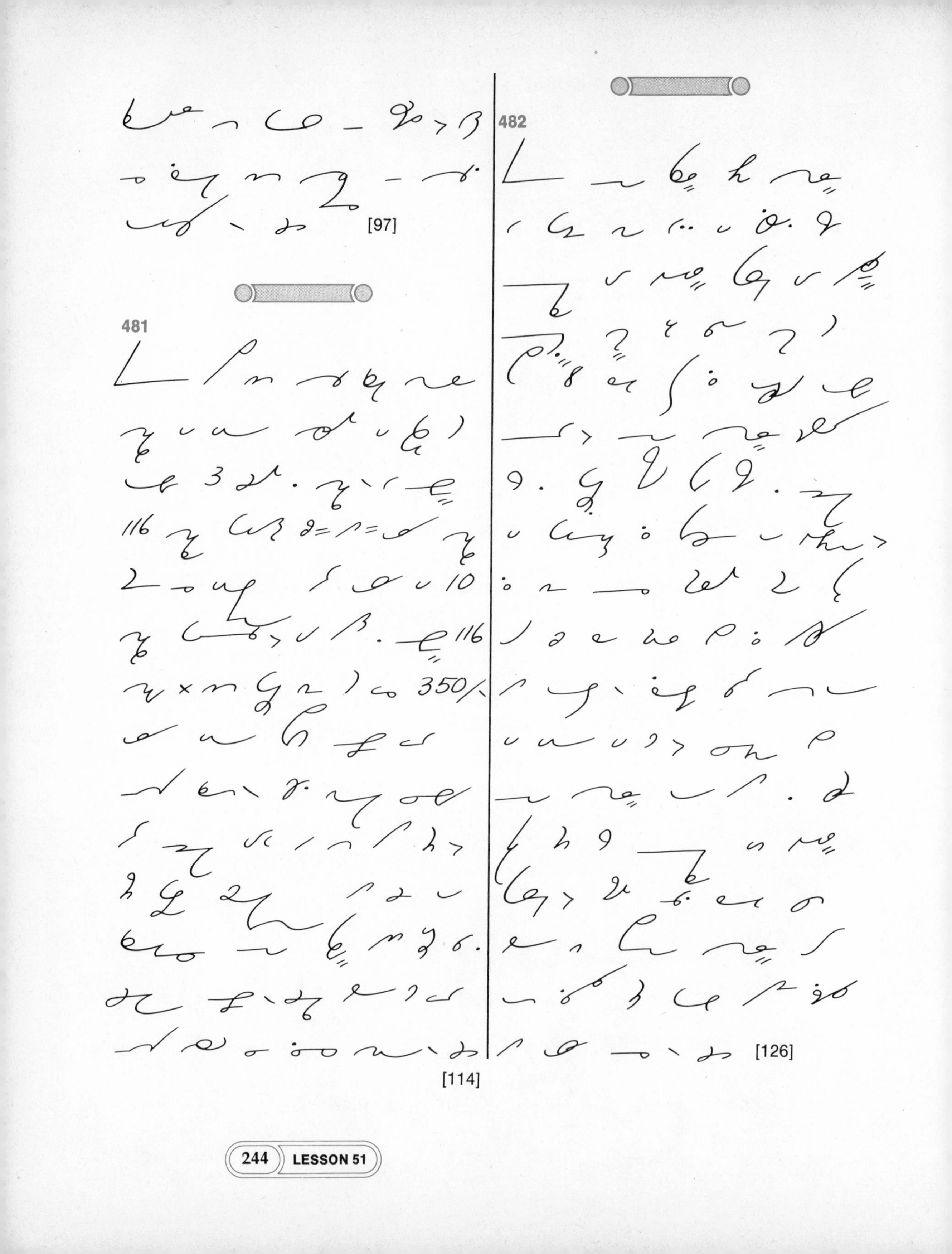

[97]

481

[114]

482

[126]

In this lesson you will receive a concentrated review of the shorthand principles you studied in Chapter 4.

483 BRIEF FORMS AND DERIVATIVES

1. *Presently, presents, part, parted, partly, advertise, advertisement, Ms., immediately, opportunities.*
2. *Advantage, advantages, suggestions, several, out, outside, ever-every, whenever, very.*
3. *Time, timed, acknowledgment, acknowledged, generally, questions, organization, overdue, overtime.*

Building Transcription Skills

484 SPELLING FAMILIES silent e dropped before -ing

Words in Which Silent E Is Dropped Before -ing

ad·ver·tis·ing	**en·clos·ing**	**in·creas·ing**
de·sir·ing	**ex·am·in·ing**	**pro·duc·ing**
de·cid·ing	**forc·ing**	**pur·chas·ing**
dic·tat·ing	**guid·ing**	**re·ceiv·ing**

485 Business Vocabulary Builder

occur Happen.

appropriate *(adjective)* Especially suitable or fitting.

competent Able.

Reading and Writing Practice

486

dic·ta·ting

whether

sim·ply

de·cid·ing

ac·knowl·edge

[158]

487

per·son·nel

ad·ver·tis·ing

30

[117]

488

me·di·um

pur·chas·ing

po·ten·tial

[128]

489

healthy

sur·geon

[121]

490

years

con·fi·dent

de·rived

re·new·al

[100]

491

gra·ti·fy·ing

[55]

492

an·nounce

back·ground

re·or·ga·nize

[96]

SPELLING AND PUNCTUATION CHECKLIST *Are you careful to punctuate and spell correctly when—*

- **1** You write your compositions in English?
- **2** Prepare your reports for your social studies classes?
- **3** Correspond with friends to whom you must write in longhand?

In short, are you making correct spelling and punctuation a habit in all the longhand writing or typing that you do?

In Lesson 53 you will practice many words and phrases that are written according to the principles you studied in Chapter 5.

493 BRIEF FORMS AND DERIVATIVES

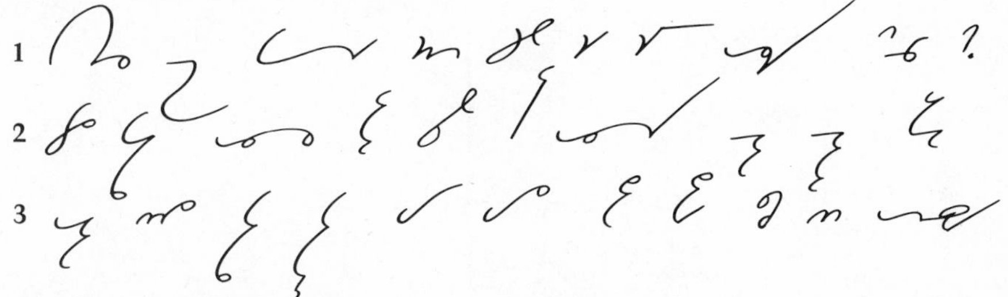

1. *Difficulty, envelope, progressed, success, satisfy-satisfactory, state, statement, requested, underneath, wishing.*
2. *Particularly, probably, regularly, speaks, ideas, subject, regarded, newspaper, newspapers, opinions.*
3. *Responsible, worthy, publicly, publications, ordinary, ordinarily, experience, experienced, usually, world, recognized.*

Building Transcription Skills

494 Business Vocabulary Builder

pressman The operator of a printing press.

petition A formal written request.

depot A building for railroad or bus passengers or freight; a station.

● Reading and Writing Practice

495

rec·og·nized

prob·a·bly

ap·pre·ci·ate

en·ve·lope

[116]

496

120

ar·ea

de·pot

shop·ping

Coun·cil

[113]

497

le·gal

whose

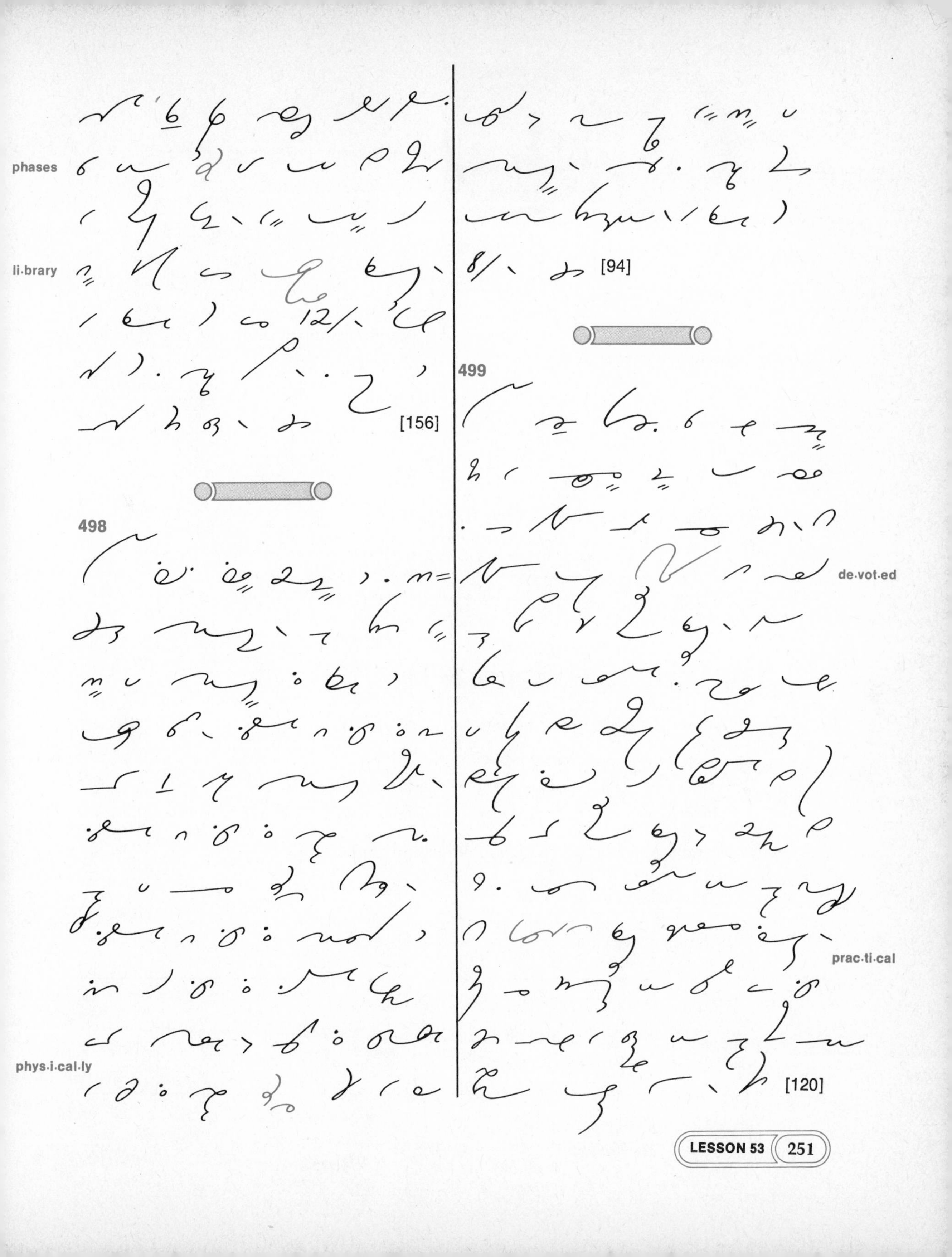

phases

li·brary

[156]

498

phys·i·cal·ly

[94]

499

de·vot·ed

prac·ti·cal

[120]

In this lesson you will have an opportunity to brush up on shorthand principles you studied in Chapter 6.

500 BRIEF FORMS AND DERIVATIVES

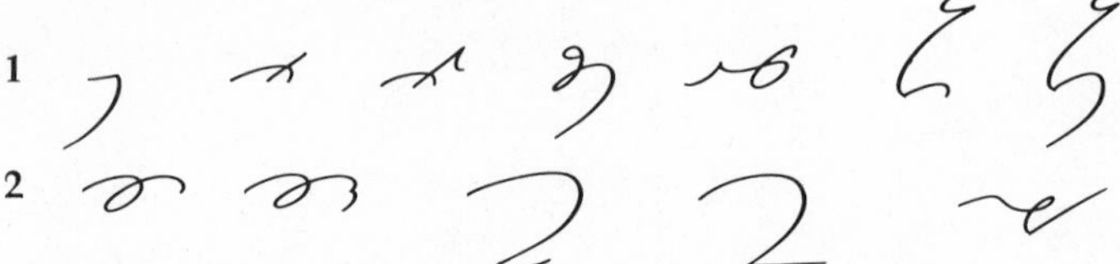

1. *Never, quantity, quantities, executive, throughout, object, objective.*
2. *Character, characters, governor, government, corresponded.*

Building Transcription Skills

501 SIMILAR-WORDS DRILL vacation, vocation

vacation A holiday; a period devoted to rest or relaxation.

I will take a short vacation *in June.*

vocation A regular occupation or profession.

My vocation *is teaching.*

---

502 Business Vocabulary Builder

creative Imaginative.

novel Original; new.

sites Places; locations.

Reading and Writing Practice

503

Phoe·nix

vo·ca·tion par

wheth·er

de·scribed

ap

knowl·edge
cre·ative ser

par

ref·er·ence [144]

504

cop·ies
ap

de·spite

par

par

re·ceive

[94]

505

par

nov·el

va·ca·tion

ser sites

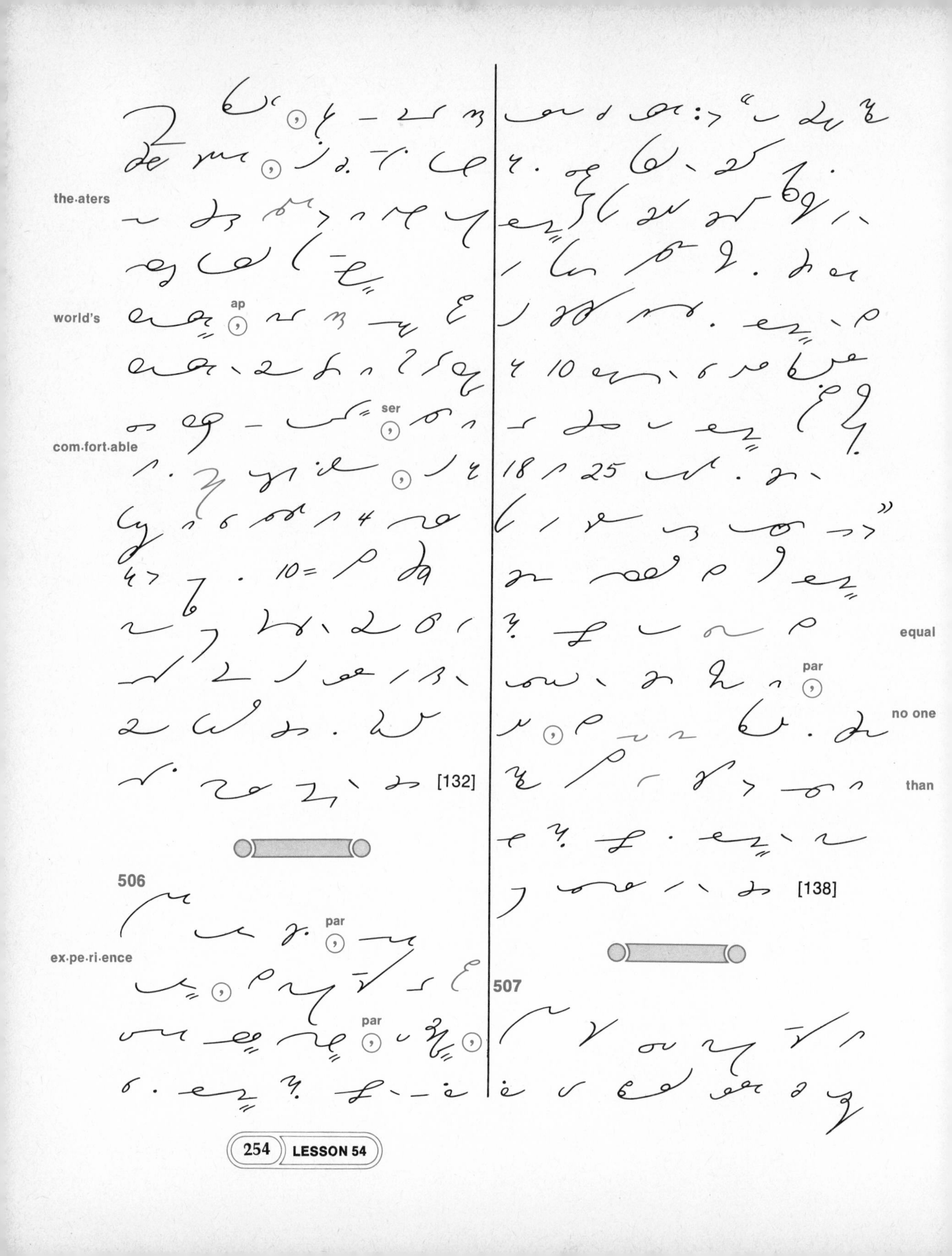

the·aters

world's

ap

ser

com·fort·able

[132]

506

par

ex·pe·ri·ence

par

equal

par

no one

than

[138]

507

ap

mod·ern

ad

par

sched·ule

[108]

508

ap

par

par

fur·ther

[103]

SHORTHAND NOTEBOOK CHECKLIST

Your shorthand notebook is another important tool of your trade. Do you:

- **1** Use a notebook with a spiral binding so that the pages always lie flat as you write?
- **2** Write on the front cover your name and the first and last dates on which you use the notebook?
- **3** Place a rubber band around the used portion of your notebook so that it opens automatically to the first blank page?
- **4** Date the first page of each day's dictation at the bottom of the page for quick and convenient reference—just as a stenographer in an office would do?
- **5** Check before class to see that there are sufficient pages remaining in your notebook for the day's dictation and, if not, supply yourself with a second notebook so that you will not run out of paper in the middle of dictation?

In Lesson 55 you will review shorthand principles you studied in Chapter 7.

509 BRIEF-FORM DERIVATIVES

1. *Suggested, corresponded, timed, organized, governed, manufactured.*
2. *Particularly, successfully, immediately, presently, gladly, partly, generally.*
3. *Sooner, manufacturer, speaker, sender, governor, timer, shorter.*

Building Transcription Skills

510 GRAMMAR CHECKUP the infinitive The infinitive is the form of the verb usually introduced by *to—to see, to be, to have, to do.*

Careful writers try to avoid "splitting" an infinitive, that is, inserting a word or phrase between *to* and the following verb.

no

To properly do *the job, you need better tools.*

yes

To do *the job properly, you need better tools.*

no

He was told to carefully prepare *the report.*

yes

He was told to prepare *the report carefully.*

511 Business Vocabulary Builder

durability Ability to withstand wear; sturdiness.

inherited Received property by will.

reality The quality of being actual or true.

Reading and Writing Practice

512

trans·fer·ring

if

be·com·ing

ap·ti·tude ser

re·ceive if

phase

sal·a·ry

par

ex·ceed·ing·ly ser

if

ser

pho·to·graph

[154]

513

intro

intro

sta·tis·ti·cal

de·pend·abil·i·ty ser

du·ra·bil·i·ty

pur·chase

when

intro

[130]

514

as

in·her·i·ted

intro

div·i·dend

trans·mit·ting par

par

ti·tle

[123]

515

intro

re·al·i·ty

18 ser 19

20

if

grat·i·tude

priv·i·lege

ap 19 [158]

intro

clas·si·fied

[137]

516

es·tate

ser

517

an·nu·al

ap

dy·nam·ic

415-1177

10 [63]

The practice material in Lesson 56 will give you an opportunity to review shorthand principles you studied in Chapter 8.

518 BRIEF-FORM DERIVATIVES

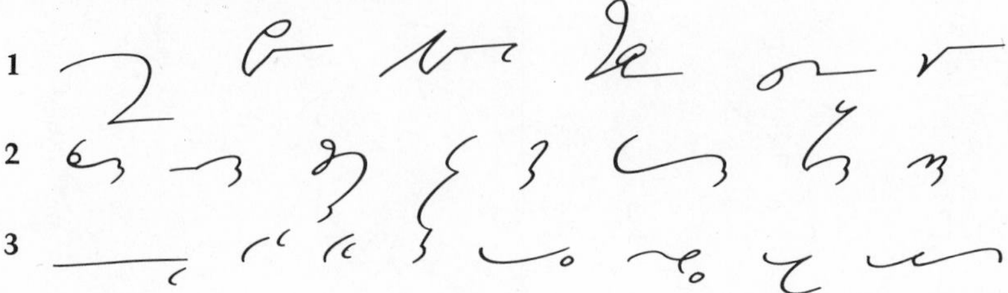

1. *Government, apartment, departments, advertisement, acknowledgment, statement.*
2. *Circulars, encloses, executives, publications, wishes, progresses, objects, worlds.*
3. *Mornings, thanks, thinks, willingly, correspondingly, represent, reorganize.*

Building Transcription Skills

519 COMMON PREFIXES super- In the English language there are many common prefixes. An understanding of the meanings of these prefixes will often give you a clue to the meaning of words with which you may be unfamiliar.

For example, you may never have encountered the word *superfluous.* However, if you knew that *super* meant *more than,* you probably could figure out that *superfluous* means *more than enough.*

In each "Common Prefixes" exercise you will be given a common prefix, its meaning, and a list of words in which the prefix is used.

Read each definition and study the illustrations that follow. Several *super* words are used in the Reading and Writing Practice of this lesson.

super- over, more than

superior Over in rank; higher.

supervise To oversee.

supervisor One who oversees.

superfluous More than enough.

520 **chore** A routine task or job.

Business Vocabulary Builder **clarification** The act of making clear or understandable.

Reading and Writing Practice

521

tedious (as) (and o)

chore

(par) (,)

kitchen

(ser)

(,) (conj)

[124]

522

(ap) local

(,)

(par) (,) confident

(if)

(ser) (,)

neighborhood

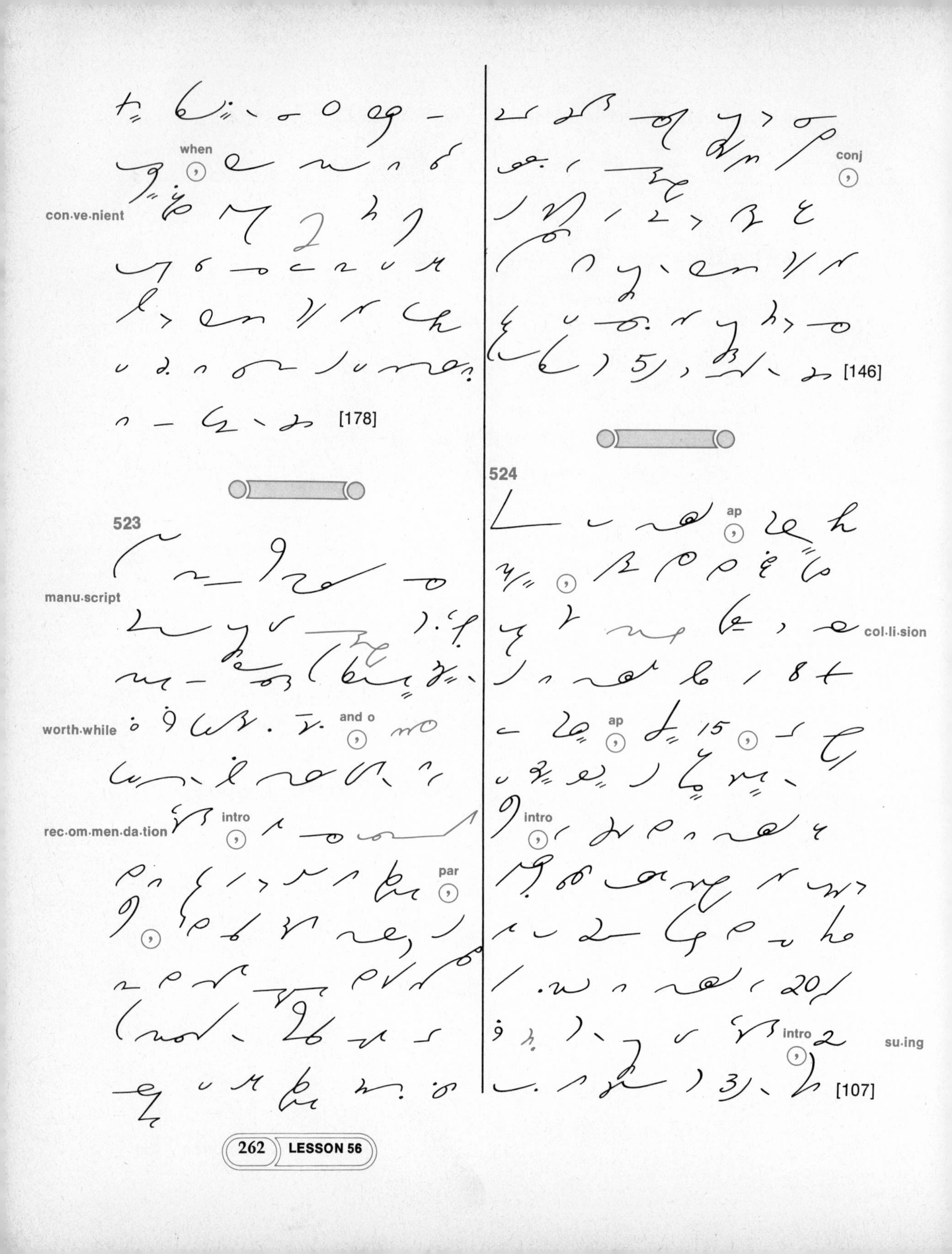

when

con·ve·nient

[178]

conj

[146]

523

manu·script

worth·while

and o

rec·om·men·da·tion

intro

par

524

ap

col·li·sion

ap

intro

intro

su·ing

[107]

PART

Shorthand & Transcription Skill Building

CHAPTER

The Secretary Advances

Your first job is important because it will give you an opportunity to use the skills you have developed and to gain experience in making them work for you. Your ability to handle more important responsibilities will be gauged by the way you handle the duties assigned to you. In order to move up, you must first earn a reputation for reliability.

Promotion in secretarial work consists of moving up to jobs that are successively more important. A secretary may begin to work for a junior executive, advance to be secretary to a department head, then become secretary to a corporate officer, and finally, advance to a position of secretary to the president of a company or chairman of the board of directors.

From the outset it is important to establish a good record. Remember, you are your own best friend when it comes to progressing on the job. By doing your best work on every assignment, by sharpening and improving your skills, and by welcoming new responsibilities as chances to prove your abilities, you will open doors for promotion for yourself.

In order to generate new opportunities for yourself, you must keep adding to your inventory of professional abilities. Continue to learn, and you will increase your value to your employer. Improve your

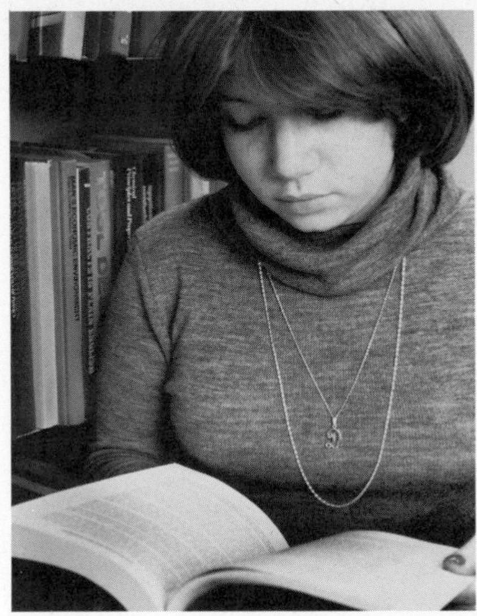

work procedures and accuracy, and take advantage of opportunities for extra service.

Keep up with changes in the business world. Participate in professional activities outside the job by taking additional training and joining a professional secretarial association. These and similar activities will enhance your value in the office and in the company.

If you want to move ahead, you have to think ahead. Achieving excellence and earning promotions rarely occur by chance; they are likely to occur when you look ahead, choose your goals, and then work hard to achieve them.

Lesson 57 is a "brief form" lesson. It contains one or more illustrations of *every* brief form in Gregg Shorthand. Counting repetitions, there are 452 brief forms or derivatives. Because you have seen and written all of these brief forms many, many times, you should be able to complete this lesson in record time!

Building Transcription Skills

525 SPELLING FAMILIES -able, -ible A difficult spelling problem for stenographers is deciding whether a word ends in *-able* or *-ible.* Unfortunately, there is no rule that tells us when to use *-able* and when to use *-ible.* In a majority of English words the ending is spelled *-able,* but it is spelled *-ible* in a sufficient number of words that you should think twice before you type an *a* or an *i.* In the following list dots are placed in the words where they may be divided on the typewriter.

Words Ending in -able

avail·able	**prob·a·ble**	**re·li·able**
com·fort·able	**prof·it·able**	**suit·able**
de·sir·able	**rea·son·able**	**valu·able**

Words Ending in -ible

de·duct·ible	**im·pos·si·ble**	**re·spon·si·ble**
flex·i·ble	**pos·si·ble**	**sen·si·ble**

---

526 Business Vocabulary Builder

defray To provide for the payment of.

administer Supervise; manage.

forcefulness Effectiveness.

Reading and Writing Practice

527

chil·dren

fam·i·ly

suc·cess·ful

re·spon·si·ble

if

if

and o

and o

suit·able

re·quest

when

intro

par

fu·ture

[177]

528

ap

Op·por·tu·ni·ties

busi·nesses

siz·able

ser

intro

com·pa·ny's

par

im·me·di·ate·ly

par

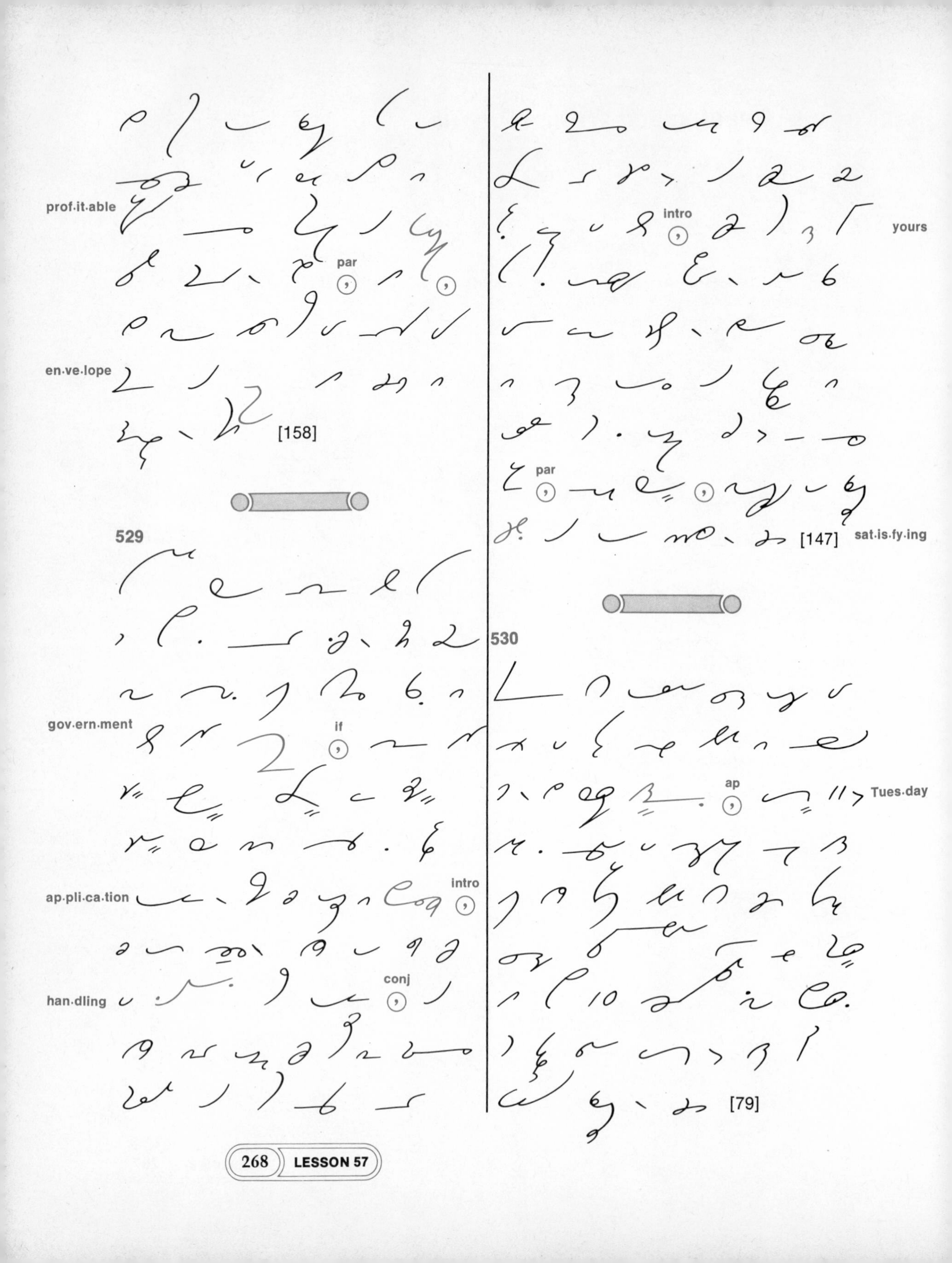

prof·it·able

par

en·ve·lope

[158]

529

gov·ern·ment

if

ap·pli·ca·tion

intro

han·dling

conj

intro

yours

par

[147] sat·is·fy·ing

530

ap

Tues·day

[79]

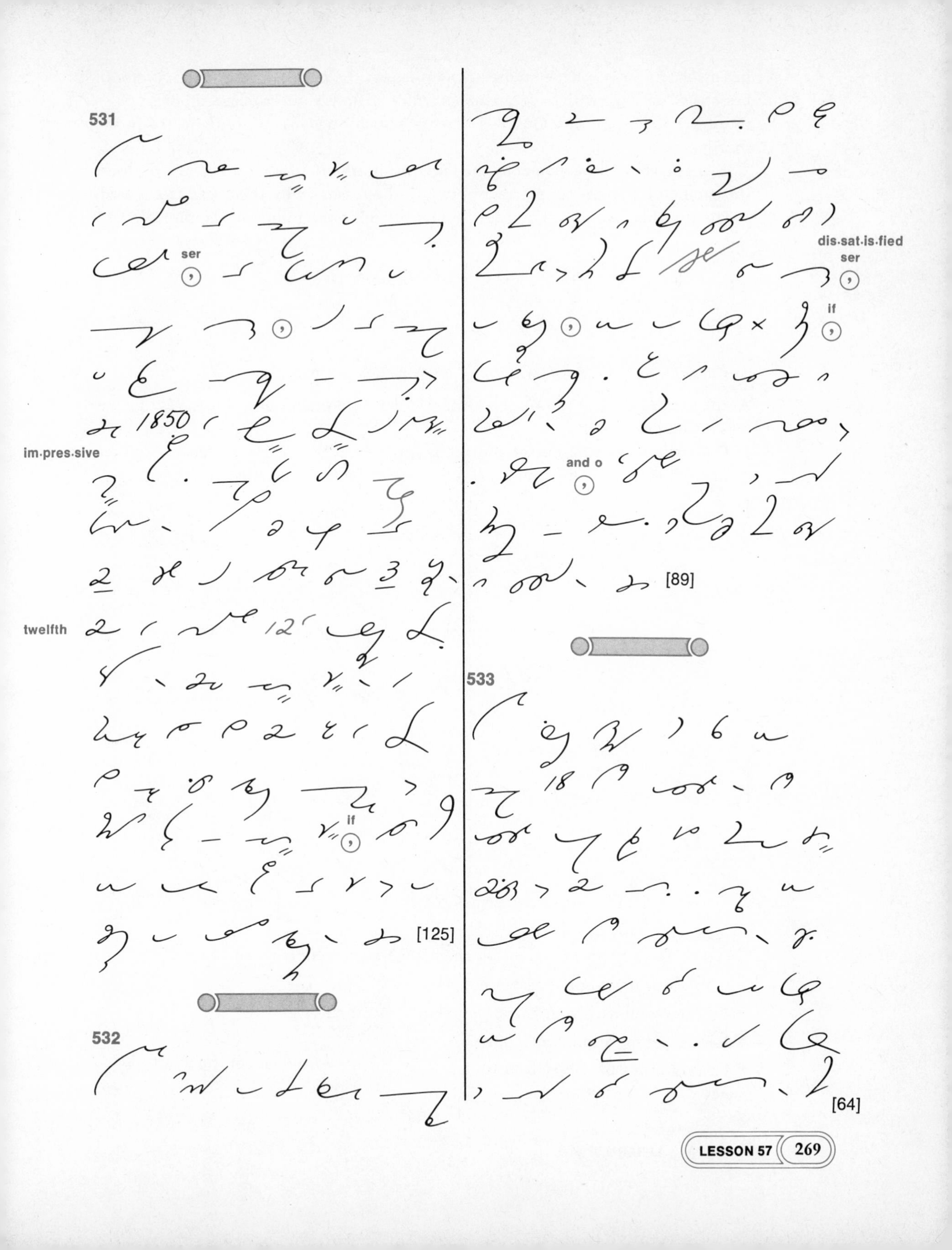

531

ser

1850

im·pres·sive

twelfth

12

if

[125]

532

dis·sat·is·fied

ser

if

and o

[89]

533

18

[64]

534 **Transcription Quiz** In Lessons 31-56 you have studied nine rules for the correct use of the comma. In Lessons 57-69 you will have an opportunity to test your mastery of these rules through a "Transcription Quiz"—a letter in which no commas are indicated in the shorthand.

It will be your job, as you copy the letter in shorthand in your notebook, to insert the commas in the proper places and to give the reasons why the commas are used.

The shorthand in your notebook should resemble the following example:

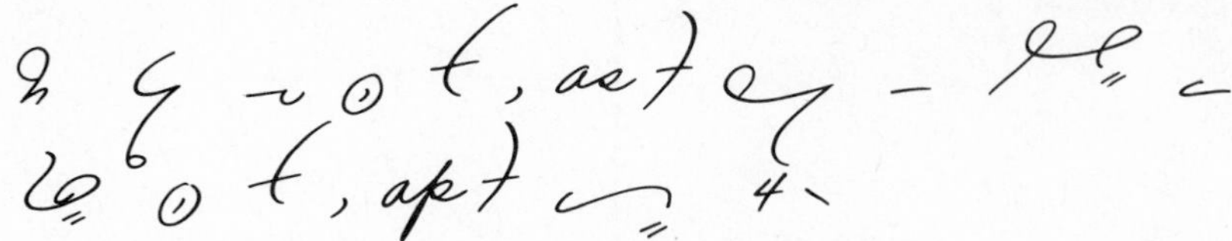

As you probably know, (, as) I will be in Dallas on Friday, (, ap) August 4.

At the head of each Transcription Quiz you will find the number and types of commas the letter calls for.

The correct punctuation of the following letter calls for 5 commas—1 comma *as* clause, 1 comma conjunction, 2 commas series, 1 comma *if* clause.

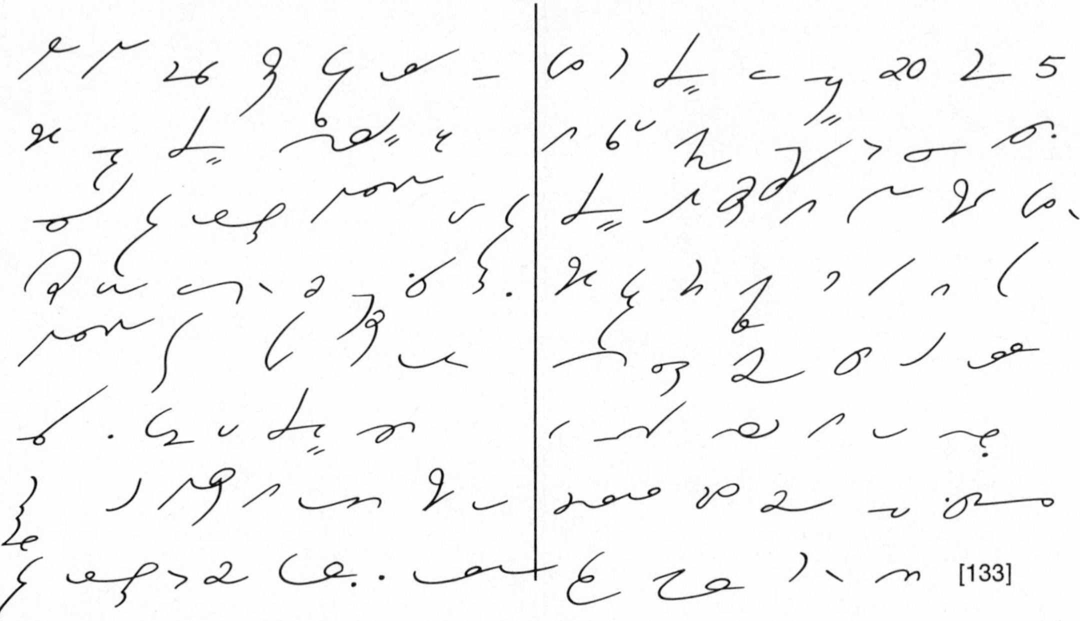

PERSONAL-USE CHECKLIST *Do you substitute shorthand for longhand wherever possible when you—*

- **1** Take down your daily assignments?
- **2** Correspond with your friends who know shorthand?
- **3** Draft compositions and reports?
- **4** Make notes to yourself on things to do, people to see, appointments to keep, etc?

This lesson provides you with an opportunity to increase your phrasing skill. It contains many illustrations of the phrasing principles of Gregg Shorthand. All told, it contains 102 phrases, counting repetitions.

Building Transcription Skills

535 GRAMMAR CHECKUP sentence structure

Parallel ideas should be expressed in parallel form.

no

I hope our relationship will be long, pleasant, *and* of profit *to both of us.*

yes

I hope our relationship will be long, pleasant, *and* profitable *to both of us.*

no

As soon as we receive the necessary information, your account will be opened *and* we will ship your order.

yes

As soon as we receive the necessary information, your account will be opened *and* your order will be shipped.

It is especially important to keep parallel all ideas in a tabulation.

no

The secretary's main duties were:

1. *Taking dictation and transcribing*
2. *Answering the telephone*
3. *To take care of the files*

yes

The secretary's main duties were:

1. *Taking dictation and transcribing*
2. *Answering the telephone*
3. *Taking care of the files*

536 **Business Vocabulary Builder**

complications Difficulties.

county A territorial division for local government within a state.

geared Adjusted in order to satisfy something.

Reading and Writing Practice

537

Christ·mas

par

par

as

owe

pur·chased

en·ve·lope

and o

[127]

538

when

115-1118

conj

cour·te·ous

shipped

40,

if

per·son·al

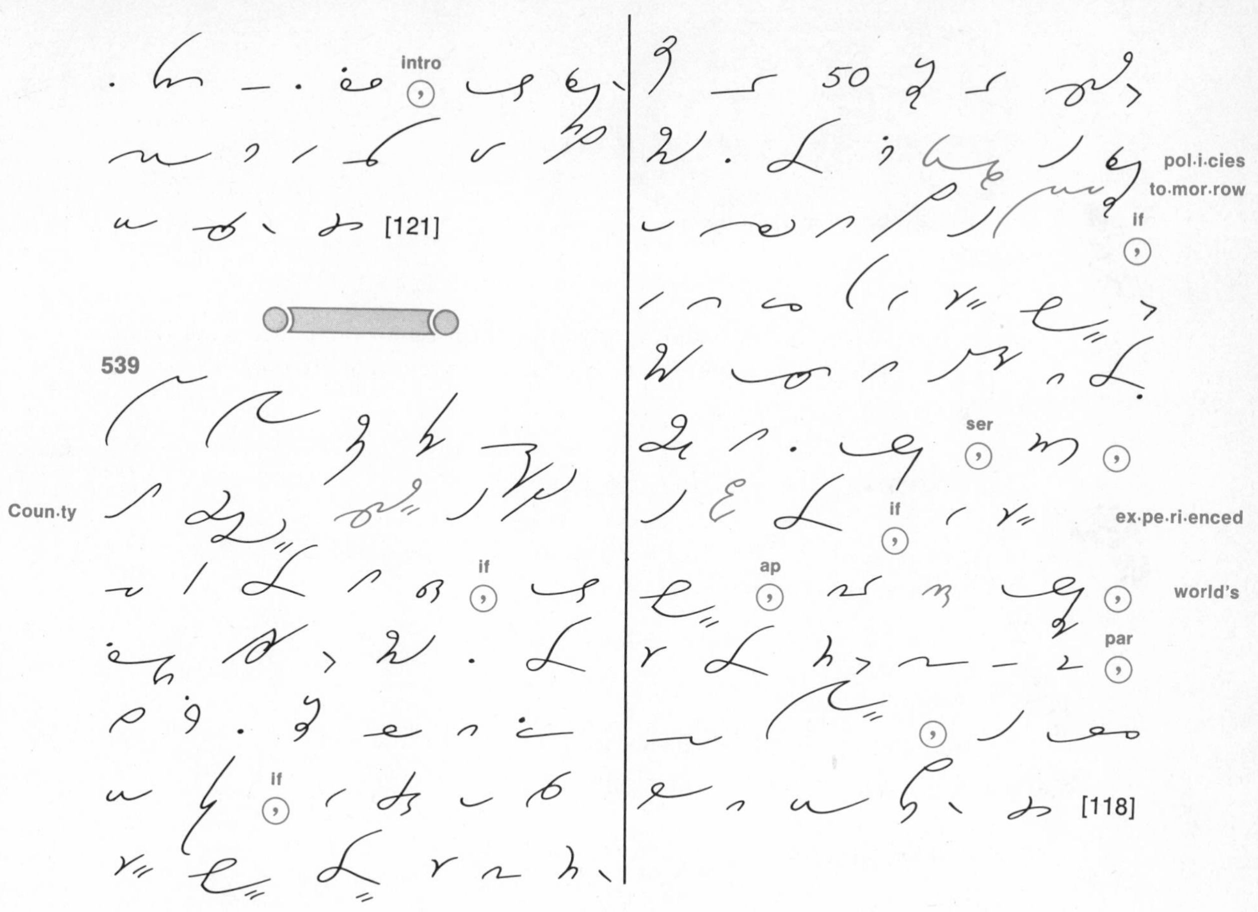

540 Transcription Quiz The correct punctuation of the following letter calls for 5 commas—1 comma *when* clause, 2 commas parenthetical, 2 commas series.

[102]

Lesson 59 provides an opportunity for you to brush up on the joined word beginnings of Gregg Shorthand. In the letters of this lesson there are 80 words containing joined word beginnings.

Building Transcription Skills

541 SPELLING FAMILIES -cial, -tial Be very careful when you transcribe words ending in the sound of *shul*. The ending is sometimes spelled *-cial*, sometimes *-tial*.

Words Ending in -cial

ben·e·fi·cial	**fi·nan·cial**	**so·cial**
com·mer·cial	**of·fi·cial**	**spe·cial**

Words Ending in -tial

es·sen·tial	**ini·tial**	**po·ten·tial**
in·flu·en·tial	**par·tial**	**sub·stan·tial**

542 Business Vocabulary Builder

conversion Something changed from one use to another.

colleagues Associates; co-workers.

convalesce To recover health gradually after sickness.

Reading and Writing Practice

543

par

un·for·tu·nate·ly

ap

23.

conj

de·spite

em·ploy·ees

intro

sub·stan·tial

and o

en·cour·ag·ing

if

com·mer·cial

con·ver·sion

when

apol·o·gize

[153]

544

ap

li·brary

thor·ough·ly

conj

de·light·ed

par

[100]

545

spe·cial

ap

ini·tial

intro

ex·haust·ed

par

per·son·al

conj

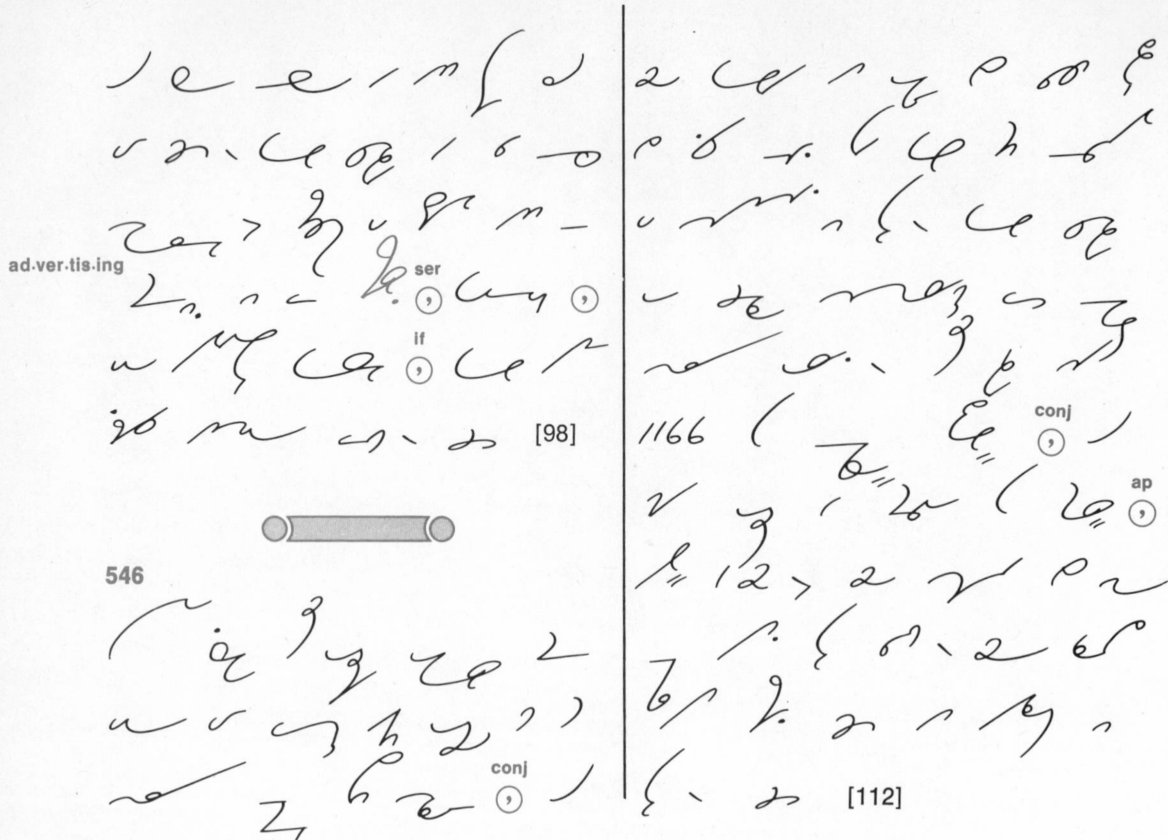

547 Transcription Quiz The correct punctuation of the following letter calls for 6 commas—2 commas conjunction, 2 commas parenthetical, 1 comma *as* clause, 1 comma introductory.

[108]

Lesson 60 concentrates on joined word endings. There are 88 words containing them in this lesson.

Building Transcription Skills

548 COMMON PREFIXES re-

re- again

replenish To fill or supply again.

repeat To say or do again.

reconsider To take up again.

reconfirm To assure again.

renew To make like new again.

549 Business Vocabulary Builder

mark down *(verb)* Reduce the price of.

portable Capable of being carried or moved about.

humid Moist.

Reading and Writing Practice

Reading Scoreboard Here is your chance to determine how much your reading speed has increased over your first score in Lesson 18.

Lesson 60 contains 767 words

If you read Lesson 60 in **17 minutes** your reading rate is **46 words a minute**
If you read Lesson 60 in **19 minutes** your reading rate is **40 words a minute**
If you read Lesson 60 in **22 minutes** your reading rate is **35 words a minute**

If you read Lesson 60 in 25 minutes your reading rate is 31 words a minute
If you read Lesson 60 in 27 minutes your reading rate is 28 words a minute
If you read Lesson 60 in 30 minutes your reading rate is 26 words a minute

---

550

rep·u·ta·ble

debt

cred·i·tors

leath·er

re·plen·ish

ward·robe

[157]

551

rep·e·ti·tion

hu·mid

de·pend·able

won't

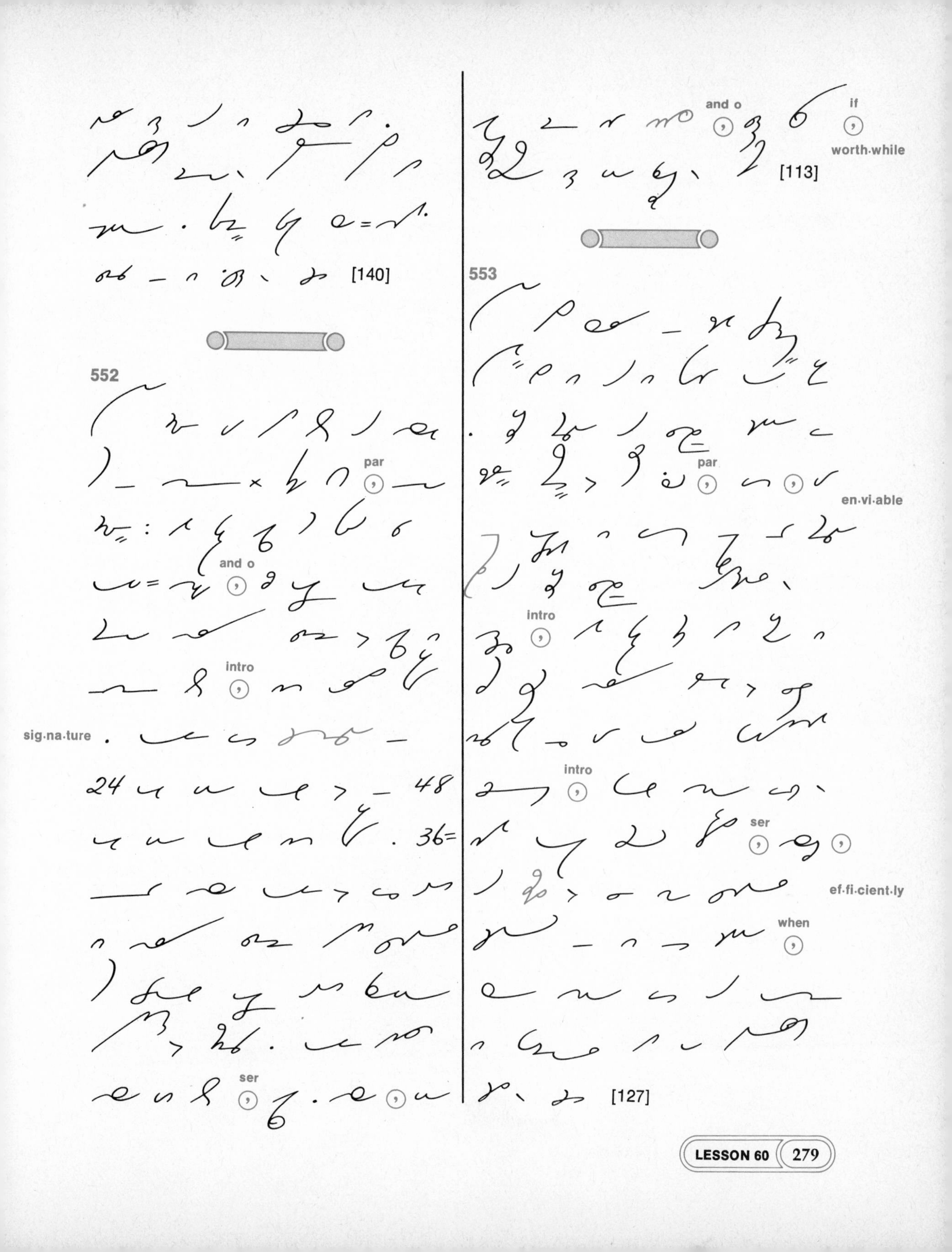

[140]

552

par

and o

intro

sig·na·ture

24 48

36=

ser

and o

if

worth·while

[113]

553

par

en·vi·able

intro

intro

ser

ef·fi·cient·ly

when

[127]

554

un·sealed

con·fi·den·tial

grate·ful

par

intro

ne·ces·si·tates

[104]

555 **Transcription Quiz** As you copy the following letter in your notebook, be sure to indicate the necessary commas at the proper points and to indicate the reason for the punctuation.

The letter calls for 5 commas—2 commas series, 1 comma apposition, and 2 commas parenthetical.

[126]

The disjoined word beginnings of Gregg Shorthand are treated extensively in Lesson 61. In the Reading and Writing Practice of this lesson, you will find 47 words containing disjoined word beginnings.

Building Transcription Skills

556 GRAMMAR CHECKUP subject and verb A verb must agree with its subject in number.

Our representative is *taking care of your needs.*

Your bills *for April* are *enclosed.*

The inclusion of a phrase such as *in addition to, as well as,* or *along with* does not affect the number of the verb. If the subject is singular, use a singular verb; if the subject is plural, use a plural verb.

Our representative, *as well as our managers,* is *looking forward to the pleasure of serving you.*

Your canceled checks, *along with your statement,* are *mailed to you each month.*

---

557 Business Vocabulary Builder

effects *(noun)* Physical property; goods.

buffet A counter for refreshments.

frustrating Disappointing.

Reading and Writing Practice

558

ap

re·cent·ly

su·per·vi·so·ry

if

ap

ed·i·to·ri·al

[134]

559

ap

adopt·ed

de·sir·able

when

ser

ef·fects

as

em·ploy·ee

[114]

560

buf·fet

par

bro·chure

as

1940

intro

ap

intro

oc·ca·sion

cit·ies

[138]

de·scribes

561

par

man·u·al

[134]

562 Transcription Quiz In the letter that follows you must supply 4 commas to punctuate it correctly—1 comma conjunction, 1 comma introductory, 1 comma *and* omitted, 1 comma *if* clause.

[148]

LESSON 62

Here is an opportunity for you to improve your grasp of disjoined word endings in Gregg Shorthand. In this lesson there are 47 words containing disjoined word endings.

Building Transcription Skills

563 SIMILAR-WORDS DRILL their, there, they're

their Belonging to them.

Some people make their *own clothes.*

there In or to that place.

The students went there *at my request.*

they're Contraction for *they are.*

They're *always ready to serve you.*

---

564 Business Vocabulary Builder

discomfort Annoyance.

purification The act of cleaning.

impartial Fair; showing no favoritism.

Reading and Writing Practice

565

their

neigh·bor·hood

ap

jus·ti·fied

conj

and o

rec·om·men·da·tions

intro

par

pro·ceed

they're

conj

par

when

[157]

566

conj

veg·e·ta·ble

conj

whole

chem·i·cals

as

pu·ri·fi·ca·tion

if

en·gi·neers

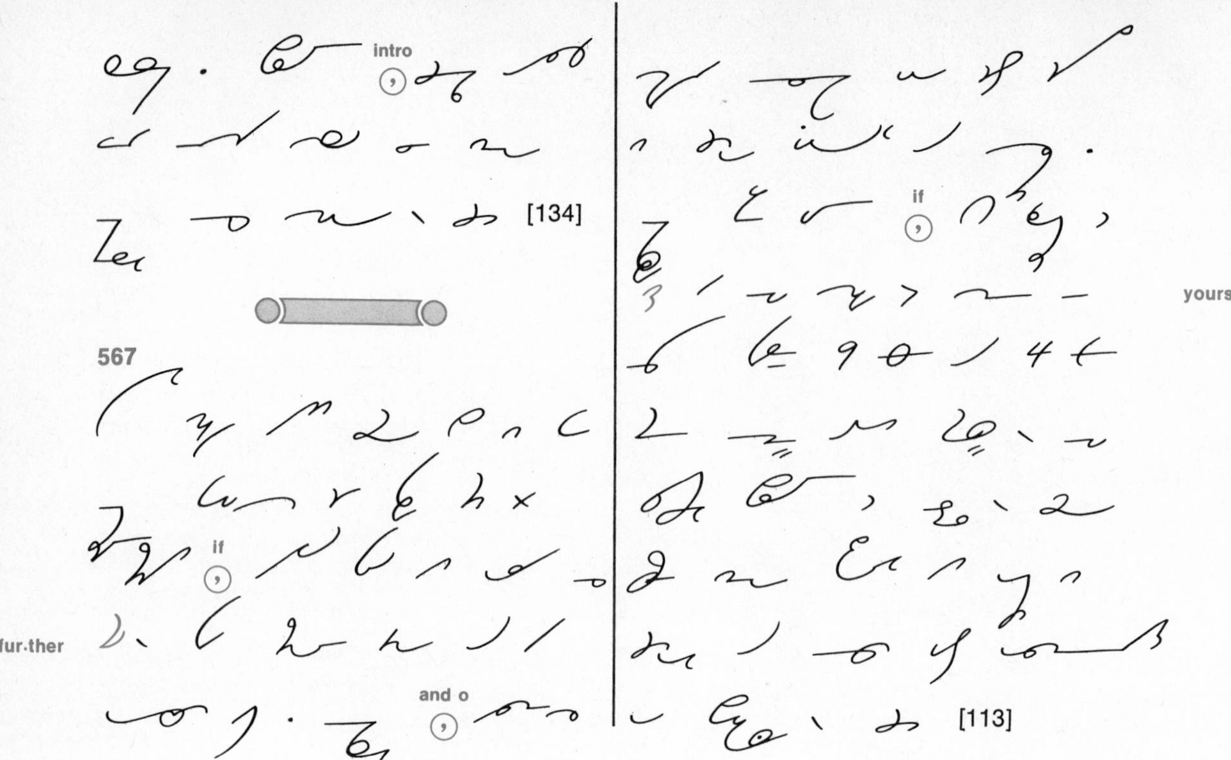

568 Transcription Quiz The following letter requires 6 commas–2 commas parenthetical, 2 commas series, 1 comma apposition, 1 comma introductory. Can you supply these commas?

[107]

In dictation your employer will frequently use numbers. Because of the great importance of accuracy in transcribing numbers, you should take special care to write numbers legibly in your notes. The material in this lesson will help you fix more firmly in your mind the various devices for expressing numbers and quantities in Gregg Shorthand.

Building Transcription Skills

569 COMMON PREFIXES un-

un- not

- **unusual** Not ordinary; rare.
- **uncertain** Not sure.
- **unprecedented** Not having been done before.
- **unnecessary** Not needed.
- **unquestioned** Not disputed.

---

570 Business Vocabulary Builder

processed *(verb)* Moved along.

pledged Guaranteed; promised.

depressed *(adjective)* Suffering from low economic activity.

Reading and Writing Practice

571 Tons of Food

weight

loaves

ser

ser

her·ring

ser

veg·e·ta·bles

ser

intro

ad·di·tion

ser

cheese

[144]

—*Your Health*

572

ap

pro·cessed

as

conj

pur·chased

ser

par

plea·sure

and o

pleas·ant

[136]

573

un·ques·tioned

pledged

intro

when

un·prec·e·dent·ed
achieve·ment

par

[144]

574 Transcription Quiz The following letter requires 6 commas—1 comma *if* clause, 4 commas parenthetical, 1 comma *when* clause. Remember to indicate these commas in your shorthand notes and to give the reason for their use.

[125]

As you learned during the early stages of your study of Gregg Shorthand, vowels may be omitted in some words to help you gain fluency of writing. In this lesson you will find many words illustrating the omission of vowels.

Building Transcription Skills

575 SPELLING FAMILIES -er, -or, -ar

Words Ending in -er

bak·er	cus·tom·er	re·mind·er
con·sid·er	of·fi·cer	speak·er

Words Ending in -or

col·or	gov·er·nor	op·er·a·tor
doc·tor	ma·jor	pro·fes·sor

Words Ending in -ar

dol·lar	pop·u·lar	schol·ar
gram·mar	reg·u·lar	sug·ar

---

576 Business Vocabulary Builder

enviable Highly desirable.

dynamic Forceful.

constructive Promoting improvement or development.

Reading and Writing Practice

577

wheth·er

if

ide·al

ad·di·tion

ser

ap

if

intro

par

cour·te·ous

and o

[133]

578

en·vi·able

of·fer·ing

ser

intro

stretch

intro

and o

gen·u·ine

ap

par

conj

aware

com·pli·ments

when

[133]

579

as

guest

for·tu·nate

ap

par

ap

dy·nam·ic

for·ward

[144]

580 Transcription Quiz For you to supply: 5 commas—1 comma *if* clause, 1 comma introductory, 2 commas series, 1 comma *when* clause.

[131]

One of the reasons why Gregg Shorthand can be written so fluently and rapidly is its blends—single strokes that represent two or more sounds. In the Reading and Writing Practice of this lesson you will find 113 words containing blends.

Building Transcription Skills

581 SIMILAR-WORDS DRILL brought, bought

brought The past tense and past participle of *bring*.

They brought *the books back after they had read them.*

bought Purchased.

Thousands of companies have bought *our Model 116 computer.*

116

582 Business Vocabulary Builder

intense Considerable.

refineries Plants for purifying oil.

commendation Praise.

Reading and Writing Practice

583

en.er.gy

ex·am·ple

intro

de·vel·op·ment

ser

intro

as

mer·chants

com·men·da·tion

bought

ap

intro

brought

conj

lo·cal

when

if

par

vi·tal

ur·gent·ly

and o

[136]

conj

ex·cel·lent

[118]

584

585

res·i·dence

par

au·to·mat·i·cal·ly

ap

par

151–1161 [109]

586

114

intro

hours

114

intro

enough

de·spite

ser

intro

114

114

brought

intro

bought

if

114

[173]

587

Man·age·ment

ap

intro

wit

[130]

588 Transcription Quiz For you to supply: 7 commas—2 commas apposition, 4 commas series, 1 comma *if* clause.

[120]

This is another lesson that concentrates on brief forms. Counting repetitions, it contains 267 brief forms and derivatives.

Building Transcription Skills

589 COMMON PREFIXES pro-

pro- in many words *pro-* means *before, ahead, forward,* or *future.*

proceed To go ahead.

progress A forward movement.

prospect A possible future customer.

promotion The act of moving ahead.

procedure A manner of going ahead.

---

590 Business Vocabulary Builder

anticipation The act of looking forward.

in arrears Behind in payment; overdue debt.

Reading and Writing Practice

591

its

intro

conj

im·me·di·ate·ly

intro

intro

and o

log·i·cal

trans·fer·ring

[146]

592

ac·knowl·edge

15

ap

pro·ceed

conj

re·mit·tance

any·one

when

ar·rears

en·ve·lope

if

pro·ceed

[134]

593

as

prob·a·bly

ap·pli·cants

conj

qual·i·ties

ser

par

conj

duties

worth-while

and o

chal·leng·ing

conj

[178]

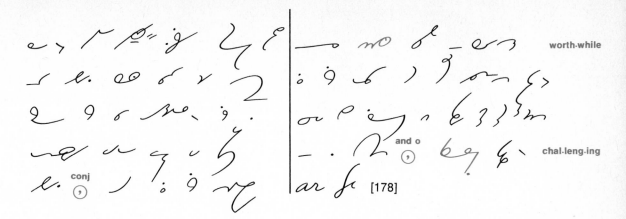

594 For you to supply: 5 commas—3 commas introductory, 1 comma conjunction, 1 comma *if* clause.

Transcription Quiz

[141]

Here is another opportunity for you to increase your skill in writing phrases. In this lesson there are 114 phrases.

Building Transcription Skills

595 GRAMMAR CHECKUP verbs with "one of"

In most cases, the expression *one of* takes a singular verb, which agrees with the subject *one.*

One of *the people on the staff* is *ill.*

One of *our typewriters* does *not work.*

When *one of* is part of an expression such as *one of those who* or *one of the things that,* a plural verb is used to agree with its antecedent in number.

Kay solved one of the problems that have (*not* has) *been annoying us for years.*

Lee is one of the students who drive (*not* drives) *to school.*

---

596 Business Vocabulary Builder

bearable Capable of being borne.

eventful Momentous; full of events.

milestones Significant points in development.

Reading and Writing Practice

597

bi·cy·cle

par

re·lieved

as

con·va·les·cence
bear·able

if

[87]

598

ap·pre·ci·ate

ap

15

conj

re·ceive

when

else·where

par

par

im·pressed

than

[130]

599

ap

an·ni·ver·sa·ry

15

16

par

conj

mile·stones

ser

suc·cess·ful

conj

intro

won't

[134]

600

as

par

and o

pros·per·ous

[104]

601 Transcription Quiz For you to supply: 6 commas—1 comma conjunction, 1 comma *as* clause, 1 comma apposition, 1 comma *and* omitted, 2 commas parenthetical.

[129]

Lesson 68 contains a general review of many of the major principles of Gregg Shorthand.

Building Transcription Skills

602 SIMILAR-WORDS DRILL some, sum

some A portion.

Have some *of our services displeased you?*

sum Amount; total.

You owe us the sum *of $500.*

---

603 Business Vocabulary Builder

incredibly Hardly believable.
judicious Having sound judgment; wise.
net income Earnings remaining after expenses.
frankness Honesty.

Reading and Writing Practice

604

par

in·cred·i·bly

sum

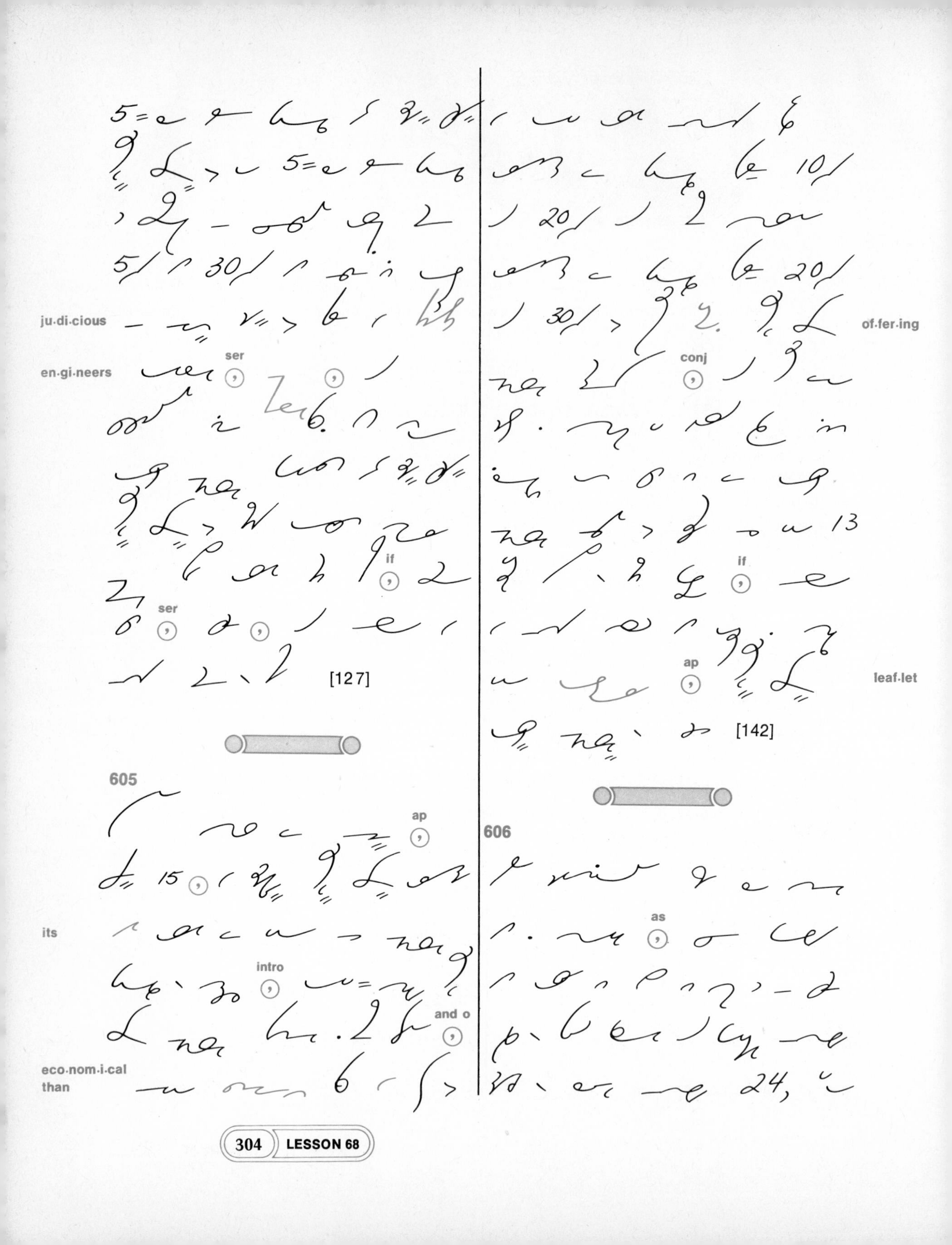

ju·di·cious

en·gi·neers

ser

conj

of·fer·ing

if

if

ser

ap

leaf·let

[127]

[142]

605

ap

606

its

as

intro

and o

eco·nom·i·cal
than

607

[130]

[87]

when

intro

re·ceive

sum·ma·ry

608 For you to supply: 4 commas—3 commas parenthetical, 1 comma *if* clause.

Transcription Quiz

[101]

You probably won't be able to refrain from chuckling as you read the "hotel" letters in the Reading and Writing Practice. They are an exchange of letters by the manager and a guest with a sense of humor.

Building Transcription Skills

609 COMMON PREFIXES pre-

pre- before; beforehand.

- **predict** To tell beforehand; to prophesy.
- **preliminary** Coming before the main business.
- **premature** Happening before the proper time.
- **presume** To assume to be true before proof is established.

---

610 Business Vocabulary Builder

- **desolated** Sad; unhappy; disappointed.
- **conceivably** Possibly.
- **establishment** Place of business.

Reading and Writing Practice

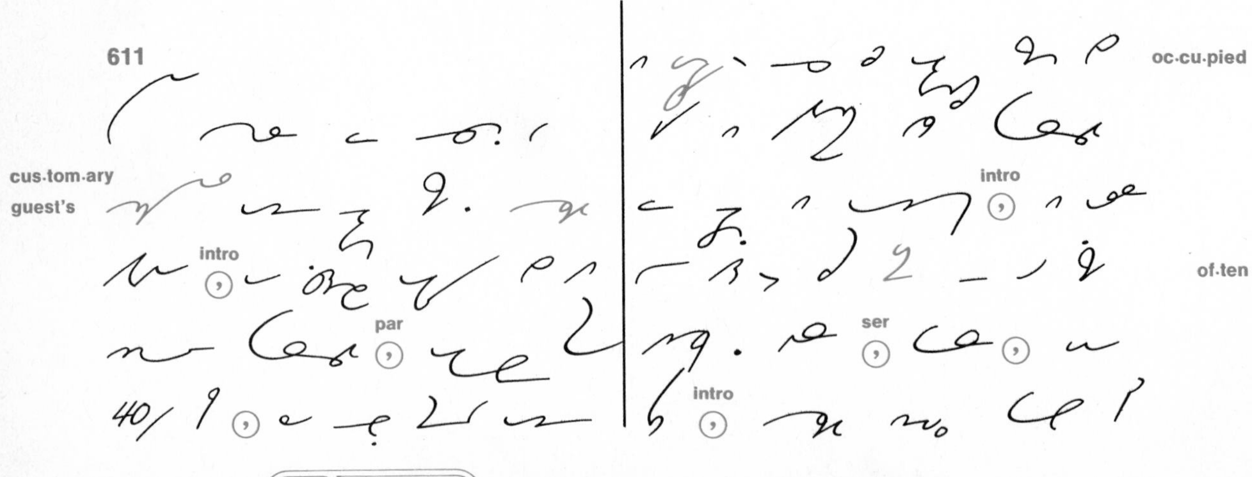

par

[95]

612

des·o·lat·ed

ap

sou·ve·nirs

vis·i·tor

zoo

con·ceiv·ably

par

par

run·ning

as

thought·ful·ly

draw·er

intro

maid

when

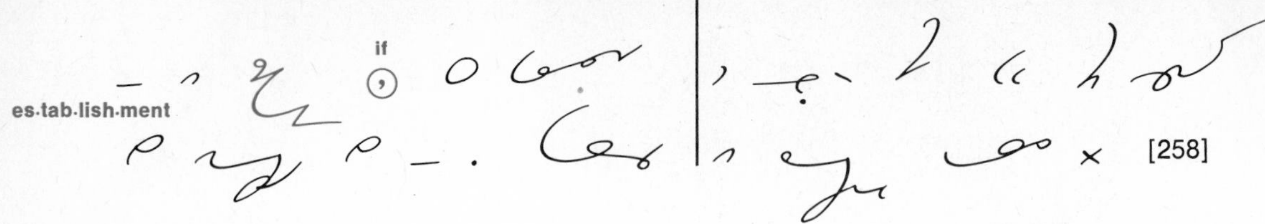

613 Transcription Quiz For you to supply: 5 commas—1 comma *and* omitted, 1 comma introductory, 1 comma conjunction, 2 commas parenthetical.

[141]

VOCABULARY CHECKLIST *Has your command of words improved since you began your study of Gregg Shorthand? It has if you—*

- ■ 1 Studied all the words in the Business Vocabulary Builders and added them to your everyday vocabulary.
- ■ 2 Paid careful attention to the Similar-Words Drills, so that you know the difference between *addition, edition; some, sum,* etc.
- ■ 3 Learned the meanings of the common prefixes presented in a number of the lessons of your textbook.

When you are employed in a business office, you will have occasion to use the telephone frequently. The information in the Reading and Writing Practice will help you use the telephone efficiently.

Building Transcription Skills

614 SPELLING FAMILIES -ize, -ise, -yze Be careful when you must type a word ending with the sound of *iz*. The ending may be spelled *-ize, ise, or -yze*.

Words Ending in -ize

apol·o·gize	**re·al·ize**	**uti·lize**
or·ga·nize	**rec·og·nize**	**vi·su·al·ize**

Words Ending in -ise

ad·ver·tise	**com·prise**	**rise**
ad·vise	**en·ter·prise**	**su·per·vise**

Words Ending in -yze

an·a·lyze	**par·a·lyze**

615 Business Vocabulary Builder

moderate *(adjective)* Reasonable.

offensive *(adjective)* Giving unpleasant sensations.

visualize To form a mental image of; to see.

commending Praising.

Reading and Writing Practice

Reading Scoreboard Now that you are on the last lesson, you are no doubt very much interested in your final shorthand reading rate. If you have followed the practice suggestions you received early in the course, your shorthand reading rate at this time should be a source of pride to you.

To get a picture of how much your shorthand reading rate has increased with practice, compare it with the reading rate in Lesson 18, the first time you measured it.

Lesson 70 contains 778 words

If you read Lesson 70 in **15 minutes** your reading rate is **50 words a minute**
If you read Lesson 70 in **19 minutes** your reading rate is **41 words a minute**
If you read Lesson 70 in **22 minutes** your reading rate is **35 words a minute**
If you read Lesson 70 in **26 minutes** your reading rate is **30 words a minute**
If you read Lesson 70 in **29 minutes** your reading rate is **27 words a minute**
If you read Lesson 70 in **32 minutes** your reading rate is **24 words a minute**

616 The Telephone

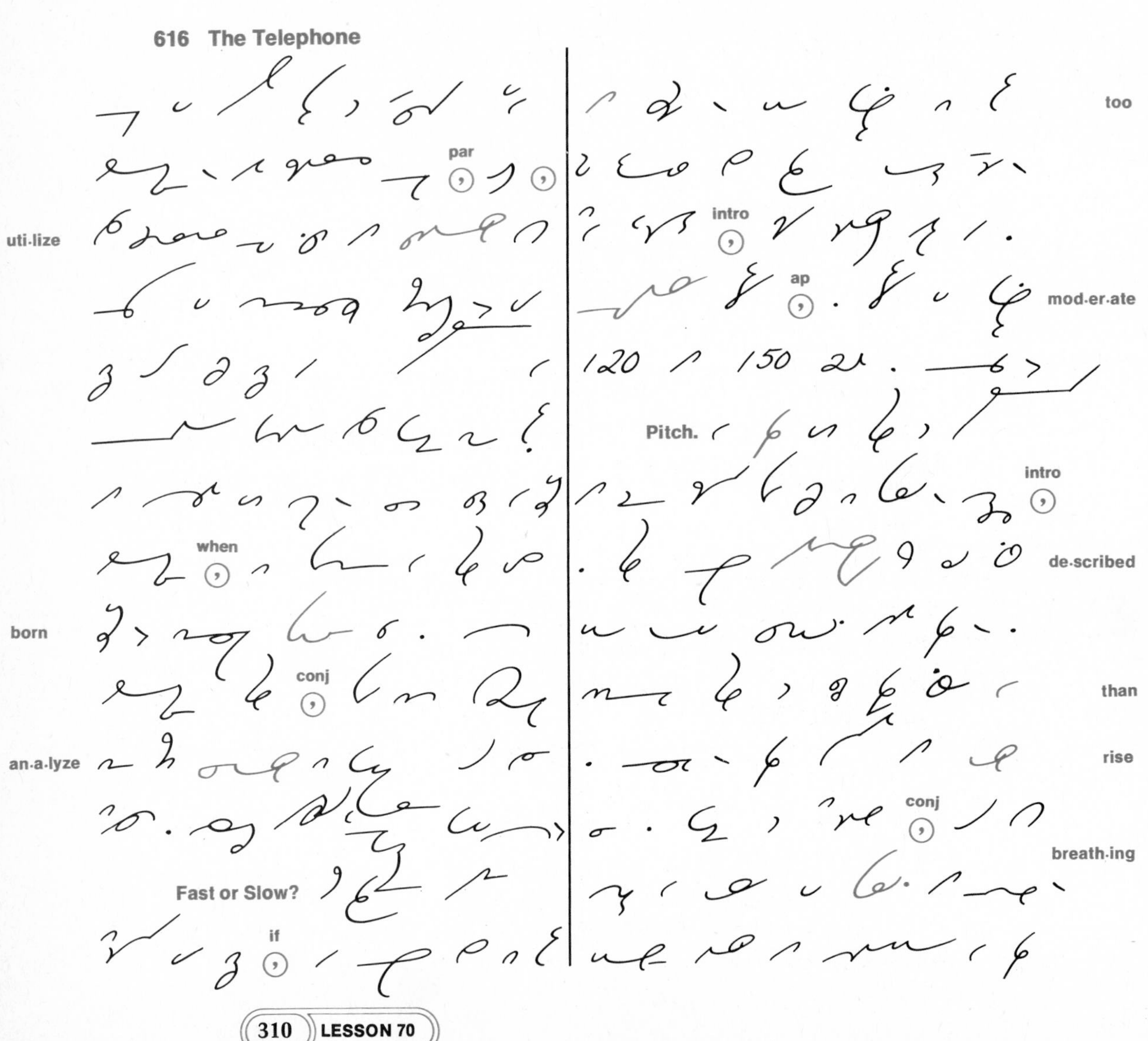

Volume.

of·fen·sive

intro

em·pha·sis

A Pleasant Voice.

par

and o

agree·able

Telephone Courtesy.

re·al·ize

ex·ten·sion

if

than

vi·su·al·ize

ser

in·ter·rupt

rec·og·nize

if

Receiving Calls.

when

track

when

when

Transferring Calls.

qual·i·fied

if

dis·turb·ing

as

al·ready

ir·ri·tat·ing

fur·ther

intro

[680]

617 Appreciation

praise

par

when

[98]

Appendix

States

The abbreviations in parentheses are those recommended by the Postal Service.

Alabama [AL]

Alaska [AK]

Arizona [AZ]

Arkansas [AR]

California [CA]

Colorado [CO]

Connecticut [CT]

Delaware [DE]

Florida [FL]

Georgia [GA]

Hawaii [HI]

Idaho [ID]

Illinois [IL]

Indiana [IN]

Iowa [IA]

Kansas [KS]

Kentucky [KY]

Louisiana [LA]

Maine [ME]

Maryland [MD]

Massachusetts [MA]

Michigan [MI]

Minnesota [MN]

Mississippi [MS]

Missouri [MO]

Montana [MT]

Nebraska [NE]

Nevada [NV]

New Hampshire [NH]

New Jersey [NJ]

New Mexico [NM]

NewYork [NY]

North Carolina [NC]

North Dakota [ND]

Ohio [OH]

Oklahoma [OK]

Oregon [OR]

Pennsylvania [PA]

Rhode Island [RI]

South Carolina [SC]

South Dakota [SD]

Tennessee [TN]

Texas [TX]

Utah [UT]

Vermont [VT]

Virginia [VA]

Washington [WA]

West Virginia [WV]

Wisconsin [WI]

Wyoming [WY]

Selected Cities of the United States

Akron
Albany
Anchorage
Atlanta
Baltimore
Baton Rouge
Birmingham
Boston
Bridgeport
Buffalo
Cambridge
Camden
Charleston
Charlotte
Chattanooga
Cheyenne
Chicago
Cincinnati
Cleveland
Columbia
Columbus
Dallas

Dayton
Denver
Des Moines
Detroit
El Paso
Fairbanks
Fargo
Fort Worth
Grand Rapids
Hartford
Honolulu
Houston
Indianapolis
Jacksonville
Jersey City
Kansas City
Knoxville
Laramie
Las Vegas
Lincoln
Little Rock
Los Angeles

Louisville
Memphis
Miami
Milwaukee
Minneapolis
Montpelier
Nashville
Newark
New Orleans
New York
Norfolk
Oakland
Oklahoma City
Omaha
Philadelphia
Phoenix
Pittsburgh
Portland
Providence
Richmond
Rochester
Sacramento

St. Louis	*Shreveport*	*Toledo*
St. Paul	*Spokane*	*Trenton*
Salt Lake City	*Springfield*	*Tucson*
San Antonio	*Syracuse*	*Tulsa*
San Diego	*Tacoma*	*Washington*
San Francisco	*Tallahassee*	*Wichita*
Seattle	*Tampa*	*Wilmington*

Common Geographical Abbreviations

America	*England*	*Canada*
American	*English*	*Canadian*
United States	*Great Britain*	*Puerto Rico*

The Metric System

If you take dictation in which there are many occurrences of metric measurements, you will have frequent use for the abbreviated forms given below. It is not wise to attempt to learn these forms until you know you will have use for them.

The metric system was devised by France and adopted there by law in 1799. Since that time its use has become almost universal except in Great Britain and the United States. It is rapidly coming into use in those two countries and, therefore, it is possible that you will need these special outlines. If the terms occur only infrequently in your dictation, it is better to write them in full.

The following abbreviations will be useful to those who must frequently take metric measurements in dictation.

		meter	liter	gram
kilo-	1,000			
hekto-	100			
deka-	10			

		meter	liter	gram
deci-	1/10			
centi-	1/100			
milli-	1/1,000			
micro-	1/1,000,000			
nano-	1/1,000,000,000			

ADDITIONAL METRIC MEASUREMENTS

Celsius
centigrade
cubic centimeter
kilobit
kilocalorie
kilocycle
kilohertz
kiloton
kilovolt

kilowatt
kilowatt-hour
megabit
megahertz
megaton
megawatt
megohm
micromicron
micron

microsecond
milliampere
millibar
millifarad
millihenry
millimicrosecond
millivolt
milliwatt
nanosecond

Index of Gregg Shorthand

In order to facilitate finding, this Index has been divided into six main sections—Alphabetic Characters, Brief Forms, General, Phrasing, Word Beginnings, Word Endings.

The first figure refers to the lesson; the second refers to the paragraph.

BRIEF FORMS

GENERAL

PHRASING

WORD BEGINNINGS

WORD ENDINGS

INDEX OF BRIEF FORMS

The first figure refers to the lesson; the second to the paragraph.

INDEX OF BUILDING TRANSCRIPTION SKILLS

The first figure refers to the lesson; the second figure to the paragraph.

Brief Forms of Gregg Shorthand

IN ORDER OF PRESENTATION

A	B	C	D	E	F	G
3						
		5				
				8		
						11
	13					
			15			
					17	
						19
					21	
				23		
			25			
					27	
29						
		31